Pikes Peak Backcountry

The Historic Saga
of the Peak's West Slope

for Tracy —

"Nigeria Luka!"

Pikes Peak Backcountry

The Historic Saga
of the Peak's West Slope

Celinda Reynolds Kaelin

CAXTON PRESS
Caldwell, Idaho
1999

Cover painting by Richard Thomas.

Library of Congress Cataloging-in-Publication Data

Kaelin, Celinda Reynolds
Pikes Peak Backcountry: the historic saga of the peak's west slope / Celinda Reynolds Kaelin.
p. cm.
Originally published: Colorado : C.R. Kaelin, 1995.
Includes bibliographical references (p.   ) and index.
ISBN 0-87004-391-9 (paper)
1. Pikes Peak (Colo.)—History. 2. Pikes Peak Region (Colo.)—History. I. Title.
F782.P63K34 1999
978.8'56—dc21   98-18189
                                                                          CIP

Lithographed and bound in the United States of America
CAXTON PRESS
Caldwell, Idaho
164923

Dedication

This book is dedicated to my dear friend
Leo Kimmett
and to his great-grandfather
Judge James Castello

CONTENTS

ILLUSTRATIONS

Photo courtesy Sanborn Western Camps
Vast forests of ponderosa pine define the valleys and streambeds of Pikes
Peak backcountry. The peak commands the entire eastern horizon.

INTRODUCTION

I fell in love with the Pikes Peak backcountry the moment I saw it. I found the area totally by accident, when my husband and I took a pleasure drive west, into the mountains, while visiting my brother in Colorado Springs. At the time, we were looking for a place to retire, and had almost decided to buy a ranch in my home state of New Mexico. However, Pikes Peak cast an irresistible spell upon us. One oldtimer echoed my sentiments exactly when he told me that he "fell in love with that Peak" when he first set eyes on her, and he had to live where he "could see her first thing every day."

I was mesmerized by her clear, frothy streams with great ponderosa pines marching along flower-strewn banks. I was enchanted by hillsides studded with magnificent granite boulders piled precariously atop one another in frozen pantomimes of turtles and frogs and Indians. Most of all, I was enthralled by Pikes Peak which commanded the entire horizon in her robe of dazzling white snow. I *had* to live in this Pikes Peak backcountry.

Certainly, there are many historians better qualified than I to write this book. And I know that there are many gifted writers who could do a better job of putting just the right words together. I doubt, however, that there is anyone who has a greater passion for the history of this area, or who has found greater joy than I have in probing the mysteries of this history.

I first stumbled onto the story of Pikes Peak backcountry while in a bookstore in Reston, Virginia. Harold and I had just bought Twin Creek Ranch and were contemplating our move to Colorado. I stopped into the bookstore for something to read during the drive across country, when a stack of old books on the floor caught my eye. I picked up the top book and was blowing the dust from its cover when it fell open. Will Drannan's account of trapping beaver in the Tarryall River Valley leaped off the page. I knew that the Tarryall River was very near our new ranch. The entire stack of books was of Colorado history, so I bought them all. Ironically, an estate in Pueblo, Colorado, had just sold them to the bookstore and now I would be taking them back to Colorado.

My daughter Jessica and her friend (also Jessica) read Drannan's book aloud during the three-day cross-country drive to our new ranch. The miles flew by as we listened spellbound to Drannan's stories of trapping beaver with Kit Carson and fighting in the Indian wars.

During the restoration of our old homestead, west of Florissant, I began to research the history of our ranch. No murder mystery could have been more intriguing or exciting. So, of course, I joined the Florissant Heritage Foundation. Then, about 1993, Leo Kimmett approached me and asked if I would like to collaborate with him on a new history of the area. I had devoured every word of his book, *Florissant, Colorado*, and eagerly agreed.

My original plan was to simply augment and revise Kimmett's *Florissant*. However, as each historic fact was unveiled it became very clear that the scope of the work had to include the area north, west, and south of Pikes Peak, to the edge of South Park. Much has been written about the Cripple Creek Mining District, but many of the best stories about Pikes Peak backcountry have never been told. I studied all of Kimmett's earlier research as it offered tantalizing clues, and then my further research revealed the untold stories of the entire backcountry.

Kimmett's great-grandfather, Judge James Castello, established what is now Florissant, in 1870, as a Ute trading post. He was successful mainly because of his integrity and his excellent rapport with the Ute Indians of the area. Later, he rented rooms to road-weary travelers and gained a reputation along the Ute Pass Wagon Road as a genial and gracious host to his guests. Leo Kimmett provides living testimony to these same endearing qualities, faithfully handed down several generations. Each of our working sessions began with a sumptuous luncheon of fresh produce from his garden, lovingly prepared by his charming wife, Julia. This Pavlovian conditioning ensured a positive reaction from me; every time that I worked on the manuscript I salivated.

Conventional wisdom has long decreed that "possession is nine-tenths of the law," and politicians have pragmatically sought to implement this logic. Spain knew that land grants, ensuring occupancy, were vital to validating their ownership of the vast expanses that they claimed in the New World. The United States also understood this principle, and passed the Homestead Act. American Indians had a different understanding of their relationship to the landscape. In their nomadic lifestyle, they harvested the fruits of the land in a cycle of successive camping grounds, and their Mother Earth unfailingly nurtured her people. It was unthinkable to view this relationship as "owning" a possession. Instead, the Ute people felt that *they* belonged to the *land*. This was diametrically opposed to the Euro-cultural concept that the *land* belonged to the *people*. The stage for conflict was set, for the land to which the Ute people belonged was the key to breaching the Rocky Mountains.

In order to understand a large complex issue, it is almost always easier to examine the smaller, component parts. The micro defines the macro. Fears and desire, passions and prejudices of every person combine to create the fabric of history. Each Ute Indian, mountain man, gold seeker, and homesteader who lived in Pikes Peak's backcountry provides unparalleled insight to the westward expansion of the United States. Each of their stories tells how and why the West came to be possessed by the dominant culture, and how the Rocky Mountains were finally conquered. We are incredibly fortunate that so many descendants of these people are still living and are so willing to share their family stories and vintage photographs. We are deeply indebted to them for their generosity.

Celinda Reynolds Kaelin
Twin Creek Ranch

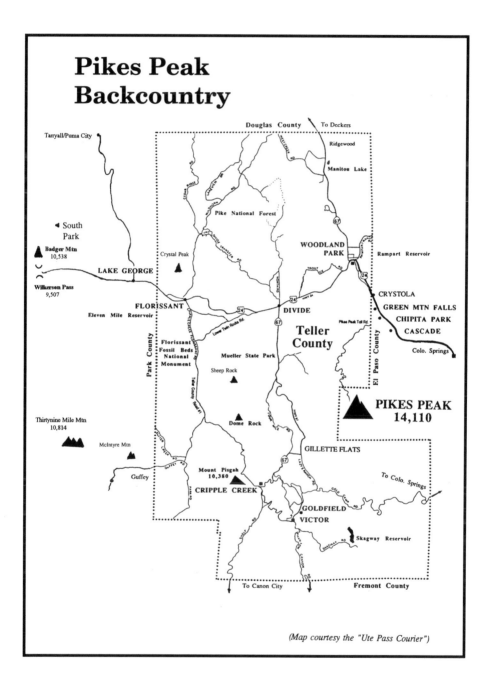

Pikes Peak
Backcountry

Douglas County   To Deckers

Tarryall/Puma City

Ridgewood

Manitou Lake

Pike National Forest

◄ South
Park

Badger Mtn
10,538

Crystal Peak

WOODLAND
PARK

Rampart Reservoir

LAKE GEORGE

Wilkerson Pass
9,507

TROUT

CRYSTOLA

FLORISSANT

Eleven Mile Reservoir

DIVIDE

GREEN MTN FALLS
CHIPITA PARK

Pikes Peak Toll Rd.

CASCADE

Teller
County

Colo. Springs

Florissant
Fossil Beds
National
Monument

Mueller State Park

Sheep Rock

El Paso County

Park County

Tarryall/Puma City

PIKES PEAK
14,110

Thirtynine Mile Mtn
10,814

Dome Rock

McIntyre Mtn

GILLETTE FLATS

Guffey

Mount Pisgah
10,380

To Colo. Springs

CRIPPLE CREEK

GOLDFIELD
VICTOR

Skagway Reservoir

To Canon City

Fremont County

(Map courtesy the "Ute Pass Courier")

Important dates in the history of Pikes Peak's West Slope

Prehistoric to 1800s — Paleo Indians inhabit Pikes Peak area beginning 11,000 years ago. Tabeguache Utes claim the area as their hunting grounds in historic times.

1779 — August 29. Spanish Governor of New Mexico, Juan Bautista de Anza camps at Florissant while in pursuit of Comanche Chief Cuerno Verde, then proceeds down Ute Pass.

1806 — November 27. Zebulon Pike climbs either Greyback or Blue Mountain, believing he is ascending Pikes Peak. He cannot reach the summit.

1820 — July 14. Dr. James, a member of Major Long's topographical survey party, ascends Pikes Peak.

1846 — George F. Ruxton, a young English adventurer, explores the Pikes Peak region via the Ute Pass Indian Trail.

1857 — Gold is found in the Colorado Rockies, and 100,000 prospectors rush to "Pikes Peak or Bust."

1858 — El Paso City (Colorado City) is founded at the base of Ute Pass.

1858 — The city of Denver is founded at the mouth of Cherry Creek.

1859 — Gold is discovered at "Fair Play".

1859 — Ute Trail is first used as a wagon road.

1861 — February 26. Colorado becomes a territory of the United States, by presidential proclamation.

1862 — United States Congress passes the Homestead Act.

1863 — Chief Ouray and ten other Ute chiefs negotiate the Hunt Treaty to ensure their traditional hunting grounds "forever."

1868 — Gold is discovered in the Central Rockies.

1868 — The Hunt Treaty is modified, and the Utes cede their hunting grounds in the central Rockies and the San Luis Valley. Their remaining lands are ensured "forever."

1870 — June 1. Judge James Castello leaves Fairplay and establishes a Ute trading post on the banks of Twin Creek.

1871 — Gold is discovered near Silverton, in the San Juan Mountains.

1871 — July 31. General Palmer plats Fountain Colony (Colorado Springs).

1872 — September 2. Colorado Springs is incorporated as a town.

1872 — December 21. Judge Castello establishes the Florissant Post Office at Twin Creek.

1873 — September 1. Ferdinand Vandeveer Hayden begins his historic survey of Colorado.

1873 — In the Brunot Treaty, the Utes cede San Juan County (San Juan Mountains) to the United States. Their remaining lands are ensured theirs "forever."

1876 — Colorado becomes a state, thanks to the excitement generated by Hayden's survey.

1879 — September 29. Utes rise up against Agent Meeker on the White River, killing Meeker and nine of his men.

1881 — September. The last of the Utes are forced to leave their ancestral hunting grounds in Colorado for their new reservation assigned under the Ute Agreement of 1880.

1886 — July 16. Construction begins on the Colorado Midland Railroad.

1886 — Cascade is established as a town along the path of the Colorado Midland Railroad.

1890 — The town of Chipita Park is established along the path of the Colorado Midland Railroad.

1890 — Green Mountain Falls is incorporated along the path of the Colorado Midland Railroad. It is named for a series of cascades down the side of nearby Green Mountain.

1890 — October 20. Cowboy Bob Womack discovers gold in Cripple Creek.

1891 — April 5. Florissant's cowboys organize the Cripple Creek Mining District.

1891 — January 21. Summit Park, the stagecoach stop, is formally incorporated as Woodland Park.

1891 — July 7. Florissant becomes an incorporated town.

1891 — A post office is established at George's Lake, and is named Lake George.

1892 — June 9. Hayden Placer is formally incorporated as
Cripple Creek.

1894 — Victor is incorporated the year following its founding
by the Woods brothers, virtually on top of their Gold
Coin Mine.

1895 — Guffey is founded after 1894 labor strike in Cripple
Creek District.

1899 — Crystola is organized by a group of psychics who claim
to locate gold mines by using a crystal.

1969 — August 20. Florissant Fossil Beds National Monument
is established.

1991 — Mueller State Park is established.

CHAPTER ONE

Geography and geology

Nestled in a small valley at the western base of Pikes Peak, about thirty-five miles west of Colorado Springs, eighteen miles north of Cripple Creek, and 8,600 feet above sea level, lies the little mountain town of Florissant, Colorado. It was the first community established in Pikes Peak's backcountry, and sits picturesquely framed by the Peak's western face. Deep green forests of Ponderosa and lodgepole pine drape themselves like a buffalo robe around the bottom of the great mountain. The 14,110-foot summit of the Peak appears much broader from this western perspective. It reveals itself by a sharp, snow-capped, demarcation at timberline— looking very much like a white-cowled chieftain with head bowed and arms outstretched above its pine-treed robe.

Hugging the northern perimeter of the Peak are the towns of Woodland Park (elevation 8,464), Crystola (elevation 7,981), Green Mountain Falls (elevation 7,800), Chipita Park (elevation 7,602), and Cascade (elevation 7,421). They are shadowed by the most dramatic face that the Peak presents; a giant cirque carved by an ancient glacier, with sheer rose-granite walls cloaked in purple shadows most of the year. Newcomers are often surprised that this dome-shaped side view of the chieftain's head is the same mountain they viewed from the 6,000-foot level of Colorado Springs, for it now appears to be all alone. It is a common mistake, for when it is viewed from each new direction, the Peak assumes an entirely different profile. Cheyenne Indians, disoriented after a raid into the Ute's mountain stronghold in the late 1860s, kidnapped early pioneer Sam Hartsel so that he could help them find their way back down Ute Pass.

On the opposite, southern side, of the Peak are the towns that made the Peak notorious—Cripple Creek and Victor, with elevations ranging from 9,494 to 9,780, respectively. But the Peak hides from view in this area, as though unwilling to acknowledge the man-made gashes in its southern girth where its gold-laden rocks spilled fortunes onto now-barren slopes.

Called "El Capitan" by the Ute people, this geographic chieftain dominates the profile of the front range with its lofty pinnacle. There is a price for this prominence, however, for every single drop of rain that falls and every single snowflake that melts searches for the lowlands, leaving their granite birthing place forever. Numerous backcountry streams collect this liquid gold on its journey from the Peak, and thereby provide a natural roadway for the four-leggeds and two-leggeds into the backcountry, for water was indispensable to travel before the automobile.

On the west face, these streams converge in the Florissant Valley to water its grassy meadows and give life to a multitude of high mountain flowers. Principal among these western streams is Twin Creek, which originates above (Hayden) Divide and then carves a dramatic path through the granite walls and boulder fields of Florissant Canyon. In the 1800s, it was known as East Twin Creek, and Witcher Creek (which joins it from north of Florissant) was known as West Twin Creek. Several other streams join the torrent of Twin Creek as it flows westward, until it finally empties its waters into the silvery threads of the South Platte River at Lake George.

On the north face, a small southeasterly creek named Fountain is born in Woodland Park, and is soon joined at Crystola by a new creek of the same name. "Fountain Creek" is the English derivative of the name originally given by French explorers in the late 1700s, "Fountaine Que Bouille" or the Stream that Boils. North and South Catamount creeks then race down the steeply treed north walls of the Peak as they all join in the now rapidly descending Fountain Creek. Various gulches emitting from the steep canyon walls of Ute Pass contribute their collections of water until Fountain Creek tumbles and roils out of the mountains, turning southward at Colorado Springs for an ultimate union with the Arkansas River at the town of Pueblo.

Cripple Creek is perhaps the most famous of the water courses on the south side of the Peak, giving name to the town that has virtually obscured the creek itself. Early pioneers seem to have been hard pressed for original names as they sought to christen the other major water ways draining the Peak's southern slope. East Fourmile Creek (named for its length) gathers the moisture from Mueller State Park, then winds and carves its way south to the Arkansas River. In a seeming act of ingratitude, it is demoted to simply "Fourmile Creek" after carving a path that now hosts the precipitous Shelf Road and providing entree to the rich cache of dinosaur bones at Garden Park, less than twelve miles south of Cripple Creek. Its sister creek, West Fourmile Creek (named for its length), suffers the same ignoble fate after carrying the waters from Thirtynine Mile Mountain (named for its estimated length) and joining East Fourmile below Wright's Reservoir.

Numerical Naming Fever also afflicted the dramatically beautiful Eightmile Creek, host to the Phantom Canyon Road. It, nonetheless, had the good manners to escort the road beneath the towering canyon walls until it freed itself of the mountains and found the plain above Florence, then it emptied itself in the Arkansas River. West Beaver Creek, Middle Beaver Creek, and East Beaver Creek drain the mountainous areas east of Victor and parallel Eightmile Creek on its trip to the Arkansas River. They also reflect a faint, half-hearted recovery from the Numerical Naming Fever.

Florissant Valley rests at an elevation ranging from 8,200 to 9,000 feet, and was formed from prehistoric lake beds. Lake Florissant was formed when the lava and mud flows from the volcano Mt. Guffey (about sixteen miles southwest of Florissant) dammed a south-flowing stream around thirty-five million years ago. (This same volcano also created a caldera similar to Cripple Creek, and now is home to the quaint mining village of Guffey.) The primeval Florissant Valley area is rimmed on the south and west with other ancient volcanos in addition to Mt. Guffey. Among these volcanoes are Mt. Pisgah, Castle Mountain, Saddle Mountain, Thirtynine Mile Mountain, and Black Mountain. Eruptions from these volcanoes were probably short and violent, but they continued over thousands of years, filling the air with dense clouds of dust and fine particles of volcanic ash.

These great ash clouds were swept northwest-ward by the prevailing winds, and much of the ash fell into Lake Florissant, carrying ancient flying insects and foliage to the lake bottom as it settled. As one ash fall succeeded another, layers of paper-thin shale accumulated on the lake bottom, resulting in the excellent array of fossils which can be found there to this day. The perimeter of the lake was also inundated with these deep layers of ash. This silt, coupled with mud flows from the volcanoes, buried the trunks of giant trees from the immense sequoia groves that surrounded the lake thirty-five million years ago. Over the centuries, this mud and silt became shale, with layers up to forty-five feet thick in some places.

As the centuries passed, mineral solutions in the ground water filtered through the silt into the buried trees, silicifying and preserving them for aeons to come. According to the *New York Times*, one of the trees from this "petrified forest" measured seventy-four feet in circumference (at the base) and was sixty feet high when it was discovered in 1874. Experts estimated that the tree was over 500 years old when buried in ash, and that it originally stood about 350 feet high. Early settlers reported that there were as many as sixty of these petrified trees still standing. They also reported that it was difficult to drive a wagon through the "forest" because of the numerous standing and fallen petrified trees. Experts labeled this prehistoric lake and its petrified forest "the greatest fossil field in the world." (This national treasure is now the Florissant Fossil Beds National Monument, detailed in a later chapter.)

In addition to the thousands of fossilized insects, birds and tree foliage, the fossilized remains of an ancient opossum, an oreodont (an extinct family of hoofed mammal), and a primitive horse have also been found at the Florissant Fossil Beds. In her autobiography, early resident Atlanta Long Thompson wrote that in the 1870s her father "was driving across the country one day when he saw some bones sticking out of a big ditch that paralleled the road. He dug them out and found them to be a rib, a tusk, and a tooth of a mastodon [This may actually have been a mammoth]. Scientists said the animal had been thirty feet high." The excitement of the 1994 twenty-fifth anniversary celebration of the Fossil Beds National Monument culminated in the discovery of the remains of a fossilized mammoth that was probably deposited during the Ice Age, and is much younger than the other Florissant fossils. Coupled with the dinosaur remains at Garden Park, these are the only documented instances of large extinct animals in Pikes Peak backcountry, but the area was certainly populated by many other great prehistoric beasts.

Just as the geology and geography of Florissant dictated the amassing of this fossilized wealth of thirty-five million years ago, it has also been the determining factor in the more recent history of Pikes Peak backcountry. About 300 million years ago, most of present-day Colorado lay buried by the waters of a huge inland sea spawned in the Pacific Ocean. These seas retreated about sixty-five to seventy million years ago as the restless earth shifted and thrust upward, creating the great mountain ranges of the American West, including the Rocky Mountains. Colorado's front range, and Pikes Peak, are only a part of this upthrust. Wind, rain, and snow patiently attacked these granite monoliths, and the eroded rock debris was carried hundreds of miles and deposited along the lowlands. Glaciers along the north and east face of Pikes Peak collected billions of snowflakes over thousands of years. Then these powerful snow packs began to sculpt the contours of Pikes Peak around 75,000 years ago. As they crept toward the lowlands, carrying tons of boulders in a frozen, scouring embrace, they ground and carved the fault lines created by the upthrust. This combined action resulted in the steep canyons at the entrance to present-day Ute Pass. Beyond this entrance, the glaciation provided gentle u-shaped valleys leading to the summit of the pass at present-day Divide.

Soil in Pikes Peak's backcountry is granular and red-rust in color, and is flecked with tiny specks of mica. When the winds carry these granules in their twirling dances, the sun catches the mica and gives it the appearance of swirling gold dust in the air. This unique soil is known as Pikes Peak Granite. It is the product of a large bubble of magma which boiled to the earth's surface about one and a half billion years ago. It came to rest about one to three miles below the surface where it cooled and was gradually exposed by erosion.

Then, during what scientists call the Tertiary period, about ten to fifty-five million years ago, a series of explosions from within the earth shattered the granite crust of the Rockies. Pikes Peak was again the center of intense and powerful volcanic activity. Colorado College's late Professor Henry Lamb wrote that "When the eruption occurred, boiling hot water from deep in the Earth percolated to the surface, carrying gold tellurides in a salt solution mixed with quartz and lava. As the substance was disbursed, molten gold was caught in the cracks."

As these series of massive eruptions blew the quartz and lava from the heart of the earth, they gradually built an enormous cone which later collapsed, forming a basin-shaped crater, or caldera, at Cripple Creek. Some scientists estimate the depth of this caldera to be at least 5,000 feet. Later, minor eruptions created a network of channels throughout the area, and these openings became host to the molten gold in the form of the tellurides sylvanite and calaverite. Sylvanite, a silvery telluride of gold mixed with silver, was first found in Transylvania in eastern Europe. Calaverite, named for Calaveras County, California where it was first found, is another of the tellurides of gold mixed with silver.

As the early geographer Ellen Churchill Semple wrote "Geographic conditions influence the economic and social development of a people by the abundance, paucity, or general character of the natural resources, by the local ease or difficulty of securing the necessaries of life, and by the possibility of industry and commerce afforded by the environment." And so the story of Pikes Peak's backcountry is the story of its geography.

Ute Pass (the glacially carved trail on the northern slope of Pikes Peak) provided a natural trail for the buffalo, the Indian, the mountain man, the prospector, the homesteader, the railroad and, later, the automobile. Rich volcanic activity in the region cached the great wealth of gold at Cripple Creek and the world-famous crystals and minerals found throughout the backcountry of the Peak. Shifting tectonic plates thrust up the great Rocky Mountain range, as the elements eroded and exposed the underlying granite. Dome Rock and other grand escarpments are now ensured for the pleasure of future generations as Mueller State Park.

Florissant's prehistoric lake bed evolved into the richly flowered and gently sloping valley of Florissant, and provides a natural passageway connecting the Ute Trail to Cripple Creek in the south. The westward thrust of the valley provides a natural access to the "hunter's paradise" of South Park. This same lake bed and its treasure of fossilized remains ensured its future as the Florissant Fossil Beds National Monument. Geography has written the history of Pikes Peak's backcountry and will, no doubt, continue to dictate her future.

CHAPTER TWO

Evolution of a buffalo track
— The Ute Trail

In the spring of 1839, F.A. Wislizenus, a German doctor who ". . . felt the need of mental and physical recreation", decided to tour the West. He traveled from his new home near St. Louis, Missouri, up the river to Westport. There he bought a horse, a mule, and provisions for his adventure. He then joined a caravan, led by Moses (Black) Harris, which was bound for the fur trappers' rendezvous on the Green River. Dr. Wislizenus kept a diary, *A Journey to the Rocky Mountains 1839* (published in 1840). At its conclusion, he wrote an eloquent prophesy of the impact of "civilization" on the Great West.

> *The ultimate destiny of these wild tribes, now hunting unrestrained through the Far West of the United States, can be foretold almost to a certainty, from the fate, already accomplished, of the eastern Indian tribes, where in the contact of races, true civilization collides with crude forces of nature, the latter must succumb. Civilization, steadily pressing forward toward the West, has driven the Indians step by step before it . . .*
>
> *So the waves of civilization will draw nearer and nearer from the East and from the West, till they cover the sandy plains, and cast their spray on the feet of the Rockies. The few fierce tribes who may have maintained themselves until that time in the mountains, may offer some resistance to the progress of the waves, but the swelling flood will rise higher and higher, till at last they are buried beneath it. The buffalo and the antelope will be buried with them: and the bloody tomahawk will be buried*

7

too. But for all that there will be no smoking of the pipe of peace; for the new generation with the virtues of civilization will bring also its vices. It will ransack the bowels of the mountains to bring to light the most precious of all metals, which, when brought to the light, will arouse strife and envy and all ignoble passions, and the sons of civilization will be no happier than their red brethren who have perished.

Pikes Peak proved to be a vital instrument in effecting the prophecy of Doctor Wislizenus. Pikes Peak is a great, granite monolith on the eastern slope of the Colorado Rockies. It presented an unfaltering beacon to Indians, Spaniards, explorers, mountain men, and early pioneers. Winding along the foot of its northern slope was the Ute Trail, a path of destiny.

A BUFFALO TRAIL

Ute Pass Trail probably had its earliest beginnings as a migratory path for the buffalo of the region, leaving their lush, grassy valleys of South Park during heavy winter snows for the milder winter pastures afforded by Colorado's eastern plains. In his *Journal of Travels Over the Rocky Mountains*, Joel Palmer wrote in 1847:

These (buffalo) *paths are remarkable in their appearance, being about 15 inches wide, and four inches deep, and worn into the soil as smoothly as they could be cut with a spade.*

Dr. Wislizenus also noted the unusual habits of the buffalo.

. . . Where a buffalo herd has grazed for some time the ground is absolutely bare; for what they do not eat is trampled with their ungainly feet. Their bellowing can often be heard for miles. It is deeper and more muffled than that of our cattle, and at a distance not unlike the grunting of a great herd of swine. To their watering places they form narrow paths, over which they leisurely move on, one behind the other. A buffalo region is crossed by such paths in every direction.

In 1820, Major Stephen H. Long, who surveyed parts of Colorado as a topographical engineer, wrote in his journal:

A large and much frequented road passes the springs and enters the mountains, running to the north of the high (Pikes) Peak. It is traveled principally by the bisons, sometimes also by the Indians who penetrate here to the Columbia.

AN INDIAN TRAIL

This trail was of great importance to the Ute Indians as it was one of their major "salt roads." This salt road was integral to trade because it connected the salt beds of the Bayou Salado (South Park) to the trading centers of Taos and Santa Fe.

There is a large body of evidence that the Great Shining Peak was also sacred to the Ute Indians of the area. On Major Long's expedition in the summer of 1820, he noted the large number of Indian beads in the bubbling springs at Manitou. This was again noted by the English explorer George F. Ruxton in 1847. Ruxton wrote:

. . . the basin of the spring (at Manitou) *was filled with beads and wampum, and pieces of red cloth and knives, while the surrounding trees were hung with strips of deerskin, cloth, and moccasons* (sic)*."*

Ute oral tradition further illustrates the spiritual nature which they attributed to Pikes Peak. According to Ute legend, the very birth of their people occurred on Pikes Peak.

In Ute language, the bear is called "quigat," and the name for the shaman or medicine man is "m'sut t'quigat"—"power of the bear." Great Spirit, God the Father, is "Sunawiv." The Bear Dance is the oldest of all the Ute ceremonies and is held each spring when the "bears wake up." Ute legend decrees that the dance was given to the people by their brother, the Bear. Bear Dance steps are an imitation of the bear as he steps forward and backward to thrust at a standing tree. Music for the dance is provided by singers who use notched sticks and a resonator to make a sound like a bear growling. The author wrote the following poem based on a Ute legend of their nation's origins:

THE LEGEND OF PIKES PEAK

Great Spirit labored, turning large stone round and round
'Til blue sky was riven by gaping hole that he had ground.

Then down thru this funnel he poured mud, snow and trees;
Thus a great mountain grew with slopes carved by breeze.

Peak's earthen flesh sparkled with tiny stars from above
And shone a deep rust red, reflecting Sunawiv's love.

Flowers danced thru meadows and bathed their face in sun,
While Cloud People hovered to be near the bright Sacred One.

Then Great Spirit smiled, as he gazed on his tall Peak
While his beautiful daughter frolicked along a lazy creek.

She gathered fragrant blossoms in a hug to her chest,
Then lay by cool, swirling waters for a sweet, dreamy rest.

Brother Grizzly Bear saw her, in tall grass where she lay
And with plans to seduce her, he slowly lumbered her way.

A dark, handsome warrior, with long, silky hair of brown,
Made love to this comely maiden in her bower on the ground.

And when he rose from her, she cried and leapt to her feet —
In horror she saw a great, dark Grizzly in a hasty retreat.

The Ute, her dusky children, all have dark and silky hair —
To walk on all fours is how Sunawiv punished Quigat, bear.

Mountaintops are thought to have strong spiritual powers among indigenous peoples, including the Utes. Modern scientists have documented highly unusual electromagnetic phenomena on these high peaks, lending further credibility to these traditional teachings. According to Ute elders, one of their principal ceremonies is the "Vision Quest," undertaken by an individual on a mountain peak for several days in seclusion and while fasting. During this quest, it is thought that the individual will be given spiritual guidance from the Great Spirit through visions. Pikes Peak was a special focal point for the Ute's Ceremonial Circle, an organization of holy people. This group made periodic journeys to nearby Crystal Peak where they collected stones thought to be imbued with spiritual properties. They then began a pilgrimage to Pikes Peak, following the trail along the mountain ridge, where they finally encamped in the area of the Pancake Rocks. Prayer Trees—pine saplings that were bent over and tied with a leather thong—still provide silent testimony to the prayers offered during the course of this pilgrimage along Cedar Mountain Road. One individual was then chosen to take all of the spirit stones to the summit of the Peak on a four-day Vision Quest.

Colorado's Ute Indians jealously guarded their buffalo trail to South Park, building a series of small, circular forts of rough rock, without mortar, and about chest high throughout Pikes Peak's backcountry. One of the best known of these is on Fortification Hill in Florissant, however there were also "forts" in the Phantom Canyon near Soda Mountain; on High Park Road near High Creek; in the Tarryall River Valley; and several near the entrance to Ute Pass.

Florissant's Ute "fort" is located on a hill within the town limits, where it is supposed that the Indians fought bloody and desperate battles years ago. In the 1889 *History of the Line*, published by the Colorado Midland Railway, it was written of Fortification Hill that:

> *All over the hill are breastworks built of rocks, just as the Indians left them, and on the side in a large rock is what has been named The Mortise. This is a deep, smooth hole cut into solid rock. It is about 18 inches in diameter and 3 feet deep, and is suppose to have been cut by the Indians to hold water during a battle in which they might be besieged for several days.*

In a story for the *Gazette Telegraph* in 1936, C.S. Dudley wrote that:

> *Early settlers reported that there was a wall around the east and northern slope of the* (Fortification) *hill part way up from the bottom. It was a dry wall of rocks, piled one*

11

upon another. Charles Fry, a pioneer farmer of the Divide-Florissant region, who came there in 1890, says he remembers this wall; that in fact, he hauled some of the rock in it away, to be used for bridge abutments. Some of this rock also probably went into buildings in Florissant.

John Felter, in his book *The Pikes Peak People*, wrote that the Utes were reported to have built many of these rock forts along the course of the Ute Trail beginning with an area near Fountain Creek. He notes that these forts had circular walls built of rough rock, without mortar, and that they were about breast-high. These fortifications were just large enough for three to four individuals. Early residents of the area reportedly found numerous Indian arrows and other artifacts in these forts.

Irving Howbert (1846-1934, *Memories of a Lifetime in the Pikes Peak Region*) wrote that there was good reason for the Utes to need such fortifications.

Every year, as far back as history or tradition goes, as soon as spring opened and grass was abundant, large parties from different tribes of the plains came marching in, and, after making their usual offerings at the "Boiling Springs," continued on up through Ute Pass into the mountains. There the Utes usually were waiting for them, whereupon a succession of battles between the contending tribes would take place, with success generally on the side of the Utes, who were the better fighters.

Kit Carson and a young man who was his foster son, Will Drannan, were to witness the final battle between the Utes and the Comanches that took place on the meadow adjacent to Fortification Hill.

In June 1870, Judge James Castello moved from Fairplay to the junction of East and West Twin creeks and established a small ranch and trading post at the western base of Fortification Hill. Judge Castello was a trusted friend of the Utes, and was well acquainted with their famous Chief, Ouray. Mrs. Castello often had fifteen or twenty Indians at her table at one time, and they gave her the name of "Heap Big Rocky

Underwood @ Underwood, circa 1860
Giant ten- and sometimes twenty-ox teams often were needed to pull supply
wagons over the most difficult sections of the Ute Pass Wagon Road.

Mountain Biscuit." Another of the Ute chiefs to call the
Castellos "friend" was old Chief Colorow, who instructed Mrs.
Castello to send smoke signals from Fortification Hill if ever
she needed his assistance. Mrs. Castello was frequently presented with blankets, buffalo robes, and tanned deerskins by
her Indian friends.

13

Wagons head east, nose-to-tail down Ute Pass. Eastbound wagons used the trail in the afternoon. Mornings were reserved for westbound traffic.

Florissant Valley was one of the favored camping grounds of the Utes until their forced relocation onto the reservations in Utah and southern Colorado in 1880. In the winter of 1874-1875, for example, Chief Ouray and his band of 600 Tabeguache Utes camped near Florissant for several months. Atlanta Long Thompson wrote that although the Utes were peaceful, their appearance would strike terror in one's heart. Their straight, black hair always had a brightly colored hawk or eagle feather in it and their cheeks were marked with a thin vertical streak of vivid yellow and flaming red paint. Mrs. Thompson noted that the Ute camps were "very colorful because every tepee had a figure of a warrior or horse painted on one or both sides of it with the bright red, green, yellow paint that only the Indians know how to make. They usually chose a level place near a little stream where they pitched their tepees . . ."

TRAIL TO THE GOLD FIELDS

Ute Trail, or the Ute Pass Wagon Road, was the principal thoroughfare to the gold and silver strikes in Central Colorado, with ample wood and water along the way. Gold strikes in Colorado's central mountains netted between 50,000 to 70,000 prospectors along the Ute Trail in 1859 alone. The Ute Trail was used primarily because the other two main roads into the gold fields were toll roads.

First among these new toll roads was the Apex and Gregory Road, constructed in the winter of 1859-60, which led to the gold fields of Black Hawk and Central City. Tolls for this road were twenty-five cents for a wagon and team, ten cents for a horse, and five cents for each head of cattle. The second of these roads was the Denver, Auraria, and South Park Road which crossed over the Platte about eight miles south of Denver, and then proceeded west into the mountains. The toll for this second road was $1.50, equivalent to the wages from a day and a half of work for the average man.

Ute Pass Trail into South Park therefore became the favored route for the prospectors headed for the gold camps. Ute Pass Trail was a very difficult road at this time, and most supplies had to be packed in on mules. Gold seekers had to leave their wagons and teams in Colorado City, at the base of the Pass,

15

then buy mules and supplies before heading up the pass to the gold fields. As a result, Colorado City experienced an economic boom.

In the summer of 1860, the Colorado (City) Town Company appointed a Mr. Bott to build a new wagon road. He was asked to build the road as straight as possible, as it sometimes took as many as twenty yoke of oxen to pull a single wagon over sections of the pass. In the fall of 1860, Governor Denver of the Kansas Territory (which included Colorado) decreed that Ute Pass would also be a toll road. A cabin and toll gate were built (some report that it was staffed by the famous "Uncle Dick" Wootton) and travelers were charged one dollar per team. The citizens of Colorado City were outraged, however, and a group of vigilantes soon ran the would-be toll keepers out of town!

Colorado Springs pioneer Irving Howbert traveled the improved road with his father in 1861, and wrote that "from Denver to Hamilton our route was the same (Ute Pass Wagon Road) that father and I had gone over the year before, but in the meantime the road had been materially improved. It was not nearly so rough, and many bridges had been put in, which made travel much pleasanter (sic)."

In 1860, a reporter for the *Rocky Mountain Herald* wrote:

The new free road lately completed from this city
(Colorado City) *to the Park, Blue and Snowy Range.*
Diggings is the choicest, the finest, the most level,
and the best constructed for horse, carriage or heavy
wagon travel that there is in the country.

Ute Pass Wagon Road was so narrow, however, and traffic on it was so heavy that only westbound horses and wagons were allowed out of Colorado Springs up until noon each day, when the directions were reversed and only eastbound traffic was allowed. In 1872, a new wagon road up the pass was completed (bypassing much of the early Ute Trail for the first thirteen miles), and it was estimated that about 12,000 horses and mules transported freight through the pass to the gold fields each year.

In addition to its use as a freight road, the Ute Pass Wagon Road was also heavily used by stagecoaches. There were at least three coaches each week that traveled the road from Colorado Springs to Fairplay in the 1870s. Among the companies operating these stage lines were the McLaughlin's, the South Park Stage Company (Spotswood and McClelland's) and Wells Fargo and Company. Stage stops for these lines were located along the Ute Pass Wagon Road about twelve to fifteen miles apart to allow for changes of horses. (These stage stations also served as polling places during elections.)

THE RAILROADS

In 1870, General William J. Palmer, who was to found Colorado Springs in 1871, organized the Denver & Rio Grande Railroad, and in 1871 began construction on that line. When the Denver & Rio Grande finally reached Leadville (by a southerly route through Pueblo and Canon City) in 1880, freighting on the Ute Pass Wagon Road declined rapidly. It was about this time that the idea of a railroad through Ute Pass was born. Colorado Midland Railroad Company (CMRR) was organized in 1883 by the owners of Aspen's Robert E. Lee Mine. Their project lay dormant until 1886, however, when James J. Hagerman (owner of Aspen's Gibson Mine) became enthused with the idea and raised the money needed to build the railroad.

Construction began on the Colorado Midland in 1886, and a heated competition with the Denver & Rio Grande ensued to see which would be the first to reach the rich silver mines of Aspen. New towns—Cascade, Chipita Park, Green Mountain Falls, and Manitou (Woodland) Park—were spawned every few miles as the railroad clung to the granite walls of Ute Pass and then climbed into Pikes Peak's backcountry. In March 1887, construction of the Colorado Midland had already reached Florissant, but it did not arrive in Aspen until January 1888, sixty days after the Denver & Rio Grande.

Colorado Midland Railroad was the first standard gauge railroad to penetrate the steep mountain grades of Colorado's Rockies. Hagerman bought twenty-two locomotives, thirty-five passenger cars, and 1,000 freight cars for his new line. The

17

Midland consisted of over 300 miles of track, with some sections of four percent grade where it crossed the Continental Divide at 12,000 feet.

In 1891, gold was discovered in Cripple Creek, and the rush was on. Until the coming of three railroads into Cripple Creek, led by the Florence & Cripple Creek Railroad in 1894, the major transportation route for the miners and their supplies was via the Colorado Midland Railroad into Florissant, and then by stage and wagon into the new mining district.

John Hundley operated the first stage line from Florissant to Fremont (Cripple Creek), and the charge was $10 for each passenger. After Hundley started his stage line, his transportation business developed into the most remarkable stage road in the world. Eight thousand pounds of express were tugged daily over the hills and through the ravines to the gold field. Each day, fifteen six-horse Concord stages transported passengers and mail eighteen miles south to the gold strike.

In addition to the Hundley Stage Line, Alonzo Welty operated a "rickety stage" to Cripple Creek, with huge quantities of beer for the miners as his main cargo. Passengers on the eighteen-mile ride to Cripple Creek were usually afforded a break at the Welty Ranch on Fourmile Creek.

In their haste to lay track for the Colorado Midland into Aspen, the engineers made an error in going over Hayden Divide, rather than going around it. This haste proved fatal to the railroad in later years. The steep three percent and four percent grades into and out of the Florissant area could have been avoided had the Midland tracks been laid in a circuitous route to the south on a more level grade. Morris Cafky, in his book *Colorado Midland Railroad,* gives a studied opinion on this error in railroad engineering.

> . . . *West of Divide, the theoretical line that should have been built probably would also have remained at a higher elevation, avoiding the steep drop into Florissant and Lake George. The maximum grade on both sides of Heyden [sic] Divide could probably have been held at 2%. But such a line was not to be. The die was cast for a steep Ute Pass location, and excessive amounts of coal and water were to*

be shot out of the stacks of laboring engines until the last flag was whistled in . . .

Pikes Peak's backcountry would have had an entirely different history if sound construction principles had been followed in the building of the CMRR tracks. As it was, a few fateful decisions by the CMRR assured its own demise nearly forty years later. The straighter tracks of the CMRR were placed so as to find their way into the Twin Creek (Florissant) Canyon, and then directly into the south edge of the town of Florissant. The railroad brought an influx of operating personnel, their families, and a need for more housing and business—all of which radically changed the little, secluded town of Florissant. Fortunately, there are a few crisp, first-hand recollections of those booming railroad days. Morris Cafky has collected some of these colorful stories, including the following by Dr. H.A. Burton, in *Colorado Midland Railroad.*

> *From the time the Midland was built until it closed in August 1918, Florissant, Colorado was a busy little village which served as a helper engine station on the railroad as well as a trading center for nearby ranchers. Six helper engines were stationed at Florissant. Two of them were big 200 series 2-8-0's and the rest were 4-6-0 freight engines. The 200's were used to help eastbound trains up the 3% grade from Florissant to Divide. The smaller ten wheelers helped westward trains—two helper locomotives to the train. Sometimes the 4-6-0's would help a west-bound freight to Bath, cut off and return light to Florissant. The freight would go on and pick up two more helpers at Wild Horse for the balance of the journey to Leadville. On other occasions, the Wild Horse helpers would be busy helping eastbound trains up Trout Creek to Bath, or on Leadville turns. In such cases, the two Florissant helpers would assist their train all the way to Leadville.*

By the turn of the century, one narrow gauge and two standard gauge railroads were transporting the majority of the freight into and out of Cripple Creek. The heyday of Florissant, and the other towns spawned by the CMRR as it climbed up

Ute Pass, was over. Florissant gradually reverted to being simply the principle depot for the CMRR for the route between Colorado Springs and Buena Vista. But Cascade, Chipita Park, Green Mountain Falls and Woodland Park tenuously held onto the economy as mountain resort towns. Divide was spared, for it had wisely played host for the Midland Terminal Line in 1895—the southern spur of the railroad into Cripple Creek.

Then, in 1907, two cataclysmic events shook the economy of Florissant. Half of the town's business district burned to the ground, and a large coal mine near Glenwood Springs was abandoned, seriously depleting the now precarious freighting business of the CMRR.

The *Gazette-Telegraph* (January 17, 1907) reported on the fire at Florissant.

Fire early last evening destroyed half the business section of Florissant, 37 miles west of Colorado Springs on the Colorado Midland railroad. Nine buildings on the west side of Castello street, the main street of the village, were burned to the ground, but the flames were stayed before they had caused further destruction. It was feared for a time that the entire town would be wiped out.

The damage is estimated at nearly $20,000. Practically all of the burned buildings were the property of Daniel Nevitt, one of the pioneers of the region. Only one of the buildings was protected by insurance, this being the residence of Robert Markle, on which there was $1,000 insurance. The fire originated at 7:00 o'clock from a defective flue in Nevitt's general merchandise store and lasted for two hours. No one was injured.

Beginning in Nevitt's general merchandise store, on the corner, the fire swept the entire block. There is no organized fire department in the town, and although most of the citizens organized themselves into a bucket brigade to fight the flames, the best they could do was to prevent the fire from spreading across the street and from reaching the residence section. All of the buildings in the block were frame and the flames consumed them rapidly. None of the merchandise or contents of the buildings were saved.

20

*The buildings burned were Nevitt Mercantile company
store, containing a stock invoiced at $7,000, the Florissant
hotel, a billiard hall, restaurant conducted by Mary Engle,
livery barn, saloon and three dwelling houses, besides a
couple of barns. These compose the entire block opposite
the Midland station. On the other side of the street were
the buildings of the Florissant Mercantile company, owned
by F.F. Castello of this city and managed by Charles
McLaughlin and James Horrigan; Allen's drug store and
the post office. None of these buildings were damaged.*

*Mr. Nevitt, who is the heaviest sufferer from the fire, is
well known in Colorado Springs and throughout El Paso
and Teller counties. He is one of the earliest settlers in the
Pikes Peak region, having lived here for the last 37 years.
. . The fire destroyed the largest part of Mr. Nevitt's property in Florissant, although he still owns other property in
the vicinity . . .*

*F.F. Castello, who is largely interested in the town, but
whose interests were not harmed by the fire, last night
expressed great regret upon learning the news of the disaster. "I am particularly sorry for Mr. Nevitt," he said. "He
is one of the pioneers of the region, and the loss will be a
hard one both for him and for the town.*

In addition to the devastating fire and the closing of the coal
mine at Glenwood Springs, there was more bad news for
Florissant. The Denver & Rio Grande Railroad installed an
improved standard gauge system into central Colorado. This
eliminated the expensive process of transferring freight from
their narrow gauge line onto and off other standard gauge lines,
and greatly increased the Denver & Rio Grande's share of business. Previously, this had been one of the biggest advantages of
shipping freight through the mountains on the CMRR. With
this triple blow, the CMRR now began to experience serious
financial difficulties.

On April 21, 1917, A.E. Carlton (of Cripple Creek fame) and
his business associates bought the Colorado Midland Railroad
at a receiver's sale for $1,425,000. Carlton began an ambitious
rehabilitation program for the line in an attempt at

revitalization. In the midst of this plan, the United States became embroiled in World War I. It was at this point that a governmental agency—the United States Railroad Administration—charged with controlling all railroad transportation, supplied a fatal overdose of "medication" for the ailing CMRR. Government officials had determined that the short route, from Colorado Springs to Grand Junction over the CMRR line, would provide the most efficient route for transporting troops and military supplies through Colorado.

In January 1918, the government plan was put into operation. It was doomed from the start, however, by that fatal design flaw of the too-steep grades. Colorado Midland Railroad engines were already overtaxed by the grueling mountain terrain, and could not effectively pull the added freight cars. By the middle of 1918, both ends of the CMRR line, and all side trackage between, were literally choked with stranded rolling stock. The government reacted by utilizing more reliable, though longer, railroad lines. Secretary McAdoo decreed that the railroad must cease operations, as it was uneconomical and unnecessary during the then all-out war effort. The last CMRR passenger train ran from Grand Junction to Colorado Springs on August 14, 1918. Carlton vainly tried to save at least the tracks, but a legal ruling required that they be pulled to satisfy debtors. Therefore, all of the rails were pulled in 1921. It now became necessary for the citizens of Florissant, and other towns along the abandoned line, to revert to the use of wagons and wagon roads for communication and transportation.

Once again, nature seemed to conspire with the ill fate of the CMRR as it had done in 1907, and in that same year (1921) Florissant was devastated by severe snowstorms and an ice over-flow from the normally placid Twin Creek. This ice flow destroyed most of the homes situated along the northern bank of the stream. The snows were so deep that year that Florissant was snowbound for nearly sixty days.

C.S. Dudley of the *Gazette-Telegraph* (4/18/1937) wrote of that terrible winter in 1921:

> . . . *South of the present Divide-Florissant road, which is the abandoned Colorado Midland grade, is the old*

highway (now Upper Twin Rocks Road) *where Charles Fry, one of the oldest residents left in the Florissant district, one winter kept the town of Florissant in provisions when a terrific storm had it all but snowbound for sixty days, by freighting from Divide with a three-horse spike team and farm wagon over packed snow, and with banks on each side so high he could hardly see over them. At Divide lives George Pierce, the only other man who traveled that snow-banked road at that time, carrying the mail, and going on horseback when he could not get his wagon farther, often arriving at Florissant many hours overdue, exhausted and all but frozen. There used to be snowstorms that were snowstorms in the region of upper Ute Pass.*

With these crippling blows from Mother Nature, coupled with the demise of the Colorado Midland Railroad, Florissant and her sister towns once again slipped into near oblivion. In 1939, the state highway department built Highway 24 along much of the old Midland railbed. Despite this improved access, however, most of the towns along the Ute Pass Wagon Road languished. Florissant even allowed its once-cherished incorporated status to lapse about this same period.

Little happened in Pikes Peak backcountry for over thirty years. Then, in 1969, the Florissant Fossil Beds National Monument was established. And in 1991, the 12,103-acre Mueller State Park was created just a few miles east of the Fossil Beds. These two attractions alone draw over 400,000 visitors up Ute Pass each year. Florissant's sister cities—Cascade, Chipita Park, Green Mountain Falls, Crystola, Woodland Park, Divide and Lake George—along the Colorado Midland railbed were reinvigorated in 1991 when limited gaming was approved for the old mining town of Cripple Creek. Then, in 1993, Florissant was designated as the northern gateway for the Gold Belt Scenic Byways Tour.

It is the geography of Pikes Peak backcountry that has generated this rebirth. And there is little doubt that geography will dictate the future of the area, just as it has written the past.

Pikes Peak Library District

Colorado Midland locomotive No. 14 races a Model T Ford up Ute Pass Canyon. The train probably won the race but the automobile eventually replaced it. Highway 24 was built on the old railroad roadbed in 1939.

CHAPTER THREE

Prehistoric and indigenous people of west Pikes Peak

PREHISTORIC MAN

In an archaeological survey of the Florissant Fossil Beds performed in 1974, numerous prehistoric projectile points were recovered—some dating from at least 10,000 years ago. In a similar survey in 1981 of Mueller State Park, a prehistoric "manufacturing" site was found. Lithic, or stone, scatter consisting of hammer stones, projectiles, and scraping tools was found, giving evidence of prehistoric (about 11,000 years old) stone tool manufacture. This is in addition to a prehistoric rock shelter found nearby, complete with its ancient fire pit and remnants of the meals cooked there.

Through these surveys, and the presence of various fossilized animal remains, we know that prehistoric man was hunting mammoth, bison, and horse on the west slope of Pikes Peak about 5,000 years before the Egyptians even thought of building the great Pyramid at Giza.

Scientists are just beginning to understand that prehistoric man not only traveled through the high mountains of Colorado, but also lived at these altitudes. Geologist Ernst Antevs has proposed that this high-altitude living was the result of what he termed an "altithermal" period in the earth's weather patterns. During this period, the climate became much drier and warmer than at the present time, making life at high altitudes (such as Florissant) more attractive than life on the dry, dusty plains. Many noted anthropologists agree with this theory.

In October 1993, the Colorado Springs *Gazette Telegraph* reported that the skeleton of a prehistoric man, about 8,000 years old, had been found in a cave on the White River in Northwestern Colorado. In the story, the *Telegraph* quoted Dr. Patty Jo Watson, an anthropologist, as saying that " . . . it's becoming apparent from this discovery and other archaeology that some of these ancient people had learned to live and work at extremely high altitudes."

Prehistoric people were hunters and gathers. They subsisted on a diet of wild game and whatever edible wild plants were indigenous to their current area of occupation. These early inhabitants depended on the herds of large animals not only for food, but also for sinew (used in sewing animal hides and fashioning weapons), and animal hides (used for clothing and shelter.) During the "altithermal hiatus," the Florissant Valley, Fourmile and Woodland Park areas, as well as other nearby high mountain valleys, would have provided all of these things, in addition to another key element for survival—quartz.

Quartz was the primary resource for making projectile points, knives, scrapers, awls and other Stone Age tools. Quartz has a hardness of seven on the mineral scale of hardness ranging from one to ten. Quartz is harder than the best grades of ordinary steel, which register at only about six on the scale. Quartz does not break easily, and is very tough under impact. Because of these attributes, quartz made an ideal projectile point for the deadly spears launched by early man's atlatl. This spear had a quartz projectile on one end. A short stick was then fitted with a hook made of antler or bison tooth, creating the atlatl. The flat end of the spear shaft was fitted into this hook. A flick of the hunter's wrist and arm while holding the atlatl would then send his spear hurtling toward its target much as a slingshot hurtles a stone.

Quartz, composed of silicon and oxygen, is an igneous material, resulting from volcanic activity. Pikes Peak's backcountry was a virtual cauldron of volcanic activity, resulting in numerous quartz outcroppings throughout the area. A number of prehistoric quartz quarries and workshops have been documented north of the Florissant Fossil Beds National Monument. In 1935, archaeologist Etienne B. Renaud (of the University of Denver) conducted a survey of the area and reported that the "most common type of site is the old campsite, with frequently an adjacent workshop."

Renaud also documented workshop sites within the Fossil Beds itself, "primarily on the sides of the main valley. They are frequently located on open terraces above drainages and, generally, provide a good view of the valley." Renaud reported that the lithic scatter at these sites was basically all "pure quartz, smoky quartz, quartzite, chert (a variety of crystalline silica), petrified wood, and chalcedony (milky or grayish quartz)." Since the soil in the Florissant Valley consists primarily of volcanic welded tuff material, prehistoric man must have collected this quartz from nearby quarries and then carried it to his scenic workshops to be fashioned into arrowheads, spear heads, hide scrapers, and knives.

Unfortunately, there has never been a comprehensive archaeological survey of the Pikes Peak area as a whole. However, archaeologists have documented other, similar, high-altitude quartz quarries throughout Colorado. The most recent of these was a site near Steamboat Springs where artifacts indicated mining activity from at least 8,000 years ago (according to the September 1993 *Gazette Telegraph* story).

Near the dawn of the Christian Era, the life of prehistoric man began subtly changing as new influences filtered up from Mexico, New Mexico and Arizona. Contemporaneous with the Anasazi culture—whose beautiful architecture can be seen in the ruins of Mesa Verde, Bandelier, and Chaco Canyon—are the Fremont Indians. The Fremont culture manifested itself around 650 A.D., and then mysteriously disappeared around 1250 A.D. In *The Archaeology of Colorado*, Cassells speculates that the Fremont man probably melted into the Ute Indians. Fremonts are thought to have occupied most of Utah and Northwestern Colorado. Scientists speculate that the 8,000 - year-old body of the prehistoric man found in the White River National Forest (referred to in an earlier paragraph) was possibly a Fremont ancestor of Colorado's Ute Indians.

Fremont Indians practiced horticulture to some extent, although hunting and gathering were still an integral part of their lifestyle. One fascinating aspect of the Fremont culture is the use of rock shelters. These consisted of dry-laid masonry granaries, shelters, and fortifications. The chest-high, circular rock structures of four- to five-foot diameter bear a striking resemblance to the remains of similar structures on Florissant's Fortification Hill. Archaeologists have not documented the presence of Fremont people any further east of Utah than Grand Junction, but the similarities are intriguing. Only a full archaeological survey of Pikes Peak's backcountry will reveal the truth.

THE UTE INDIANS

According to archaeologist E. Steve Cassells, the Utes were probably the earliest historic inhabitants of western Colorado, including Pikes Peak's backcountry.

> ...A probable reference to them by the Spanish in 1626 and a treaty in 1680 make them the earliest historically documented aboriginal group in western Colorado. An early history of New Mexico by Fray Pasados places them on the plains with the Apaches and probably in the area north of the San Juan (in the region west of Pikes Peak) and as far west as the Great Salt Lake. There is little reason to doubt subsequent accounts, including that of Dominguez and Escalante in 1775-76, which portray the Utes as the sole aboriginal inhabitants of western Colorado in historic times.

Ute legend further corroborates the prehistory of their tribe as outlined on the preceding pages, verifying the theories of anthropologists, archaeologists, and historians. This legend was recorded by T.F. Dawson and F.J.V. Skiff in the book *The Ute War*, first published in 1879.

> This legend is to the effect that the forefathers of the tribe, long years ago, lived near a vast warm lake northeast of the Big River (the Colorado); that the country was warm, full of big trees and big deer and big oxen with white horns (mammoths?); that big fishes and snakes as long as an hundred lodge poles abounded in this lake; that one day all the big oxen began to roar together, and that

they raised such a steam from their nostrils that the earth reeled and the sun was obscured; that suddenly the lake fell, and continued falling for three moons, and then became so much reduced that they knew it not any more, but that the big lake they found had been drained away to the south, and that its warm water had gone out through the mountains, the present canyon of the Green River and of the Big River (the Colorado); *and that this old bed in the Toom-pin-to-weep, as they call the stream, is where the lake waters were drained. They also say that the story goes on that all the big deer and the big oxen with white horns strayed away eastward, and all perished in the mountains from cold or by the arrows of the Ute hunters; that soon after a big flood formed Grand River Canyon, and after this flood came a small race of people who had skin canoes, and who brought seed corn of a small kind, called in Spanish chiquito maze; that these people were almost white, and that they taught the Utes how to make good spears and bows and earthenware; that they built stone houses in the cliffs, and cultivated pumpkins, corn and beans; that they had silver and gold in abundance, and iron tools that they had obtained in the mountains to the northeast; that afterwards, from the northwest, came big red Indians over to this country and killed and drove off the little people, who finally all went south, as well as the big red men, who are the Apaches, Navahoes and Kiowas. They also say that the big oxen with white horns, the grande lagarios* (probably alligators), *were found down among the Apache and Navajo Indians, but that by and by the country became dryer and colder, and the Utes only were left on the Big River and its branches; that melted rocks were poured out everywhere and left the country desolate, and that the little people had told their forefathers that where they came from were big waters, and in these waters were men with bodies like a fish. They say that in this old river bed is plenty of gold, but that it is sure death for any one to go into the canyon to get it.*

Prior to the settling of New Mexico's San Juan Pueblo by the Spanish in 1598 (nine years before the British established the Plymouth and Jamestown colonies), the Ute were a nomadic people who subsisted on roots, berries, fish and game. They lived in small family groups, spread across most of Colorado, eastern Utah, and northern New Mexico. This widely dispersed population did not mandate a cohesive political structure, and so there was none. Long before they discovered the many uses of Spanish horses, the Utes used domesticated dogs to transport their goods as they followed the migrating herds of buffalo, or to carry their goods to the different trading centers such as Taos. *The Southern Utes*, a tribal history, records the observations of an early Spaniard (1500s), Vicente de Zaldivar, who wrote of the colorful scene presented by the Utes and their dogs of burden:

> *It is a sight worth seeing and very laughable to see them* (the Utes) *traveling, the ends of the* (tepee) *poles dragging on the ground, nearly all of them* (the dogs) *snarling in their encounter, to load them the Indian women seize their heads between their knees and thus load them or adjust the load, which is seldom required, because they travel along at a steady gait as if they had been trained by means of a rein.*

Colorado's high mountain valleys and lush green plains were connected by a web of migratory trails developed by the buffalo. Certain of these trails were highly frequented by the Utes as they carried meat, hides, tallow, suet, and salt to trade with other Indians at the continental crossroads of Taos and Santa Fe. These primary trails were called "salt trails," and knowledge of their routes was a vital commodity. (Proper usage of salt was the only means that early people had of preserving their food over long periods of time.) These salt trails were noted by their unique landmarks, and their precise courses were committed to verses called "Journeysongs," a verbal type of trail map. These Journeysongs had a worth of their own, and so were traded along with other valuables of the Indian buckskin economy.

30

The hunting and gathering lifestyle of the Utes changed dramatically, however, with the acquisition of the horse from the early Spanish settlers. In 1637, there was an armed conflict between the Utes and the Spanish which was fought by both parties on horseback. The Spanish prevailed, and about eighty Utes were taken prisoner and held as slaves in Santa Fe. This seems to be the earliest documented use of the horse by the Utes. Later, in 1659, Ute raiding parties captured more than 300 horses from Spanish settlements in northern New Mexico. These horses were driven to the Ute strongholds in the Shining Mountains of Colorado. Both of these instances would seem to argue that the Ute had become expert horsemen by the first half of the 1600s. Some historians argue that the Ute did not acquire the horse until the 1700s. However, these two well-documented instances attest to their acquisition of the horse much earlier. In fact, it would appear from this documentation that the Utes were probably the first of the North American Indians to acquire the horse. It is even quite probable that the Utes had mastered the horse much earlier—in the late 1500s.

This hypothesis is supported by a legal agreement between the Utes and the Spanish within the terms of an interesting land control system, the *encomienda*. Encomienda was introduced by the first Spanish Governor of New Mexico, Don Juan De Onate, in 1598. Under this system, certain prominent Spaniards were granted authority over large sections of land. Their responsibility was to take care of the indigent Indians and to teach them Catholicism. They, in turn, were to supply men and *horses* when military protection was needed. This agreement, then, would imply that the Utes were already proficient at breeding and riding horses by 1598.

The Utes were noted as superb horsemen, and it was this love of horses that later proved so calamitous in the events of 1879. Marshall Sprague writes in *Massacre* of the Utes' horse mastership.

No less authorities on equines than Frank Gilbert Roe and J. Frank Dobie have written that the Colorado Utes were among the first, if not the very first, North American horse Indians. Roe has stressed that most Indians who took on horses were not intrinsically altered by them. But in contrast to most, the imaginations of the Utes were fired by horses to such a pitch as to completely change their tribal personality . . .

It was wonderful how well it worked out for the Utes. Decade by decade, the use of horses passed from Ute family to Ute family, northwesterly along their Rocky Mountain corridor, across the magnificent divides of Western Colorado and over the Uncompahgre-Tabeguache Plateau into Utah. In the process, they made a discovery; the high valleys which nobody else had wanted contained grasses of very high protein content. Using these grasses for forage, they developed a pinto pony fourteen hands high—wiry, self-supporting, sure-footed, requiring no care, and so strong as to wear out two Rio Grande horses.

There was another nutrient in these high mountain grasses that proved even more desirable than protein. It was silica. Silica is one of nature's building blocks, a mineral that vitalizes the body of horse and man by strengthening the connective tissue, skin, hair, nails and hooves. This same silica, produced by volcanic activity, is the mineral responsible for petrifying the giant sequoias in the Florissant Valley. With the ingestion of silica-rich native grasses and water, these Indian ponies became noted for their sinews and hooves of steel, and their great strength and endurance.

There were numerous conflicts between the Indians and the early Spanish settlers, and the Indians that escaped sought the safety of the mountains of Southern Colorado. In addition, the Ute began to raid the Spanish villages in New Mexico. Blooded Spanish horses were the highly valued bounty from these raids. Horse "stealing" imparted an entirely different cultural meaning among the Ute than in the Euro-American culture. Utes considered that Great Spirit placed the four-leggeds upon the earth first in order to teach two-leggeds how to live. Therefore, the same natural law that compelled bull elk to "steal" cows from one another compelled the Utes to "steal" horses, for they were the "things by which men live."

Although the Spanish gave spirited pursuit, they were not always successful in recapturing their livestock. It was probably during these skirmishes between Indian and Spanish, and between Indian and Indian, that many of the prized Spanish horses were set free upon the mountain meadows of New Mexico and Colorado. Our modern horse is not indigenous to North America, even though the remains of prehistoric horses have been found all over the continent. Therefore, some of Colorado's beautiful wild mustangs are most probably the progeny of these wild blooded Spanish horses. In fact, the term mustang is derived from the Spanish word *mesteno*, which means an unbranded horse.

These mustangs thrived in the mountains and on the plains of Colorado. General Palmer, the founder of Colorado Springs, wrote of seeing three large herds of these wild horses on his trip to the Pikes Peak area in 1869. Irving Howbert, another of Colorado Springs' founding fathers (1846-1934) wrote with a pioneer's appreciation of the wild mustangs in his *Memories of a Lifetime in the Pike's Peak Region.*

> *Up to the time of the founding of Colorado Springs, there were large herds of wild horses in the eastern part of El Paso County and adjacent country. Many attempts were made from time to time to capture them by use of pitfalls and other devices, but these efforts seldom were successful. One method tried with some success was to have mounted men stationed in relays at intervals of several miles over a long distance, to run down the wild horses. One of the horsemen would start the herd running at full speed in the intended direction and follow it; as the herd passed by the first relay man, the pursuer would drop out and the other, with a fresh horse, would take his place. This continued until the end of the line was reached. Then, if possible, the herd was turned back and the men who had dropped out would take up the pursuit again. This would be continued for hours with the hope of tiring the wild animals until they could be lassoed, but it never was entirely successful, for as a rule only weaklings were captured, and they were of little value.*

33

In his memoirs, *Black Mountain Cowboys*, author and rancher Paul L. Huntley reminisces about the mustangs of the South Park area (including Pikes Peak backcountry) in the early 1900s. The most prized of these wild horses were those found at Black Mountain, on the south edge of South Park, near Guffey—just about thirteen miles south of Florissant. These "were good horses, some of the best winded and sure footed horses that ever walked." Huntley notes that these horses were also extremely difficult to catch due to the high altitude and the extremely rocky condition of the mountain. Most of the cowboys' saddle horses were kept on ranches about 5,000 feet above sea level. Black Mountain was about 9,000 feet above sea level, and this gave the mustangs a great advantage, as the saddle horses became easily winded at that altitude. Huntley recounts some of the adventure and challenge of trying to capture these wild horses.

Most saddle horses, with a saddle and packing a man, just couldn't keep up with the wild horses. The only way was for two or more men to get after them. When you first jumped them they would run five or six miles just for the fun of it, down one ridge, then, near the end, cross over the gulch or draw then run back up. They could keep this up all day.

One of the most famous of Colorado's mustangs was a wiry little bay ridden by the Englishwoman, Isabella L. Bird, in 1873. Bird and her horse, Birdie— "a little beauty, with legs of iron, fast, enduring, gentle, and wise"—traveled over 700 miles alone on a sightseeing tour of Colorado. Bird wrote fondly of her little mustang companion.

Birdie amuses every one with her funny ways. She always follows me closely, and to-day got quite into a house and pushed the parlor door open. She walks after me with her head laid on my shoulder, licking my face and teasing me for sugar, and sometimes, when any one else takes hold of her, she rears and kicks, and the vicious bronco soul comes into her eyes. Her face is cunning and pretty, and she makes a funny, blarneying noise when I go up to her. The men at all the stables make a fuss with her, and call her "Pet." She gallops up and down hill, and never stumbles even on the roughest ground, or requires even a touch with a whip.

Unlike their counterparts in the dominant culture, Ute warriors carefully studied the habits of their four-legged brother, the wild horse. With this knowledge, then, they knew to surround the watering holes of the mustangs in the spring, just as the heavy snows were melting. As the herds quenched their thirst after feasting on the new spring grass, they became vulnerable. Their full bellies kept them from running at full speed. At this critical moment, a mounted warrior flashed into their midst, yelling and waving a blanket. The frightened herd now scattered in every direction. Now, without cohesion, each member was confused and vulnerable, and wildly plunged into the rawhide loop of its new Ute master. These clever "savages" found it quite easy to capture a wild mustang when you used your brain.

Ute assimilation of the horse into their nomadic way of life had a dramatic effect on their economy and lifestyle. Now mounted, rather than on foot, they were able to pursue bison out onto the eastern plains at the base of their Shining Mountains (the Rockies). Without the benefit of the white man's iron horse shoes, the Ute invented their own, very portable, horse shoe. First, they collected sap from the plentiful pine trees. Then they fashioned horse shoes from this sap by using a hot stone to evenly spread a gooey barrier over the horse's hoof. They were therefore able to ride their rugged ponies throughout the Rocky Mountains with little risk of lameness.

Use of the horse not only increased the Utes' food supply, but also provided a surplus of skins and byproducts for trade. They enjoyed an abundance of food and also a thriving "buckskin" economy. However, the structure of Ute society changed as a result. Land could now support them in higher densities. Also, their mounted lifestyle required larger numbers of people to work together in cooperation. Many family groups now began to band together.

Origins of the Ute name reflect their lifestyle prior to the advent of the horse. Ute people call themselves "Nuntz" (also spelled Nuche) which means "people." However, they consider the name of their tribe to be sacred, and so it is seldom if ever used in conversation. The Shoshone called these same people "Tsiuta" which means "rabbit hunters." (John Wesley Powell wrote a detailed description of the Ute method of rabbit capture in his journal.) Early settlers and Mountain Men changed the pronunciation to "Yutas." Later usage shortened the name even more to the current "Ute."

In the late 1700s, the Ute Nation was divided into a confederation of Seven Nations: the Mouache, the Capote, and the Weeminuche, (all called Southern Utes); the Grand, the Yampa and the Uintah, (all called the Northern Utes); and, finally, the Tabeguache or Uncompahgre Utes. Tabeguache Utes claimed central Colorado, including all of Teller County, as their hunting grounds. The name "Tabeguache" is a Ute word meaning "People who live on the warm side of the mountain." "Uncompahgre" is a Ute word meaning "red water" or "red lake."

Each band, or tribe, of Utes was governed by several chiefs. Usually there were war chiefs, peace chiefs, and the all-important medicine man, whose authority was comparable to a chief. Within the context of Native American spirituality, the most minute details of daily life offered a constant interaction with the Great Spirit, Sunawiv. It was understood that the Great Spirit was everywhere present, and that all things were filled with this spirit. It was further understood that all of life sprang from the earth, and therefore the land was seen as Mother Earth, and all creatures—four-legged, two-legged, winged, and water-dwelling were related as brothers. Even stones and trees and the wind were considered relations, or brothers. Ute life way underscored the understanding of a symbiosis of the entire universe. The medicine man was the link in communicating and understanding this symbiosis, this Oneness.

This philosophy of Oneness fomented a true democracy within the Ute social structure. When council was held, each man was given a full opportunity to discuss the question at hand.

Usually, no decision was made without first reaching a consensus of opinion in council. In this way, each person's concerns and opinions were incorporated in the final plan of action.

Ute society was organized into a system of government similar to that of any contemporary American town with a mayor, city council, police force, and heads of departments. The position of head chief was analogous to the office of mayor. The head chief was generally an older and wiser man, chosen for his wisdom, courage and compassion. He usually retained his position for life. His duties were complemented by those of the war chief who functioned as the head of a police-type force. The war chief was usually a younger man who had proven his abilities in battle. In the event of any conflict, the war chief asserted his authority. However, any instigator could assemble a war party by simply informing the war chief. In other matters, however, the war chief served as the enforcer, or policeman, for the head chief. There were also numerous other subchiefs who were involved in governing of the tribe. Central to all tribal policy, however, was the shaman, or medicine man.

Spirituality was an immanent, or intrinsic, facet of daily life. The Great Spirit controlled the roaming of the buffalo, the winds and rains, each person's health, and all subsidiary spirits—for everything possessed spirit. The medicine man therefore had the final say, after appropriate rituals, on any undertaking; for the medicine man was the communicating link with the Great Spirit.

Pikes Peak backcountry still bears numerous cultural landmarks from these first citizens of the land. Prayer trees stand as silent sentinels along Cedar Mountain Road northeast of Divide, marking the route of the holy people who took their sacred stones from Crystal Peak for a Vision Quest and blessing on Pikes Peak. These prayer trees evidence a unique chair-shape, showing where the people bent pine saplings parallel to the ground and tied them to a stake with a rawhide thong. As the sapling grew, it reached toward the sky and its bark encased the leather thong, leaving a tale-tell, finger's-width groove as the rawhide deteriorated. Medicine trees abound at the Florissant Fossil Beds National Monument and nearby

Sanborn Western Camp. These upright pine trees carry scars where bark was peeled away for use in healing ceremonies. They are easily identified by a straight horizontal cut, usually about six to eight inches long, used to insert a prying stick which then peeled a two- to three-foot section of bark from the tree. Stone tepee rings near Victor are testimony to the large encampments in that area. Pike also noted the remnants of a large Ute encampment that he found near Lake George in 1806, now buried by the waters of Elevenmile Dam.

Florissant was a favorite camping ground of one of the greatest of the Ute chiefs, Ouray. An 1886 map of Florissant shows an area designated as Ouray's campground at the western base of Fortification Hill. In the 1800s, this site would have presented an excellent campsite. It was strategically located on the northern bank of Twin Creek, with its crystal clear water and lush green meadows for the ponies. Fortification Hill lay just a few feet away, where it could facilitate the sending of smoke signals and the defense of the two trails at its base. Marksmen could be quickly placed in the rifle pits and behind the rock ramparts on top of the hill to thwart the advance of any hostiles from the North-South Oil Creek Trail, or the East-West Ute Trail. Smoke signals or mirror signals sent from Fortification Hill could be seen from Mount Pisgah (originally Signal Mountain) in the south, Signal Butte in the north, Badger Mountain in the west, or Gold Hill in the east. (There are unconfirmed reports that the Ute may have referred to the nearby Fossil Beds as the "Valley of Shadows.")

The same 1886 map also shows the open meadow east of Fortification Hill and labels it "Ute Battleground." This label was probably in reference to a fierce battle recorded in the journal of Will Drannan, the foster son of Kit Carson. Carson, Drannan and Johnnie West had been trapping in the Tarryall during the winter of 1852. Carson learned there was to be a battle between the Ute and the Comanche, and arranged to be a spectator. Carson's friend, the Comanche Chief Kiwatchee, had hoped to engage Carson and his men on behalf of the Comanche. Carson declined, however, probably because of his long friendship with the Ute. It is also highly probable that

Carson's Ute friend from Taos, Ouray, was present at this battle. Ouray had left Taos to join his father and the Tabeguache Ute band in 1850. It is also very logical to assume that the battle with the Comanche was led by the Tabeguache Ute, as it was held in their hunting grounds.

This was to be a final battle between the Utes and the Comanches over the hunting right to the South Park "hunter's paradise." Drannan reports that the fight took place on the banks of a creek (probably Twin Creek) "about two miles from where it empties into" the South Platte. He also noted that this creek "heads in the Pike's (sic) Peak . . . . and runs almost due west." Some authors have placed this battle in South Park. However, Twin Creek is the only creek in the area that meets the description set forth by Drannan—originating on Pikes Peak, flowing due west, and emptying into the South Platte. This description, coupled with the 1886 map of Florissant, seems to place the battle at Fortification Hill in Florissant.

Comanche warriors and their families encamped on the south side of Twin Creek, and the Utes encamped on the north side. Each morning at sunrise, the warriors of each tribe met along the banks of the creek to do battle, and at sunset they carried off their dead and wounded. Through the night, neither tribe made any attempt to molest the other. But the night was "hideous with the shrieks and cries of the squaws and children of the warriors who had been killed or wounded during the day." This battle lasted four days, with hundreds of dead and wounded on each side.

Drannan assumes the Comanche were the victors of this battle. However, there is no corroborating evidence to show that there was ever a Comanche presence in the area. It is more probable that the Ute prevailed—as usual. Historically, South Park's "hunter's paradise" and the Ute Pass Trail remained their domain until the relentless press of white miners and settlers forced them onto reservations.

Chief Ouray ensured his place in history as perhaps the greatest Indian peacemaker of all time. He safely led his people through the most turbulent period of his people's history—the westward expansion of the United States. The Utes had a long history of diplomatic relations with the Europeans, beginning with the Spanish in the 1500s. Ouray capitalized on this tradition, and was instrumental in maintaining most of his peoples' lands, peacefully, from the days of the first gold strikes in 1858 until the final, climactic, Ute Agreement of 1880. While other Indian leaders in the West such as Sitting Bull and Crazy Horse, fought fierce battles and lost many lives in their bid to maintain their traditional lands, Ouray instead launched an effective diplomatic defense.

Among the Ute, however, Ouray remains a somewhat controversial figure. When the United States signed its first major treaty with the Utes in 1863—the Hunt Treaty, which wasn't fully ratified until 1868—Ouray was designated by the whites as the principal chief of the Utes. Tabeguache (or Uncompahgre) Utes, of which Ouray was the chief, were the most numerous of all the bands at the time (numbering approximately 1,500). The northern Utes were not present for the treaty negotiations, and many of the other bands did not wish to participate. Tabeguache-Uncompahgre Utes claimed most of the area in dispute, and their band represented the greatest numbers of Ute. Therefore, the United States cavalierly designated them as the "owners" and accepted Ouray's signature as legally binding for all Utes.

Chief Joseph of the Nez Perce had a similar experience with the United States government. He very eloquently explained the Indian viewpoint of such illegal tactics. Joseph likened this method of "purchase" of land to the purchase of his personal horse from his neighbor, who did not participate in the ownership of the horse in any way, and who illegally sold Joseph's horse after he had refused to sell.

Ouray, however, saw such treaties as a means to survival. In 1860, Kit Carson had urged his Ute friends to secure their lands from white encroachment by negotiating a treaty. Consequently, Chief Nevava sent Ouray to assess the impact of the white men seeking their fortunes in the Ute's Shining Mountains. Ouray traveled up the Oil Creek Trail into Florissant, then down the Ute Trail into Colorado City and Denver, and returned to Conejos through the Arkansas Valley.

On this trip, Ouray found nearly 100,000 such gold-hungry men already in the Shining Mountains. He was convinced that it was only a matter of time before these crazed white men would take over all Ute territory. Total Ute population at this same time numbered about 4,000, and their territory encompassed all but the eastern plains of Colorado. Any reasonable person would consider these unfavorable odds. Besides, their territory was simply too large to defend against such massive encroachment. This was quite different from fighting small bands of hostile Pawnee or Comanche.

Ouray's early life provided him with a combination of skills and experiences necessary to lead his people through the traumatic transition from a free and wide-roaming nomadic people to a reservation-incarcerated people.

A spectacular meteor shower, called the most brilliant such display in history, filled the night skies above the Rockies on November 13, 1833. This became known as the Year of Shooting Stars. It was also the year of Ouray's birth in Taos, New Mexico. He was the son of a Jicarilla Apache father, Guera Murah (also called Salvador), and a Tabeguache/Uncompahgre Ute mother, whose name is not known. Ouray's mother bore a second son, Quenche, a couple of year's after his birth, and she died soon thereafter. Guera Murah remarried, and he and his new wife left the two brothers with a Spanish family in Taos when Ouray was about ten or twelve years old. Guera Murah had been captured by the Utes when he was a child, and was raised as a Ute. Therefore, when the Tabeguache Ute Chief, Nevava, sent for Guera, he loyally responded, leaving his young sons behind.

Ouray and his brother, Quenche, lived with their Spanish foster family until 1850. They earned their keep by herding sheep, hauling firewood, and packing mules for the many trading caravans through Taos. At the time, Taos was a bustling, cosmopolitan town on the Santa Fe Trail. It had a colorful population of a little over 500 Spanish, Indians, French, English, American and Mexicans. Kit Carson had made his home there since 1843. It was probably during this period that Carson and Ouray began what would become a life-long friendship. Ouray received a Catholic education while in Taos, and spoke fluent

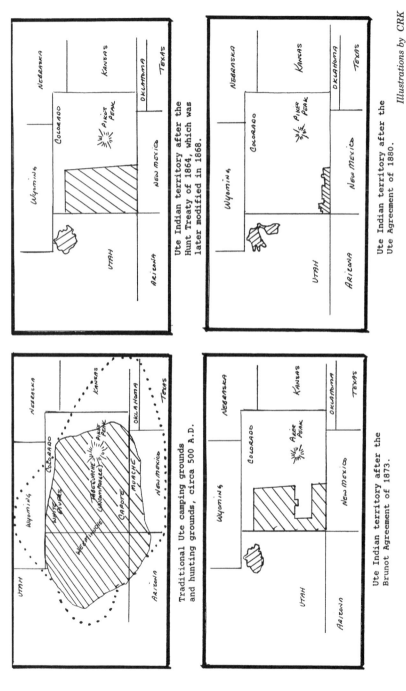

Ute Indian territory after the Hunt Treaty of 1864, which was later modified in 1868.

Ute Indian territory after the Ute Agreement of 1880.

Traditional Ute camping grounds and hunting grounds, circa 500 A.D.

Ute Indian territory after the Brunot Agreement of 1873.

Illustrations by CRK

Vanishing Ute lands. Ancient Ute lands slipped from their control with each treaty they signed. Ute hunting grounds originally included virtually all of the western two-thirds of Colorado. After 1880, the Utes were confined to reservations in southern Colorado and eastern Utah.

Tutt Collection, Colorado College
Ute encampment at Florissant, in the meadow just east of Fortification
Hill. The large tepee on the right is the chief's. This is probably
a winter hunting camp, as everyone is wearing blankets.

Spanish in addition to Ute, Apache, English, and Indian sign
language.

Ouray left Taos in 1850, joining his father and Chief
Nevava's band of Tabeguache. (It was probably Nevava's band,
including Ouray, that fought the Comanche on the banks of
Twin Creek in 1852.) Sadly, it was only a short time after their
reunion that Ouray's father died. However, Ouray soon became
Nevava's enforcer (similar to chief of police) and rose to the rank
of sub-chief.

Ouray was thoroughly alarmed by the number of whites he
found in his fact-finding tour of 1860. Therefore, in 1862, he
convinced the Tabeguache/Uncompahgre to ensure their territory against further encroachment from the whites. His negotiations with the United States government resulted in the Hunt

Treaty which guaranteed the Utes the western third of Colorado "forever," but shrinking their territory by fifty percent. With this Hunt Treaty, the Utes lost access to their sacred Suniwiv at Pikes Peak, along with the healing waters of Manitou Springs. Many of the Utes felt that Ouray had betrayed them. However, they continued to hunt the vast elk and deer herds of the Pikes Peak region until their final removal to the Ute Reservations in 1880-1881.

In 1869, Hunt was replaced as governor of the Colorado Territory by General Edward M. McCook. McCook tried to use this intra-tribal enmity against Ouray by establishing one of the lucrative Ute agencies in Denver. Any Ute who so desired could draw his or her annuity in Denver rather than at the remote mountain Ute agencies. Teller County's north-south Oil Creek Trail gained new importance as the anti-Ouray Utes found their way to McCook's Denver Agency.

Each month, colorful bands of Utes wound their way through the tall grass and beautiful wild flowers of the Florissant valley, past Crystal Peak, along the South Platte River and into Denver. Early Florissant maps label Wildhorn Road, north out of Florissant, as the "Ute Trail," and early Florissant pioneers speak of frequent visits by Colorow, Piah and other Denver Utes, as well as Ouray.

Unfortunately, gold was also found in the San Juan Mountains (near Silverton) in southwestern Colorado in 1871. "Forever," liberally used in prior Ute treaties, was once again amended to mean "as long as convenient." Colorado's Utes were again coerced into signing yet another treaty, the Brunot Treaty of 1873, which delineated sacred Ute lands "forever." With this treaty, the Utes ceded the coveted San Juan Mountains. Ouray wryly noted that "Agreements that the Indian makes with the (United States) government are like the agreement a buffalo makes with the hunter after it has been pierced by many arrows. All it can do is lie down and give in."

One can only speculate on what lands the Ute might still retain in Colorado had it not been for the actions of the rigid, over-zealous White River Indian Agent, Nathan Meeker. White River Ute Agency was located in northeastern Colorado. It boasted fertile, high mountain valleys nurtured by crystal clear streams. These lush mountain valleys provided excellent forage for Ute ponies. Unfortunately, they were also ideal for Meeker's vision of a pastoral Ute Nation. Meeker developed a terminal case of tunnel vision in his quest to reform the free-spirited, nomadic Utes into farmers. Meeker blackmailed his Utes into farming by withholding their allotment of food and supplies, sent by the government as payment for their lands. Tensions escalated in the conflict over converting grazing land into farm land. Finally, the situation exploded when Meeker threatened to shoot all the Ute ponies.

For the Ute, this was tantamount to genocide. The horse was not simply a means of transportation or sport. The horse was life itself. The horse ensured success in the hunt and food for hungry stomachs. The horse ensured safety from hostile tribes. The horse defined an individual's worth. The gift of horses ensured marriage to the desired woman. Foals were made a member of the household, and brought into the tepee each night to ensure their safety. When a warrior died, he needed his best horse or horses for his spirit journey, and so they were slain at his grave. The horse and life itself were inseparable.

In September 1879, the Utes rebelled, killing Meeker and ten other whites. They took Mrs. Meeker, her daughter, a farm girl and her two children captive.

Ouray rose to the occasion immediately, preventing any other Utes from joining in the uprising. His half-sister Susan was instrumental in securing the release of the captives. She boldly interrupted the council with their rescuer, General Adams, insisting that the Utes release the captives unharmed. Ironically, Susan herself had been rescued by the U.S. Army several years before the Meeker incident. She had been taken captive by the Apaches, and was about to be burned live at the stake when a cavalry detachment gallantly raced to her rescue.

Unfortunately, the Meeker Uprising was the fatal catalyst in Colorado's smoldering cauldron of anti-Ute sentiment. General Philip Sheridan's pronouncement that "the only good Indians I ever saw were dead" was echoed in virtually all of Colorado's newspapers. Senator Henry Teller declared that Ute genocide was the only possible solution. The citizens of Greeley (of which Meeker had been a founding father) passed an anti-Ute resolution.

> *Resolved, As the sense of this people, that the Indians within the limits of our State are a hindrance to its proper development, and a constant menace to the safety of the people; that by their recent unprovoked and inexcusable depredations they have forfeited all claims to remain among us; and we insist as our ultimatum in this matter that the death penalty be inflicted upon the fiendish murderers of our friends; and that the Utes be speedily removed beyond the borders of Colorado.*
>
> *Two hundred thousand people pray for this result.*

Colorado whites, led by Senator Teller and the press, were demanding Ute genocide. Bowing to public pressure, the United States Congress passed the Ute Agreement of 1880. This "Agreement" provided for the removal of all Utes from Colorado to reservations in Utah and southern Colorado. However, Ouray's efforts to secure the release of the hostages and to prevent further bloodshed were to be rewarded according to the Ute Agreement of 1880.

> *The Uncompahgre* (Tabeguache) *Utes agree to remove to and settle upon agricultural lands on Grand River [Colorado River], near the mouth of Gunnison River, in Colorado, if a sufficient quanity* (sic) *of agricultural land shall be found there; if not, then upon such other unoccupied agricultural lands as may be found in that vicinity and in the Territory of Utah.*

This area was not only extremely fertile agricultural land, but also carried special spiritual significance for the Ute. Grand Mesa was known to the Ute people as "Thigunawat," the home of departed Ute spirits, and was considered sacred land.

Otto Mears, the infamous entrepreneur of Colorado's toll roads and high-altitude railroads, had himself appointed to President Grant's commission which enforced the treaty. Earlier treaties provided that subsequent treaties could only be ratified by a three-fourths vote of all Utes. In 1881, Mears was charged with bribery for paying two dollars in cash to every Ute that signed the treaty. However illegal, Mears did succeed in obtaining the required number of votes. Mears' treachery did not stop here. He led the commission in requiring that the Tabeguache Utes be co-located with the White River Utes on the Uintah Reservation in Utah.

Treaty provisions for a special Tabeguache reservation at the junction of the Colorado and Gunnison Rivers were completely ignored. In fact, later that same year the area was declared public land. This extremely fertile farmland then became the location of the city of Grand Junction which was incorporated in 1882. Fortunately, Chief Ouray died before this last betrayal by Mears. His efforts to bring peace and prevent further bloodshed after the Meeker uprising were ultimately repaid with treachery. The Ute Nation was conquered by lies and deceit, not valor.

Sadly and ignobly, the nomadic lifestyle of the Ute was tragically and abruptly ended. It is a bitter irony that the Ute hunting grounds on the western slope of Pikes Peak, where they valiantly fought the Comanche on the banks of Twin Creek, were later named Teller County after the strident anti-Ute politician, Senator Teller. In a further irony, the Colorado Midland Railroad wound its way through Ute Pass and along the Ute Pass Trail adorned with the image of a noble Ute warrior as the railroad's logo.

Denver Public Library

Chief Ouray and his wife, Chipeta. Ouray used diplomacy and treaties to
retain the ancient lands of his people longer than any other tribe. After
Ouray's death, Chipeta joined Chief Colorow's band, renounced the white
man's ways, and lived as a traditional Ute.

CHAPTER FOUR
Early Europeans and Americans

SPANISH ADVENTURERS

On August 29, 1779, the Spanish governor of New Mexico, Juan Bautista de Anza, camped in the Florissant Valley while in pursuit of a marauding band of Comanches. De Anza had set out from Santa Fe on August 15, with 600 men. Five days later he was joined by about 200 Utes and Apaches who begged for the chance to combine forces against the Comanche. (It was the Ute who named the Comanche. Comanche, or Komantcia, is a Ute word meaning "Anyone who wants to fight me all the time.")

29 August 1779 Sunday At eight o'clock, the weather still bad, we forged ahead to the east (from Johnson Village at Buena Vista). *In this direction and through a good country four leagues* (about twelve miles) *were made. These over we paused in a good arroyo, as much to refresh the riding beasts as to give time to all people of the expedition to prepare and dress the meat of fifty head of buffalo they had succeeded in killing in less than ten minutes from the great number which broke in on our march* (in South Park).

. . . After these scouts had been sent out at the time spoken of, we again took up our route at six in the afternoon to the east-southeast. Along it six leagues (eighteen miles) *were made through good country, with many small streams. The day's journey terminated, the night now being well advanced, at the foot of a hill which was called Los Ojos Ciegos* (in Florissant).

Los Ojos Ciegos, or Blind Eyes, probably refers to Twin Rocks, a prominent landmark along the Ute Trail in Florissant. Two house-size, oblong boulders appear as though suspended in the pine trees, visible for miles before reaching Florissant. The rocks were probably named Los Ojos Ciegos in reference to the Ute legend of a very proud coyote who thought to impress others with the trick of making his eyes leave his head on command. However, he did the trick once too often, and his eyes were left hanging in the pine trees, never to return to their sockets.

Angry Comanches had been raiding Spanish settlements in northern New Mexico during the latter half of the 1700s in an attempt to drive the Europeans back to Mexico. The fateful provocation in 1779 was led by a brash young chief, named Cuerno Verde. "Cuerno Verde" in Spanish and Ute means Greenhorn. In a skirmish at Ojo Caliente (north of Santa Fe) in 1768, the first Comanche Chief, Cuerno Verde, was killed by the Spanish. His son vowed to avenge his father's death, and so assumed his father's name and his distinctive headdress. The name was reflected by the headdress, which was made of leather and green-tinted buffalo horns.

The two adversaries—De Anza and the younger Cuerno Verde—were perhaps destined to meet. In a fate somewhat similar to that of Cuerno Verde, both De Anza's father and grandfather had been killed while fighting the Apaches in Sonora, Mexico. His resolve was a match for the notorious Comanche's aggression. De Anza noted that Cuerno Verde's own "nation accuse him, ever since he took command, of forcing them to take up arms and volunteer against the Spaniards." Cuerno Verde's own men called him by the Comanche name Tabivo Naritgant, or "Dangerous Man."

Florissant was an ideal resting spot along De Anza's campaign route. The valley was large enough to accommodate the camp needed for over 800 men in addition to providing plenty of grass and fresh water for their 2,400 horses and mules. De Anza continued his pursuit down Ute Pass, or Puerto del Sierra Almagre (Doorway to the Red-Ocher Mountains), through what is now Colorado Springs and then south along Fountain Creek, or Santa Rosa—so named by the Spanish. (The Spanish also called upper Fountain Creek, which cascades from Pikes Peak above Manitou Springs, the Rio Almagre.) After a successful skirmish just north of Pueblo, De Anza finally encountered Cuerno Verde a few miles south of Pueblo, and defeated him on the banks of Greenhorn Creek—named after this famous Comanche chief who died on its banks. Greenhorn Mountain, just east of Interstate 25 south of Pueblo also is named for the chief. With the defeat of Cuerno Verde, De Anza was able to secure an enduring peace with the Comanche.

At the time of the fateful altercation between De Anza and Cuerno Verde, the Spanish presence had been felt in the New World for over 200 years. It wasn't until 1565 that Spain established its first settlement in what is now the United States, almost seventy-three years after Columbus first encountered the Americas. This colony was established at St. Augustine, Florida. However, the first Spaniards in the American West were refugees from a failed colony in Florida, who inadvertently landed in Texas near Galveston Island in 1528. They had fled Florida, and had hoped to find safe sanctuary in Mexico, but a storm blew them off course. These Spaniards, led by Cabeza de Vaca, spent six years wandering through Texas and Northern Mexico before being reunited with their compatriots in Mexico.

In 1538, the Viceroy of New Spain, Antonio de Mendoza, sent a Franciscan monk, Marcos de Niza, to explore the region north of Mexico. De Niza returned from his quest within a year, telling incredible stories of a city of great wealth, "bigger than the city of Mexico." Incited by the fabulous wealth of the Incas in Mexico, the Spanish were all too ready to believe and to exploit. By 1598, Don Juan de Onate led a force of 129 colonists up from Mexico to establish the first Spanish settlement in the west at San Juan Pueblo, just north of Santa Fe. The Spanish Pope, Alexander VI, had given all of the "New World" to the Spanish Crown in 1493, and so the Spaniards of New Spain felt it their right and imperative to ensure ownership through colonization as quickly as practicable.

Meanwhile, in 1682, the French explorer, Robert Cavalier, sieur de La Salle, set out from Canada to explore the Great

Lakes and the Mississippi River. During this foray, La Salle laid claim to the entire Mississippi drainage for his king, Louis XIV of France. This drainage included the Platte and Arkansas rivers, which carried the waters from the eastern slopes of the Rockies down into the Mississippi.

After France ceded the Louisiana Territory (including Colorado) to Spain in 1763, necessity forced Spain to use French officials and citizens of their new territory to procure the transition. In 1794, Spain sent the Frenchman, Captain Louis Villemont, on a Mission of the Court to evaluate the new Spanish dominion. His mission was to map and investigate the Louisiana Territory. He began his journey in New Orleans, traveling north to St. Louis, Missouri, and continuing into South Dakota before turning south. He then followed the South Fork of the South Platte River into the heart of Pikes Peak backcountry, encamping at Lake George, before tracing the source of the river to Fairplay. His memoirs and topographic maps of the area left the legacy of French names such as Platte River, Bayou Salado and Fountaine Que Bouille.

When the English established their colonies at Jamestown in 1607, and at Plymouth in 1620, they claimed sea-to-sea boundaries, from the Atlantic Ocean to the Pacific Ocean.

Colorado lay in the center of this territory disputed by Spain, France and England. Spain was generally accorded ownership of all of Southern Colorado, up to the Arkansas River, and all of western Colorado, again with the Arkansas headwaters defining the boundary. Pikes Peak's backcountry, and all of eastern Colorado belonged to the French. At the end of the French and Indian War in 1763, the Treaty of Paris awarded all of Colorado to Spain. So for a brief period, Pikes Peak's west slope became Spanish territory. Then in 1800, Napoleon forced Spain to return the Louisiana Territory (including central and eastern Colorado) to France, and so the Peak's west slope was once again French territory.

However, in 1803 Napoleon sold the Louisiana Territory to the United States for $15 million, and so the slopes of west Pikes Peak finally found permanent ownership with the new Republic.

West Pikes Peak country still bears many traces of its multi-national past. Along with the colorful pioneer names such as Cripple Creek and Tarryall, there are traces of the Spanish influence in such names as Colorado (meaning "red") and El Paso (originally "El Paseo," meaning the pass) County. Teller County was part of El Paso County until 1899, when the new county was created. El Paso was the original name of Colorado City at the base of Ute Pass, for Ute Pass was originally known as "El Paseo". The Utes, however, called it El Puerto del Sierra Almagre, meaning "Doorway to the Red Earth Mountains." Pikes Peak was named "El Capitan" by the Utes and Spanish, and was used as a prominent landmark demarcating Spanish territory. French explorers and trappers named the headwaters of Fountain Creek in Manitou Springs the "Fontaine que Bouille" (meaning the Stream That Boils). South Park was first known by its French name, Bayou Salado (Salt Marshes). The Platte River was so named by the French because of its very "flat" appearance. Colorado Springs pioneer Irving Howbert writes in his *Memories of a Lifetime in the Pikes Peak Region*:

> *In corroboration of the claim that Spanish expeditions passed over the town site of Colorado Springs at a very early date, is the following incident. While digging a cellar at 529 East Pike's Peak Avenue in June, 1894, workmen uncovered, some six feet below the surface, an iron box four by six inches in size, which was rusted to the point of disintegration. This iron box held a crucifix, attached to which was a Maltese cross having a small erect cross as a pendant. The two crosses were made of dark colored stone resembling chalcedony, while the crucifix was of solid brass hammered. All these articles were hand made showing the hammer marks and filed edges. None of the three bore any inscription or date, but evidently had been lost by some priest accompanying one of the early Spanish exploring expeditions.*
>
> *Van E. Rouse, secretary of the Board of Education in Colorado Springs at the time of the discovery, happened to be watching the excavation when the iron box containing the crosses was uncovered, and obtained possession of*

them. It was Mr. Rouse's purpose to give them to the El Paso County Pioneer Association for its historical collection, but before this was done they had mysteriously disappeared. However, they had been seen by many people, myself included. The loss was most unfortunate, for these old Spanish crosses were relics of great historical value.

Pikes Peak Library District
Zebulon Montgomery Pike

ZEBULON MONTGOMERY PIKE

El Capitan, the great peak, was later to be re-named for the man whose writings made it famous, Zebulon M. Pike, rather than for the American who first climbed it, Dr. Edwin James. The swirling mists of political intrigue have obscured the historical truth of Zebulon Montgomery Pike in much the same manner that the swirling winds of snow and cloud obscure the great mountain peak that bears his name.

In July 1806, Pike was sent to explore southwestern Louisiana Territory by General James Wilkinson. Pike set out with about seventy-five men, mostly Osage Indians. Their starting point was near St. Louis, Missouri, where Pike followed the Arkansas River west into Colorado. In November, he was offered his first glimpse of the 14,110-foot mountain that would come to bear his name. Pike wrote that "At two o'clock in the afternoon I thought I could distinguish a mountain to our right which appeared like a small blue cloud." Actually, he had to travel another 150 miles over a period of twelve days before his party encountered the mountain. When they finally drew near enough, Pike and three other members of his party set out to climb the peak. On the fourth day of the attempted assault, they were forced to abandon their efforts.

27th November, Thursday. Arose hungry, dry and extremely sore from the inequality of the rocks on which we had lain all night, but were amply compensated for toil by the sublimity of the prospects below. The unbounded prairie was overhung with clouds which appeared like the ocean in a storm, wave piled on wave and foaming, whilst the sky was perfectly clear where we were. Commenced our march up the mountain and in about an hour arrived at the summit of this chain. Here we found the snow middle deep, no sign of beast or bird inhabiting this region. The thermometer which stood at 9 (degrees) above 0 at the foot of the mountain here fell to 4 (degrees) below 0. The summit of the Grand Peak, which was entirely bare of vegetation and covered with snow, now appeared at the distance of 15 or 16 miles from us, and as high again as what we had ascended, and would have taken a whole day's march to have arrived at its base, when I believe no human being could have ascended to its pinical (sic). This with the condition of my soldiers who had only light overalls on, and no stockings, and every way ill provided to endure the inclemency of the region; the bad prospect of killing anything to subsist on, with the further detention of two or three days, which it must occasion, determined us to return.

After Pike aborted his attempt to climb Pikes Peak, he led his expedition further west along the Arkansas, then up the west branch of Oil Creek Trail, through what is now Elevenmile Reservoir, and into South Park. In the Elevenmile area, Pike noted that:

One of our party found a large camp, which had been occupied by at least 3,000 Indians, with a large cross in the middle. Quere. Are those people catholics?

Actually, the "cross" that Pike found was the Ute symbol for the four sacred directions—East, South, West, and North. This symbol was placed in the center of each new encampment by a medicine person immediately prior to encampment. Sacred tobacco offerings were made to Mother Earth at this point in thanksgiving for the sustenance that she offered to the people. The people, in return, offered the choicest portions of everything harvested—meat, berries, eagle feathers, etc. at this same sacred site. In this way, each encampment was sanctified, linking the earth to the people and the people to the earth.

Pike's party left the South Park area and crossed into the San Luis Valley, Spanish territory. This caused great consternation among the Spanish, who captured Pike and his men and held them prisoner for over a year before they were repatriated.

During Pike's absence, General Wilkinson was revealed to be deeply enmeshed in the treasonous plot with Aaron Burr to create their own empire in the western Louisiana Territory. Burr was tried for treason in 1807, but was acquitted. Pike was tainted by his association with Wilkinson, but was finally cleared of any unpatriotic deeds by the War Department in 1808. In 1810, Pike published a highly popular record of his adventure, titled *An Account of Expeditions to the Sources of the Mississippi, and Through the Western Parts of Louisiana, to the Sources of the Arkansaw, Kan, La Platte, and Pierre Juan Rivers.* His book was also sold in England, France, and Germany—whetting the European appetite for the romance of the western frontier.

MAJOR STEPHEN H. LONG

The War of 1812 not only ended Pike's life, but also created a hiatus in exploration of this western frontier. It wasn't until 1820 that the Secretary of War John C. Calhoun sent Major Stephen H. Long to explore the Rockies. After exploring along the front range, the party arrived at the Great Peak. The party's botanist, Dr. Edwin S. James, together with a soldier and a wagon master, decided to climb the peak. They finally succeeded late in the afternoon of July 14, 1820. When they returned to their base camp, Major Long decided to confer the name of "James Peak." The name did not stick, however. This was probably due to the popularity of the writings of Pike that had been previously published and widely circulated.

JAMES PURCELL

Actually, Pike had been preceded in Colorado by another American, James Purcell of Kentucky, whom Pike referred to as "Pursley." Pike met Purcell in New Mexico, and recorded his story for posterity. Purcell had set out from St. Louis with a few companions in 1802. They spent three years trapping and trading with the Indians, but not without incident. Pike wrote of one such very colorful happening. Some Indians had stolen Purcell's horses, and he and his friends followed the "thieves" into their village. Pike relates that "The horses were there, but the Indians refused to give them up. Pursley saw his horse, with an Indian on him going to the water at the edge of the town, pursued him, and with his knife ripped open the horse's bowels. The Indian returned to the village, got his gun and came and snapped it at Pursley, who pursued him into the village with his knife. The Indian took refuge in a lodge surrounded by women and children. This struck the chiefs with astonishment and admiration for the 'mad Americans,' as they termed them, and they returned the other horses to the hunters."

Later, while Purcell was in the midst of trading with the Comanches and Kiowa on the Eastern plains of Colorado, they were attacked by a band of Sioux. They fled into the mountains, probably by way of Ute Pass, through Pikes Peak backcountry. Purcell remained in South Park, where sometime around 1805, he claimed to have discovered gold. He is said to have later discarded the yellow metal when it became too cumbersome, as it was of no value in the remote areas of his travels. When Pike encountered him in Santa Fe in 1807, Purcell was working as a carpenter. He apparently was immune to the metallic fever which ruined so many lives during the second half of the 1800s.

GEORGE FREDERICK RUXTON

One of the most remarkable American travelers through the Pikes Peak backcountry was a young Englishman, George Frederick Ruxton. Born near Oxfordshire, England, Ruxton's spirit of adventure was thwarted and stifled by the conservative atmosphere of English society and countryside. He wrote in *Adventures in Mexico and the Rocky Mountains* that "I was a vagabond in all my propensities. Everything quiet or commonplace I detested and my spirit chafed within me to see the world and participate in scenes of novelty and danger."

When just seventeen, Ruxton fought in the Spanish Civil War, winning the Cross of the Order of San Fernando. He then returned to England and enlisted in Her Majesty's Eighty-ninth Regiment. When shipped for duty in Canada, he became bored with barracks life and sold his lieutenant's commission. He then reveled in the life of a hunter in the deep forests of upper Canada. After a brief visit to England, he set off on two separate trips to Africa. Ruxton could not resist the romance of the Mexican War, and so in 1846 set sail for Veracruz. From there he journeyed up to Santa Fe, and thus began his two-year adventure in the mountains of Colorado. He traveled extensively, up Ute Pass, into Woodland Park, Florissant, Lake George and throughout the Pikes Peak area, writing of this primitive freedom:

> *Although liable to an accusation of barbarism, I must confess that the very happiest moments of my life have been spent in the wilderness of the Far West; and I never recall, but with pleasure, the remembrance of my solitary camp in the Bayou Salade (South Park), with no friend near me more faithful than my rifle, and no companions more sociable than my good horse and mules, or the attendant cayute [coyote] which nightly serenaded us. With a plentiful supply of dry pine-logs on the fire, and its cheerful blaze streaming far up into the sky, illuminating the valley far and near, and exhibiting the animals, with well-filled bellies, standing contentedly at rest over their picket-fires, I would sit cross-legged enjoying the genial warmth, and pipe in mouth, watch the blue smoke as it curled upwards, building castles in its vapoury (sic) wreaths, and, in the fantastic shapes it assumed, peopling the solitude with figures of those far away. Scarcely, however, did I ever wish to change such hours of freedom for*

all the luxuries of civilised (sic) *life; and, unnatural and extraordinary as it may appear, yet such is the fascination of the life of the mountain hunter . . .*

Young Ruxton died in St. Louis in 1848 of epidemic dysentery at the very young age of twenty-seven. Fortunately, Ruxton provided vivid accounts of adventures of the Mountain Man in both *Life in the Far West* and his autobiographical *Adventures in Mexico and the Rocky Mountains.* Ruxton was the first author to write extensively of the Mountain Man. His colorful and authentic portrayals of fictional La Bonte and Killbuck created a new romance of these heroes in fringed buckskin.

MOUNTAIN MEN

Dr. LeRoy Hafen, former Director of the State Historical Society of Colorado, wrote that "Trappers and traders were the trail makers and path finders of Colorado, the real pioneers of the rocky Mountain West . . . . It was the trapper's persistent search for beaver and the trader's urge to barter with red men, that unlocked the geographical secrets of the western wilds and eased the way for official explorers and for settlers."

There were a few impediments, however, which precluded the rich beaver pelts of South Park and Pikes Peak backcountry from the fortunes of would-be trappers. The Louisiana Purchase of 1803 loosely defined the new American borders as laying north of the Arkansas River. The area south of the river was still claimed by Spain, which actively discouraged incursions by "foreigners" into its territory. Santa Fe and Taos—centers of Spanish commerce—were also the closest trade centers for any would-be trappers to exchange their beaver pelts for cash. This exchange, however, required a grant, or license, from the Spanish government. These grants were sparingly awarded, and were usually given only to Spanish citizens. Without access to the markets in Santa Fe and Taos, trappers were forced to travel east, the full distance of the Arkansas River, to the bustling markets in St. Louis.

Beaver hats were the height of style, however, in both the Eastern United States and in Europe, and fashionable, monied society was prepared to pay handsomely to indulge its tastes. At one time a single beaver pelt brought as much as thirty dollars; thirty dollars represented an entire month's salary for the common man of this period. The extreme profitability of this luxuriantly furred, web-footed rodent spawned the golden age of the Mountain Man, from the early 1800s until the middle of that century.

The demise of this golden age was foreshadowed by legislation passed by the United States Congress, the "Trade and Intercourse Act" of 1834. This law was intended to preserve the resources and way of life of the American Indian from further encroachment by the white man. Among these protected resources was the beaver. During the golden age of trapping, however, most conflict between the whites and the Indians was averted mainly through the proclivity of the beaver to grow its thickest fur, and therefore most valuable pelt, during the harsh Rocky Mountain winters. The American Indian, dependent upon the migrating buffalo and other seasonal sources for food, generally abandoned the deep winter snows to follow these food sources to the somewhat warmer valleys and plains at the base of the mountains.

In the way of all things since the beginning of commerce, it was economics which finally ended the romantic era of the Mountain Man. Silk top hats became the fashion and beaver pelts, which had sold for as much as thirty dollars each, fell in value to less than three dollars each in the late 1830s. The American Fur Company, organized by John Jacob Astor in 1808, ended its mountain business with a final Mountain Man rendezvous in 1839 on Horse Creek in Wyoming. The last of all the Mountain Man rendezvous was a small, dispirited affair held on Wyoming's Green River in 1840.

CHOUTEAU AND DEMUN

In the late 1700s and early 1800s, St. Louis, Missouri was a small village. Because of its strategic location, it was the fur trade center for the western frontier. It is not surprising, then, that August Pierre (A.P.) Chouteau, the grandson of one of its founding families, would be among the first to harvest the rich and abundant beaver pelts of Pikes Peak's backcountry.

A.P. Chouteau was outfitted by his younger brother, Pierre Junior (Cadet), in 1815 for a fur trading expedition into the Rocky Mountains. Cadet's company, Berthold & Chouteau, was later (in 1827) to become the sole western agent for Astor's powerful American Fur Company. A.P. Chouteau and his brother-in-law, Jules DeMun, traveled into the Rocky Mountains to the sources of the Platte and Arkansas Rivers (Teller County and South Park areas) to trade with the Comanches, Arapahos and Utes. The trip was a financial disaster that presaged further problems between the brothers. These culminated in an 1838 lawsuit wherein Cadet won a settlement against August Pierre for everything that he owned.

Cadet's business ventures into the fur business of the Rocky Mountains carried the dissonance of the brother's unhappy relationship. When Cadet sent his partner's son, Sylvestre Pratte, to Taos in 1826 to take charge of 120 free trappers, he again met with severe financial losses. These trappers ranged as far north as the Platte River and Lake Utah, exploring every tributary and stream of the Upper Arkansas drainage, which included Pikes Peak's backcountry. Though these trappers spent two years gathering their furs, they had little success, and the venture was viewed as a calamity by Cadet.

CAPTAIN JOHN GANTT

Indians of the Rocky Mountain area were first introduced to the insidious poison of alcohol by a dishonored ex-Army officer, Captain John Gantt. Gantt was dismissed by the Army in 1829 for falsifying pay accounts, and sought his fortune in trapping the headwaters of the Arkansas in the South Park area. During the winter of 1832, he and his party of trappers built a log stockade on the Arkansas River near the mouth of the Purgatory (about seventy miles east of Pueblo). He established trade with the Indians of the area, persuading them to drink his sweetened whiskey. In 1834, he moved his operations six miles east of Fountain Creek (present-day Pueblo) on the Arkansas River, and named it Fort Cass. His trade with the Indians was challenged by Bent, St. Vrain & Company who built a fort three miles further east on the Arkansas. Gantt was no match for their competition, and abandoned his fort and trading business about 1835. Bent & St. Vrain also abandoned this location, and rebuilt their fort another seventy miles east on the Arkansas River on its current location just outside of La Junta. (This fort is also a recent reconstruction, as the original was destroyed by an explosion and fire in 1848.)

One of the more famous trappers working with Gantt during this period was none other than Kit Carson. Carson and Gantt trapped the South Park area, working in the Florissant Valley and Woodland Park, then east down Ute Pass, during the winter of 1833.

KIT CARSON

Christopher "Kit" Carson began life inauspiciously as the third son—and sixth of eight children—born in 1809 to a Revolutionary War veteran and his Kentucky bride. His father was killed when Carson was but nine, and four years later his mother remarried. There was friction between the new stepfather and young Kit, so he was apprenticed to a saddlemaker in Franklin, Missouri. In 1826, at the age of seventeen, Carson ran away, joining a wagon train bound for Santa Fe. Thus began the legend of the man who was to become a Mountain Man, Indian agent, and renowned explorer—the Christopher Columbus of the West.

In 1829 Carson received his first taste of the freedom and romance of the Mountain Man when he joined Ewing Young's trapping expedition to Arizona and California as camp cook. Carson was an apt pupil, however, and was Young's trusted lieutenant by the time they arrived back in Taos two years later. He then set out with the famous trapper, Thomas Fitzpatrick, in 1832, and made what was probably his first incursion into Pikes Peak's backcountry. Later that year, he left Fitzpatrick and joined Captain John Gantt—who Carson refers to as "Captain Gaunt" in his autobiography. Carson and Gantt trapped South Park and Pikes Peak backcountry throughout the next year, 1833. Carson then spent the next ten years trapping in the company of some of the West's most famous Mountain Men—including Jim Bridger and Old Bill Williams.

It was also during this period that Carson had his first taste of battle with the American Indian. Mountain Men were the interlopers, traveling and trapping illegally in the mountains of the West, which the United States government had designated as belonging to the American Indian. Indians dealt harshly with these hairy-faced, buckskin-clad intruders, usually setting them afoot by stealing all of their horses and at other times, taking their lives. Carson soon learned that by striking back swiftly and firmly, he and his men were usually able to prevail—even when the odds were ten or more against one.

Harper's Weekly, *1862*

Kit Carson

However, Carson's later fame as a proficient and eager Indian fighter is strangely at odds with his other dealings among his unwilling American Indian hosts.

While it is true that he fought a great many battles against hostile Indians, he also was married to two different Indian women at different times. His first wife was an Arapaho girl named Waa-nibe, or "Singing Grass." She bore him a daughter, Adaline, about 1837 and then a second daughter sometime later. This second daughter died at three years of age when she fell into a kettle of boiling soap in Taos. Waa-nibe was spared the agony of seeing this helpless child die, for she herself had died shortly after giving birth.

Carson then married a Cheyenne girl known as "Making Out Road" sometime around 1841. He fought a deadly duel with another of her suitors, an overbearing French bully named Shunar. Carson killed his rival, and won the hand of this lovely Indian maiden. However, this marriage seems to have lasted only a few months, and ended with a bitter fight.

In January 1842, Carson was baptized a Catholic and, in February 1843, married Marie Josefa Jaramillo of Taos. His brother-in-law was the ill-fated governor of New Mexico, Charles Bent. It is interesting that Carson does not mention either of his Indian wives in his autobiography. However, genteel society at that period would have been outraged by anyone married to what they considered to be a "savage."

One of Carson's many foster children, Will Drannan, gives us another glimpse of Carson's relationship with the American Indian. In their travels together, Drannan wrote that they were most always met by the chief of the nearest village, and were required by frontier etiquette to attend a very specially prepared dog feast and then to smoke the peace pipe. Typical of their reception at the different villages was Drannan's description of an encounter with a band of Comanches as recounted in his memoirs *Thirty One years on the Plains and in the Mountains*.

> *We were met on the outskirts of the village by White Horse, Chief of the Comanches, who, being an intimate friend of Uncle Kit, shook hands with us and conducted us to his own wick-i-up. There we unpacked the animals and piled up our goods, and White Horse detailed an Indian to guard the packs day and night.*
>
> *After our horses had been picketed out to grass, the Chief took us into his lodge to dine with him, and here again we had boiled dog and the peace smoke.*

Carson and Ouray, chief of the Tabeguache Utes, were good friends through some of the most critical periods in Ute history. They probably knew each other from their early days at Taos— Ouray having lived there from the time that he was ten years old (1843) until he was about seventeen (1850). Carson and Marie Josefa Jaramillo made their home in Taos until they moved to nearby Rayado. In December 1853, Carson was named the Ute Indian agent at Taos and served in this capacity until his resignation in 1861 in order to enlist in the Union

Army. Ouray replaced Nevava as chief of the Tabeguache Utes in 1860, having first served as subchief for an extended period. As subchief and chief he would have worked closely with Carson.

Through this friendship, Carson urged his friend Ouray to seek a treaty with the United States government to ensure well-defined boundaries to sovereign Ute Territory. The timing of this treaty was critical, as gold had been discovered near Denver in 1858; near Leadville and in the Tarryall Valley in 1859; and near Durango in 1860. Colorado's mountains were swarming with tens of thousands of whites suffering from "gold fever." Adding to this pressure, Colorado became a territory in 1861 and then Congress passed the Homestead Act in 1862. These two actions sent additional thousands of whites into the Rockies with "land fever."

Ouray and Carson began work almost immediately on a treaty to protect Ute lands. The Ute were successful in negotiating with the Governor of the Colorado Territory, and in 1863 what would later be known as the Hunt Treaty was signed. The United States Congress did not ratify this treaty, however, and in 1868 Ouray and nine other Ute chiefs traveled to Washington for further bargaining. Ouray persuaded Carson to accompany them although Carson was seriously ill at the time. A number of changes were made to the treaty, mostly to the disadvantage of the Utes.

This treaty came about mainly through the friendship of Carson and Ouray. Through it, the Utes maintained their life-giving hunting grounds in Pikes Peak's backcountry and the South Park area, even though gold and land fever raged through the Rockies coupled with strident cries of "The Utes must go!"

The Civil War also created a complex and unfortunate climate for the Indians of the West. The Confederate government strove for strategic advantage by embroiling the Choctaws, Chickasaws, Creeks, Seminoles and Cherokees as allies in their battle with the North. In Minnesota, angry Sioux took up arms against the whites when the promised annuities of their treaties were interrupted by the Civil War. In New Mexico, militant Navajo seized the opportunity of a distracted Union military to launch fierce attacks on New Mexico settlements.

Brigadier General James H. Carleton, commander of the Department of New Mexico, was keenly aware of the vulnerability of the white settlers under his protection. With an economy of men and materials dictated by the profound battle waging between the North and the South, Carleton devised a simple and effective "scorched earth" policy in dealing with the Indians. Under Carleton's direction, Colonel Kit Carson led the First New Mexico Volunteer Cavalry, conquering both the Mescalero Apaches and the Navajo. In a final, fateful march against the Navajo in 1864, through Canyon de Chelly, Carson effected a devastating scorched earth campaign. He then oversaw the controversial and deadly Long Walk, relocating the now starving Navajo to the Bosque Redondo in eastern New Mexico. With this final blow, the Navajo Wars ended.

Carson received a final command at Fort Garland (Colorado) in 1866, and was mustered out of the Army in 1867. He joined his family at their farm near Las Animas (at Boggsville) for a much needed rest. A horse had fallen on him in a hunting accident in 1860, and he had never fully recovered from the injury to his chest. His friendship with Ouray mandated the trip with him to Washington, D.C. in 1868, to assist in the treaty negotiations. Carson returned to his ranch, exhausted, and suffering with an aneurysm in his chest. Two days after his return, Josefa gave birth, then tragically died ten days later. Kit followed his beloved wife exactly one month later, on May 23, 1868.

There were a number of Mountain Men whose exploits equaled or exceeded those of Kit Carson. However, Fate chose to cast Carson in a different light. It was Carson's service to the Pathfinder of the West, John Charles Fremont, that catapulted him into the public's eye and international fame. Carson met Fremont on a Missouri riverboat in 1842, and offered his services as guide through the Rockies. Fremont had been selected to head this expedition by his father-in-law, Missouri Senator Thomas Hart Benton. Benton had plotted for years to expand the western borders of the United States, and felt that

Fremont's reconnaissance of the area would make it more attractive to Americans. Carson led Fremont over South Pass (along what was later known as the Oregon Trail) in 1842 and again in 1843. In 1845, he joined Fremont for a third trip to California, this time remaining with Fremont to fight against the Mexicans until his return in 1848. It was Fremont's *Report*, published in 1845, that captured the imagination of the American public and launched Carson into the pages of history.

Carson's biographer, Harvey Carter, wrote in *Mountain Men and Fur Traders of the Far West*:

> ... there is less difference between the real Carson and his legend than is usually the case with frontier heroes. This is because Carson was really a man of many admirable qualities and few reprehensible traits and because he really did lead a strenuous and adventuresome life.

WILLIAM F. DRANNAN

It is generally agreed among Carson's biographers that he took under his protection as many as twenty homeless young boys. These foster children were of all races—Anglo, Spanish and Indian. This was probably his way of healing himself of the pain he had experienced when his own widowed mother remarried and he ran away from his unhappy home.

Perhaps the most famous of these foster children was William F. Drannan. Drannan was born on the Atlantic Ocean to French emigres on their way to America in 1832. They later died in the cholera epidemic of 1836, leaving four-year-old Will and his seven-month-old sister. The orphaned Will was taken in by a plantation owner by the name of Drake whose lands bordered on those of General Andrew Jackson near Nashville, Tennessee. Young Drannan was quartered with the Negro slaves, and was greatly mistreated. He never learned what became of his baby sister.

In Drannan's autobiography *Thirty One Years on the Plains and in the Mountains*, he asserts he ran away from Drake in 1847, finding his way on foot to St. Louis where he met Kit Carson. It is a controversy over this date that makes many historians question the veracity of Drannan's memoirs. They

Drannan, Thirty One Years on the Plains and in the Mountains
Captain William F. Drannan, foster son of Kit Carson, poses with his
favorite horse, Black Bess.

argue that Carson was in California with Fremont in 1847, and
so Drannan's account must be manufactured. If, however, one
views Drannan's account as having erred in the date by five
years—making it 1842—then the remaining events in
Drannan's life do appear to be logically truthful.

It was in 1842 that Carson took his young Indian daughter
to a boarding school in St. Louis, and had his fateful first meeting with Fremont. This also seems more logical in light of
Drannan's actions. He writes that he met Carson in the lobby of
a hotel where he had gone to inquire for a job. Carson took note
of him when he began to cry after his request for a job was
denied. In the 1800s, a fifteen-year-old was usually considered
a man, and to cry as a child would be unthinkable—no matter
what the provocation. Tears from a fifteen-year-old would have
hardly engendered the sympathy of Kit Carson nor induced him
to take such a soft young man as a fledgling Mountain Man.
This is, however, the more probable response from a ten-year-
old, which Drannan would have been in 1842.

Drannan's memoirs were first published in 1900, over fifty
years after his experiences with Carson. They were written
without benefit of a journal, and were composed almost

entirely from memory. Even Carson's autobiography errs in many of the dates that he assigns to events. This is a natural, but not necessarily fatal, flaw in writing from memory. Drannan's book was quite popular. It sold very well, and this sheer volume of sales subjected Drannan to broad public scrutiny and validation. His book survived this rigorous test, and was even republished several times.

Drannan's memoirs provide an interesting insight to the true character of Kit Carson, and also paint a vivid picture of their years trapping in Pikes Peak backcountry.

In October 1842 (Drannan lists as 1847), Carson, Drannan, and Johnny Hughes traveled up the headwaters of the Arkansas, where they built a winter cabin on a "stream that empties into the Arkansas." (This could have been near Currant Creek or Four Mile Creek in southern Teller County. The timing of this trip would have allowed for Carson's first trip with Fremont from June to August of 1842.)

Drannan writes that Carson's method of establishing a trapper's camp for the winter was to enter the area on horseback with plenty of packhorses for the provisions. These horses were then sent back with a hired man once the destination was reached. On subsequent trips, the horses were simply pastured nearby during the winter months. The use of pack animals allowed for a number of comforts in the winter quarters. Drannan reports that the "cabin" was sometimes made entirely of logs, and at other times was a log cabin partly bermed into the earth, and was generally about twelve feet square. Its roof was made of small pine logs, covered with brush and pine boughs, then covered again with dirt. A crude door was fashioned out of hewn logs, fastened together with crossed pieces held together with wooden pins. This whole affair was then hung on heavy wooden hinges.

A small portable wood stove was used for cooking and heating, and a crude bed was made out of a green elk hide which was fastened to a rough-hewn log frame. By immediately sleeping on the green hide, it shaped itself to one's body providing "first class comfort."

Harper's Weekly, *1862*

A Mountain Man sets his beaver traps.

Each trapper had responsibility for a dozen traps, or a "string." These traps were carried around in a "trap sack" made of stout buffalo skin. Early Mountain Man Joe Meek left a detailed account of the business of trapping beaver in his memoirs *No Man Like Joe.*

> . . . (the trapper) *has an ordinary steel trap weighing five pounds, attached to a chain five feet long, with a swivel and ring at the end, which plays round what is called the float, a dry stick of wood about six feet long. The trapper wades out into the stream, which is shallow, and cuts with his knife a bed for the trap, five or six inches under water. He then takes the float out the whole length of the chain in the direction of the center of the stream, and drives it into the mud so fast that the beaver cannot draw it out: at the*

same time tying the other end by a thong to the bank. A small stick or twig, dipped in musk or castor (an oil taken from the beaver's glands) *serves for bait, and is placed so as to hang directly above the trap, which is now set. The trapper then throws water plentifully over the adjacent bank to conceal any footprints or scent by which the beaver would be alarmed, and going to some distance wades out of the stream.*

In setting a trap several things are to be observed with care: first, that the trap is firmly fixed, and the proper distance from the bank—for if the beaver can get on shore with the trap he will cut off his foot to escape; secondly, that the float is of dry wood, for should it not be the little animal will cut it off at a stroke and swimming with the trap to the middle of the dam be drowned by its weight. In the latter case, when the hunter visits his traps in the morning, he is under the necessity of plunging into the water and swimming out to dive for the missing trap and his game.

These traps were monitored each day (some were as far as seven or eight miles from camp). The drowned beaver were removed, skinned, and the traps were reset. The skins were then stretched by making a bow of a small willow or other pliant sapling, and then pulling the hide over this frame. As the hides dried, they were removed from the frames, and packed in another frame for transport, with fifty "plews" to each bale.

Only the barest of necessities were packed in for the winter's camp—coffee, sugar and flour became only fond memories after the first few months. Trappers fed themselves with whatever game could be found within the area. Beaver tail was considered quite tasty, and if nothing else, provided diversity in an otherwise bland diet of other fresh meat. The cold mountain streams of the Rockies freeze solidly for only brief periods during the winter, usually no more than six weeks. Trappers used this forced hiatus to make enough moccasins, gloves, shirts and leggings from their elk hides for the remainder of the season. (Each trapper required at least twelve pair of moccasins each year.)

Trappers always left their camp in early spring as the snows began to leave the mountain valleys. This early departure usually insured ample separation between the return of indigenous Indians of the area and the departure of their unwelcome winter guests.

Drannan trapped for Carson for almost ten years, making numerous forays into the Rockies for the bounteous beaver skins. Their final trip together was to South Park and the Tarryall in 1852. They traveled over Ute Pass and struck South Park on the east side, probably at Wilkerson Pass. Drannan wrote glowingly of his first view of South Park.

> . . . a more beautiful sight I never saw than the region was at that time. Coming in from the direction mentioned, one could overlook the entire park, which was almost surrounded by snow-capped mountains, and the valley, several miles below, which was about eighty miles long and from ten to twenty miles wide, was as green as a wheatfield in June. When we were near the valley we could see elk in bands of a hundred or more, with small herds of bison scattered here and there in the valley, and antelope by the hundreds.
>
> I had often heard of a hunter's paradise, and when I got sight of this lovely valley, with its thousands of wild animals of almost every description known to the continent, I made up my mind that if there ever was such a place as a hunter's paradise, I had surely found it. The high mountains with scattering pine trees on the sides; the snowy white peaks above the timber line, and the many little mountain streams and rills that paid tribute to the main stream that coursed this beautiful valley, all combined to form a scene of magnificent grandeur. The quaking-asp, balm and various other kinds of small timber that grew along the streams all helped to add to the beauty of the scene.

This last winter's camp was made in the Tarryall River Valley, just north of present day Lake George. Drannan writes that this was the winter when a large herd of bison in the valley nearly trampled him to death when they stampeded. The following spring was also eventful in that he and Carson witnessed the final, decisive battle between the Ute and the Comanche in Florissant.

Carson and his friend Lucien B. Maxwell "rigged up a party of eighteen men to go trapping" on this expedition as a final farewell to their lives as Mountain Men. Besides Carson, Maxwell, Drannan, and Johnnie West, it is not known who the other members of this party were. They split into groups of three and four, and established cabins about four to eight miles apart. (A trapper's cabin dating from this period is still standing at the Twin Creek Ranch in Florissant. Another trapper's cabin, bearing Carson's carved signature and dating from this period, is located on Black Mountain near Guffey.)

Drannan writes that "Aside from my race with the bison, I put in a very pleasant winter (1852), and Uncle Kit said he had never spent as pleasant a time in the mountains as he did that winter in South Park. 'In fact,' said he, 'it was more like a pleasure trip than anything else.'

PIKES PEAK BACKCOUNTRY

CHAPTER FIVE

Judge Castello
builds a trading post

From 1852 until 1859 there was a brief respite from the white man's intrusions into Pikes Peak's backcountry. Beaver were no longer threatened by hairy-faced trappers, and so they rebuilt their dams in the gently coursing waters of Twin Creek. Great blue heron stalked the sandy stream bed, searching for food as noisy flocks of Canada Geese built their nests in the willows along the banks.

Coyotes slunk through knee-deep grama and wheat grass, pouncing on the large snowshoe hares who fed there. Golden eagles, bald eagles and peregrine falcons gently glided on thermals from the valley, preying on unwary prairie dogs and ground squirrels. Thousands of mountain blue birds searched for tiny bugs among the grasses as the sun magnified the hue of their lazurite wings.

Small herds of buffalo marched along the Ute Trail as billowing clouds of black and brown buffalo birds followed in their wake, leaving their orphaned eggs in the nests of the songbirds along the trail. A myriad of brightly colored butterflies and hummingbirds flitted among meadows choked with delicate blue wild iris and columbine.

Deer, elk and antelope calved and nourished their young on the silica-rich grasses growing among the fallen petrified trees. Bear wandered through the timbered hills surrounding the valley, feasting on a bounty of wild blackberries, cow currants, and rose hips. Mountain lions stretched lazily atop the huge boulders in Twin Creek Canyon, Painted Rocks and Dome Rock luxuriating in the warm mountain sun.

Mustang ponies whinnied to one another, periodically inter-rupting the peace of this idyllic mountain retreat as they car-ried dusky hunting parties into the valleys. Grassy banks along sparkling mountain creeks turned host to a multitude of buffa-lo-skin tepees, gently glowing like Mexican *luminaria* under the stars, as the cooking fires were kindled and succulent fresh game was roasted.

Then, in late 1857, a Delaware Indian, Fall Leaf, presented a quill of Colorado gold dust to a merchant in Lawrence, Kansas and the fate of the Rocky Mountains was sealed. During the next two years, gold seekers came swarming over the Shining Mountains. Soon the gentle tendrils of blue smoke from 600 Ute tepees were obliterated by the black smoke from 100,000 prospector campfires. This was the state of the mountains in 1860 when Chief Ouray made his fact-finding journey which resulted in the Hunt Treaty.

Twenty-year-old Charles Castello was among those with visions of gold dust in their eyes. He traveled from Florissant, Missouri to the Gregory Diggings at Central City by ox team in 1859. He must have been impressed by what he saw, for he was joined the next year by his forty-six-year-old father, James Castello. James also must have been favorably impressed, as he soon sent Charles back to Missouri for the sole purpose of returning with the remainder of the Castello family. James worked the Nevada Gulch near Central City, then moved on to the diggings near Fairplay. He was joined there in 1863 by his wife, Catherine Hughes Castello, and their five other chil-dren—Lucy Ann, James, John, Andrew, and Francis (Frank). Charles, however, chose to remain in Missouri.

It is very likely that Catherine Castello was relieved to have her husband and oldest son out of Missouri during the Civil War. Missouri, far from the bloody battlefields of Virginia, was nonetheless a hotbed of rebel guerrilla warfare. Catherine Castello told her grandchildren many stories of ambush killings, of crying Negroes who did not want to be freed, and of Missourians' deep-seated hatred of Lincoln.

Catherine Castello exemplifies the early pioneer woman in her faith, courage, and sturdy ability. Fearless and trusting, she left her comfortable home in Florissant, Missouri, at her husband's summons. Despite the rigors of winter, she gathered her five children and her household goods and boarded the train for Atchison, Kansas. James sent two trusted guides, John and Aaron Ripley, to meet Catherine at the train and accompany her by ox cart to Fairplay—a dangerous journey of sixty days through the mountains. As the wagons approached the line demarcating the Colorado Territory, Catherine lined up her children, gave each a good scrubbing, and dressed them

Photo courtesy Myrtle Dalby
Judge James Castello, circa1865

in their best. She dressed five-year-old Frank, the youngest, in a new pair of red velvet pants, which she had made for this special occasion.

The Castellos soon settled into the vibrant life of the Fairplay gold camp. By 1866, there were about 200 residents and a thriving brewery. James and Catherine established the Castello Hotel—a charming two-story log building which also hosted the town's meetings.

James, who had been sheriff in St. Louis, was soon acting as county judge. In 1865, Judge Castello became a member of the first state Senate of the Colorado Territory. In 1868, he was appointed by President Johnson as receiver at the newly established United States Land Office in Fairplay. As receiver, Judge Castello acted as "banker" for the U.S. government, collecting and depositing all federal monies. He served in this capacity until 1872.

Social life for the Castellos soon revolved around their two eligible daughters, who were quickly married off. In 1865 Lucy Ann married George W. Barrett, a freighter who later became one of the few prosperous miners at Hamilton on the Tarryall River. Then Mary Castello married William H. Beery in 1866. Beery was a teamster along the Ute Pass Wagon Road. He and Mary later established the Thirty-Nine-Mile Ranch along Currant Creek, just about thirty miles south of Fairplay.

It was during this time at Fairplay that Judge Castello became involved as an agent for the Colorado Superintendency of Indian Affairs. When Congress passed the Homestead Act in 1862, thousands of land-hungry settlers pressed in on the Indian lands. (This was in addition to the thousands already scouring the mountains for gold.) The government made hasty new treaties every few months to placate the Indians. In these treaties, the Indians were guaranteed annual supplies and monthly rations "forever" in exchange for their lands. The Indian Bureau had been established under the War Department in 1790 to control these commercial relations, but this control was later transferred to Congress in 1834. The annual budget of the Indian Bureau soared to over five million dollars. Suddenly, the fragile business of Indian relations became big business, and an excellent venue for buying votes.

This new Indian Bureau required a virtual army of contractors, agents, freighters, warehouse owners and distribution clerks. With so many jobs, and so much money at stake, the Indian Bureau became a key pawn in the game of political patronage, and abuses were rampant. President Johnson sought to lend an air of nobility and integrity to Indian relations in 1869 by placing the nomination of Indian agents in the hands of church societies. Unfortunately, most of these "godly" men proved to be as corrupt as their secular counterparts. Judge Castello, however, proved to be the exception to this rule. He became a trusted friend of the Utes and their leaders in a friendship that would grow and deepen over the years.

In 1861, an agency for the Tabeguache Utes was established at Conejos with Lafayette Head as agent. Head had been run out of his native Illinois by his neighbors when he married a twelve-year-old girl. He escaped with her to Colorado, where she later died. He then married a wealthy, vivacious Spanish widow and settled near Conejos in 1854. He became an early

cattle baron and a very powerful man. The Utes, however, accused Head of stealing
supplies intended for them
and then substituting the
shipment with spoiled provisions. Cattle that were designated for the Utes were
euphemistically called "slow
elk" and shot by hungry
miners. Otto Mears (who
later replaced Head as agent
at Conejos) derisively called
these cattle bearing the Ute
USID brand (United States
Interior Department) the
"USID—U Steal, I Divide"
beef.

Photo courtesy Myrtle Dalby
Catherine Hughes Castello, circa 1865

Agent Head shrewdly
hired Chief Ouray as his interpreter for the princely sum of
$500 a year, hoping that this would enhance his relationship
with the Utes. The winter of 1864 had been brutal for the
Tabeguache Ute people, as heavy snows prevented them from
gathering their winter supply of buffalo meat. As a result, they
were reduced to begging for food. In November, Utes and settlers had been shocked and outraged by Colonel Chivington's
ruthless attack on Black Kettle's peaceful Cheyenne encampment at Sand Creek, east of Colorado Springs. Over 150 Indian
men, women and children were killed. Chivington had censured
one of his men during this foray for trying to spare the life of an
Indian child, reminding him that "nits become lice."

It was in this highly charged environment that Governor
Evans wrote to Judge Castello one of many letters seeking his
help with the Utes:

COLORADO SUPERINTENDENCY
INDIAN AFFAIRS

Denver, August 2, 1865

Hon. James Castello
Fair Play Park Co. C.T.

Dear Sir:
    Yours is received enclosing $90.00 as per agreement.
    As for "Colorado" (Chief Colorow) he left here in perfect friendship, and said he was satisfied. I gave him some shirts and also the man who came with him together with some light articles, the only things he could carry. Agent Head was here to distribute them and his interpreter "Ouray." The Major left to go . . . the South Park, but I learn afterwards parted with "Colorado" and went to Conejos. This I presume is what he means by "vamoosing to Conejos." He and "Ouray" were professedly greatly pleased with my talk and the prospect of a distribution of one or two thousand sheep this fall and he wanted me to write to the people of Cash Creek that he was all right, which I did.
    I am astonished at your report and but for sickness, which kept me awake all night, I would come up in person to see him.
    Will you go at the government expense and see him and give him - which you are hereby authorized to purchase—twenty sheep and a couple or three sacks of flour, or a couple beefs if you cannot get the sheep.
    Tell "Colorado" that I sent them to him because he could not take them, and assure him that I am not for the Mexicans to do any harm to the Indians, but will protect both; that I have ordered a great many sheep for them and will send him word to come, and get them near the Salt Works (in South Park) when the goods come which I hope for soon.
    I have ordered Major Head to go to see him immediately and to call upon you, and if it is all right when he comes, he can return. I trust I can rely upon your utmost efforts in this matter for which I will make suitable compensation.

Very Respectfully,

Your Obt. Servt.

Jno. Evans

Gov. & Ex. Officia
Supt. Ind. Affairs.

Chief Colorow was one of the most noted hostile Indian chiefs in Colorado. He was labeled a "bully and a coward" commanding the "loathing and disrespect of both white man and Indian." Colorow and his band often threatened settlers, delighting in the terrified response he received by making gestures of scalping them. He was one of the few Utes who was adamant in his assertions that whites did not belong in Indian territory, and gained a following of like-minded warriors. He gained further notoriety for a drunken altercation with Colorado Governor McCook in 1870, and then for leading a band of fifty Utes in defeating Major Thornburgh's nearly 200 troops after the White River (Meeker) Massacre in 1879. It is no small wonder that Governor Evans was relieved to have someone such as Judge Castello able to deal with Colorow.

It became increasingly difficult for these early prospectors to remove the gold from its ore, and the thwarted miners began leaving the camps in droves. By 1865, Tarryall, Hamilton, Jefferson and Fairplay were almost ghost towns. Judge Castello decided that his future lay elsewhere than Fairplay. His son-in-laws had probably told him of the widely-used Ute Pass Wagon Road, and the lack of an adequate resting place for stagecoaches and teamsters. Chief Ouray and his other Ute friends had also probably told him of the importance of the crossroads at Twin Creek.

General Edward M. McCook became Governor of Colorado in 1869, and was quite open in his intentions of making a fast fortune. For a price, McCook furthered the business interests of railroads, mines, smelters, real estate and banks. One of his schemes toward this end revolved around Ouray's newly signed Hunt Treaty. In order to control the more than $200,000 annual budget of this treaty, McCook established the Denver Ute Agency. Under this arrangement, any Ute could register with Indian Agent James B. Thompson (McCook's brother-in-law)

Kimmett Collection

Judge Castello's Trading Post was built in June 1870 near the junction
of East Twin Creek and West Twin Creek, at the base of Fortification Hill.

and receive his supplies and annuities in Denver. The East Oil
Creek Trail (which loosely followed Teller Road #1 and
Wildhorn) soon became a highly frequented Ute trail to Denver.

In June, 1870, Judge Castello and his son arrived in Twin
Creek and began construction of a log cabin. He chose a site for
this new home at the base of Fortification Hill, north of East
Twin Creek. His home site was adjacent to the usual camping
ground of his friend, Chief Ouray. It was also propitiously located at the junction of the east-west Ute Trail Wagon Road and
the north-south East Oil Creek Trail.

Catherine Castello and the children rejoined the Judge in
November, and set up housekeeping at that isolated ranch. The
next nearest ranch was eleven miles west on the wagon road
and belonged to Milton Pulver (Pulver Mountain, on the south
side of Wilkerson Pass commemorates his homestead). Four
other families joined the Castellos that fall: E.J. Smith at the
South Platte crossing; the R. Marcott family; John Westal; and
M. Riggs who settled south of Twin Creek on Four Mile Creek.

There was no doctor in the Florissant area until the 1880s.
A feisty, independent woman whom the locals called "Dirty

Colorado Historical Society
Northern Ute Chief Colorow and some members of his band pose
for the camera about 1879. Most of the warriors pictured were
involved in the White River Uprising, later in 1879. Top row,
from left: Nicaagat (Captain Jack), Tanoa (Washington), Catz, Piah
(Black Tailed Deer), Canalla (Johnson), Unknown. Front row,
from left: Tabweah, Wanzits (Antelope), and Chief Colorow.

Woman" proffered her services as midwife and herbalist whenever needed. Nancy Ann Roberts was a large, heavy-set woman
who smoked a corn cob pipe and swore like a man. She defied
convention at every opportunity, and consequently sported a
bright red, sun-burned face through her refusal to wear a proper sunbonnet. She had thin, wispy hair which she twisted into
a tiny knot on the top of her head. Her calico dress was always
encrusted with a hefty layer of dirt and grime—which no doubt
inspired her sobriquet. In addition to her nursing services, she
owned and operated Dirty Woman Ranch and her own sawmill.

Social life for these early settlers was provided by seasonal
outings for berry picking, spring and fall roundup, and by barn

dances. For these occasions, the women spent an entire day in preparation—baking bread, assorted fruit pies, and cakes and frying chicken or roasting wild game. At dawn, the next morning, large hampers of bread, pastries, meats, and preserves were loaded into the wagon along with assorted quilts and blankets, to be used both during the journey and for the usual overnight stay. Then the whole family piled into the farm wagon and the oxen slowly plodded to the destination. Once arrived, the children ran wildly as the adults mingled and exchanged the latest gossip and news. At mealtime, everyone shared their food, which was served accompanied by rich, thick campfire coffee or cool and aromatic wild mint tea.

Judge Castello's modest cabin was soon expanded to include a trading post, general store, and hostelry for overnight lodging. Travelers along the Ute Pass Wagon Road were thankful for the accommodations provided at the Castello Trading Post. Judge Castello was a "genial" man and a gracious host, and Catherine was famous for her hearty home cooking, especially her biscuits. Her table was always graced with her elegant silver and Bohemian glass casters, family heirlooms.

Anna Dickinson was one of these travelers. Anna was born into poverty in Philadelphia in 1842. However, she soon proved herself a child prodigy. She gained national recognition as a very popular anti-slavery lecturer when she was only eighteen. For many years, she averaged 150 lectures, and earned approximately $20,000 a year. In September 1873, she met up with Hayden's survey party and succeeded in climbing Long's Peak with Doctor Hayden. Anna then rode the Denver & Rio Grande down to Colorado Springs. Of course, she did this in style also— perched out front of the engine on the cow catcher! Of course, Pikes Peak had to be climbed before she headed west into South Park. (This was very much the same itinerary that Lady Isabella Bird would follow several months later.) Fortunately, Anna left a charming record of her travels up the Ute Pass Wagon Road. In her journal, *A Ragged Register*, (published in 1879) Dickinson gives a vivid account of her stay at Castello's in Florissant.

Ute Pass Historical Society
A group, that appears to be made up of city folk, enjoy a Sunday afternoon in the mountains. Entertainment included fishing and target practice.

Photo courtesy Rose White
Settlers climb aboard farm and ranch wagons and an early automobile for a picnic and afternoon of berry picking.

(We) *Got a pair of good beasties and comfortable vehi-
cle, clambered into it cased in light woolen garments so
that neither sunnings nor wettings could trouble us, with
substantial hand-bags, a bucket to water the horses; some
lunch; some field-glasses, and divers odds and ends by
way of baggage—and made for the Twin Lakes and
"Derry's."*

*Rode thirty-three miles the first day. From Colorado
Springs to Manitou, up the wild Ute Pass to the beautiful
open country beyond; through Hayden's* (Divide) *Pass,
where on either side the road nature has piled a vast mass
of boulders to the height of four hundred feet, as regularly
and symmetrically as though done by a mason's hand;
across land that was rich and prolific, though we had
started at an elevation of six thousand and were uncon-
sciously moving along to an elevation of nine thousand
feet, and toward sun-setting turned a mile or so from the
line of our travel to see some petrified stumps of trees.*

And shall never forget the spot where they stood.

*A place-like an enormous basin, the sides gently sloping
up to the level brim all around. Short, soft gray grass covering the ground. Timber on the uplifted surrounding edge
miles away, each twig and leaf of which stood out soft yet
distinct as an ivory painting in one's hand. A sky and air
for which I could find no likeness save the 'pearly clearness
of the Celestial City," the coloring shot through it reflected
from the clouds and the sunken sun making a 'light that
never was on sea or land." The pallid massive stumps,
ghostly and cold, of what had been wood ages before the
deluge. Not a sound. Not a chirp of cricket, nor stir of twig
or leaf, or blade of grass, nor whisper of bird. Not a sight
or vestige of existence, human or brute. It was awful, yet
filled with enchantment.*

We carried its exalted spell till we reached Costello's
(sic) *jolly hospitable ranche, with its queer little rooms
lined with canvas and adorned with innumerable copies of
illustrated newspapers, its huge open fireplace made of*

*petrified wood, its gorgeous fire, its royal supper, and yet
more royal beds of sweet-smelling straw.*

*Don't you wish you knew Judge and Madame Costello,
and that they would let you come to their ranche, and feed
you and talk to you, and make you happy, and at depart-
ing allow you to capture from the museum on their open
veranda some antelope-horns or deer-horns, or horns of
Rocky Mountain sheep, mineral specimens or petrified
wood?*

*If you don't, it is because you are a poor benighted mor-
tal, with no knowledge of what you are rejecting.*

*We meandered away from it with reluctance, though we
had before us some long heavenly days of driving across
the South Park, and over the Arkansas Divide.*

By 1873, Catherine Castello's seclusion in the Florissant
Valley was lessened somewhat by the arrival of the Reverend
David P. Long and his family. Reverend Long surveyed the valley, and decided to settle in the "petrified forest" since no one
had yet laid claim to the area. He built a log cabin (just south
of what would later become the Hornbek homestead) which had
a magnificent view of Pike's Peak; he felt that it was the perfect
home site. Long planned to file a homestead claim as soon as
the land was surveyed. His daughter, Atlanta Long Thompson,
wrote of these early days in Florissant in her autobiography,
Daughter of a Pioneer.

*When the few scattered settlers in the region heard that
Pa was building a cabin and intended to live there, they
came and helped him. This cabin was about eighteen feet
long and fifteen feet wide. It was built of round logs and
smaller logs were used for the roof. A large ridge pole was
put across the logs when the walls were high enough and
then smaller logs were laid on this ridge pole, forming the
roof. These poles were usually covered with dirt, but Pa
found some white clay near by, and he used this instead.
This made a splendid covering for the roof until the three-
day rains of August commenced and then it began to leak.*

Photo courtesy Douglas and Virginia Pearce.
Reverend David Long and his family pose for a photo on February 2, 1895.
Long was the first white settler on what is now the Florissant Fossil Beds
National Monument. The photo was taken three years after his wife, Lydia,
died. Top row, from left: William, Eva, Rev. Long, Atlanta (Mrs. Silas
Thompson). Front row, from left: Joseph, George, Emma, Loa.

*In one side of this cabin there was a small window. The
only doorway was cut in one end and the door itself was
made of rough boards with a wooden latch that fit down
into a groove on the inside with a buckskin thong hanging
on the outside. One could pull this thong and lift the latch.
The latch string was always out. There were no locked
doors in those days. In the other end of the room was a fireplace in which we burned pitch logs. One of these logs
would burn all evening and throw out a cheery red glow.
We children thought it great fun to throw pitch logs onto
the fire. In addition to the fire place, there was a small
cook stove in one corner of the room and in another corner
were two or three shelves to hold some dishes. We had a
home-made table and a few broken chairs which Pa had
mended. There wasn't much room for furniture but we*

*always had a trundle bed which could be pushed under
the big bed in the daytime.*

*Pa could go out and kill a deer any day that we needed
meat. The cotton-tail rabbits were plentiful, too, and we
enjoyed them just as much as we did fried chicken. In this
way we always had fresh meat.*

*Since there was no school for her children, Ma per-
suaded Pa to build on another room and she taught us
children and the neighbor children, and even boarded one
little girl who could not walk so far.*

Chief Ouray and his Utes were still frequent visitors to the
Florissant area all through this period, for it remained
Tabeguache Ute hunting grounds in addition to being the cross-
roads for the East Oil Creek Trail and the Ute Pass Trail.

Atlanta Long Thompson wrote that:

*Chief Colorow was in our house many times. He was
very friendly toward the white man. He could speak some
English, and father enjoyed talking to him. Sometimes he
would come and bring some of his tribe with him. They
would sit on the floor and say, 'Heap pretty squaw,'meaning my mother, and then say, 'Me like heap biscuits.'*

In the winter of 1874-75, Chief Ouray camped near
Florissant with a band of 600 Utes. They remained there for
several months, probably hunting, gathering herbs and berries,
and trading with Castello. One day, a ranchman named J.
Pleasant Marksbery—who lived along the Tarryall River—rode
into town. He stopped at Castello's post office, tethered his
horse, and went into the building. In the meantime, Ouray's
War Chief, Shawano, recognized Marksbery's fine pony as one
stolen from his Ute friend, Antelope. A Ute brave quickly
removed the saddle and bridle, swung his leg across the pony's
back, and rode off.

Agent Thompson (no relation to Atlanta Long Thompson)
related what he recalled of the incident (over thirty years later)
in his memoirs, *Sons of Colorado*, published in 1907:

. . . Marksberry (sic) *went to the Ute camp, while the men were all out hunting, showed a paper which he said was an order from me as special agent, took the horse, and, with his boy leading the animal—he acting as rear guard—started for his home. Meantime Tab-We-Ap* (Chief Tabernash, or Tabweah), *coming in from the hunt, was told by his squaw what had occurred, and at once started in pursuit. All that could be ascertained from the boy, at the subsequent trial, was that he heard a shot, saw Marksberry fall from his horse, let fall the lariat by which he was leading the captured animal, and "streaked" it for home.*

Within a few hours the telegraph wires were burning again. The neighbors and friends of the murdered man gathered at Castello's, armed and frantic to attack the Ute camp. (They would have been wiped out in a few minutes.) *However, the influence of dear old Judge Castello prevailed to keep them in check, and through his counsel they agreed to leave the settlement of the affair to the proper authorities.*

There is a homely saying, "Blessed is the man who bloweth his own bugle," etc. I will only blow mine to the extent of saying that, with the aid of Ouray, I succeeded in capturing the wicked Tab-We-Ap, brought him to Denver, where he was confined in jail by order of the Commissioner of Indian Affairs, and every effort was made, and every opportunity offered the friends of Marksberry to convict him. No direct evidence was offered or produced, and after holding the prisoner for two months, the Commissioner of Indian Affairs at Washington ordered his release.

Tab-We-Ap was one of the party of "picnickers" that afterwards killed Jo. McLain near Deer Trail, and later was himself killed by Big Frank in the fight at Junction Ranch, in Middle Park.

These memoirs convey a markedly different tone concerning the Utes than Thompson's official reports filed at the time. In these reports, dating from 1871 through 1875, he notes repeatedly that *whites* persistently stole horses from the *Utes*. This situation becomes much clearer as R.B. Townshend's memoirs *A Tenderfoot in Colorado* illuminate this period in history. He observed that most of the gold seekers came out to Colorado by covered wagon. Six or seven men then banded together and outfitted themselves with picks, shovels, tents, and food stuff for about six months at the base camps of Denver or Colorado City. They then hired an ox team to transport themselves and their goods into the mining districts in the mountains. Unfortunately, this left them on foot once they hit pay dirt, and horses commanded the unheard of price of $125 a head.

In addition to the conflict with his own official reports, Agent Thompson's account of Marksbery's murder appears to be seriously in error when it is compared with the contemporaneous newspaper accounts of the incident. *Rocky Mountain News* ran the following story on January 21, 1875:

THE MARKSBERY MURDER. Friday last J. Pleasant Marksbery, a well-known mountaineer, was shot and instantly killed by Shewano, the war chief, whose band are encamped near Mt. Pisgah, about 20 miles south of Florissant also south and west of Pikes Peak. The circumstances are about as follows: Last spring, during the deep snows at Colorado Springs, the Utes traded off some of their ponies. A Mr. Nat Colby purchased one for $20.00 and a revolver, but shortly afterward sold (?) it to Mr. Marksbery for a yoke of cattle. Marksbery had the pony in his possession until about the 20th (of December). Ouray's band of Utes were then camped near Judge Castello's ranch. Mr. Marksbery, who resided some sixteen miles from Florissant on Tarryall Creek, came to the place for letters, goods, etc., and while in the store some Utes stripped saddle and bridle off the pony, and rode off. Mr. Marksbery did not miss the pony until he was about ready to start home. He reentered the store where he was accused by Shawano of stealing the pony, which led to some rather harsh words between them. Marksbery, in the scuffle which ensued, got possession of Shawano's gun and told him he would keep it until his pony should be restored . . .

91

The Hunt Treaty of 1868 was very specific in its provisions for treatment of "bad men among the Indians." The treaty states that such men will "deliver up the wrongdoer to the United States" once proof has been made to their Indian agent. In a followup story printed in the *Rocky Mountain News* on January 26, 1875, further light is shed upon the murder:

THE MARKSBERY MURDER. Promptly in response to telegraphic order from the Indian department at Washington, Major Thompson a few days ago dispatched Chas. A. Jockmus to Florissant with orders to bring to Denver the Ute Indian Tabweah, who is charged with the Murder of Marksbery. On arriving at the Ute camp, Ouray willingly complied with Major Thompson's order and at once surrendered Tabweah. The party arrived here last evening when Tabweah was turned to the custody of Deputy Sheriff D.J. Cook and lodged in the County jail. John Ward came up as an interpreter, as also did Antelope who claims that the killing of Marksbery was done in self-defense. Ouray states that when Marksbery entered the Ute camp in search of the pony said to have been stolen he claimed that he had an order from Major Thompson and one from Ouray as well, for the delivery of the pony, which was not true; that after Marksbery rode away with the pony he was followed by Tabweah and another Indian who tried to induce Marksbery to surrender the animal, that he refused, and made frequent threatening demonstrations with his rifle, the result of which was that Tabweah fired upon him in self-defense and killed him.

Clearly, the Shining Mountains of Colorado were not yet tamed, despite the number of new "civilized" inhabitants. They were certainly not the place for a genteel, lone woman to plan a horseback sightseeing excursion. However, that is precisely what Lady Isabella Bird decided to do in the winter of 1873. She was no novice at world travel, having begun exploring from her native England when she was but twenty years old. She had already visited Scotland, Hawaii, Canada, and the eastern United States before she reached the Rocky Mountains.

Bird was forty-two when she arrived at Greeley and rented a wiry little bay mustang pony, Birdie, who was to become her sole companion. Bird and Birdie set out, alone, in October 1873. Their 800-mile adventure carried them from Long's Peak, down the Goodnight-Loving Trail to Colorado Springs, (I-25) west through Ute Pass and into Florissant, then north through South Park to Fairplay before heading east again. She arrived in Denver in December 1873. Bird kept a record of her travels in a series of letters, which were later published. In this volume, *A Lady's Life in the Rocky Mountains*, Bird gives a colorful description of her stop in Florissant.

Sketch from Harper's Weekly, *1879*
Ute Warrior Tabweah, accused of killing Marksbery. Tabweah was killed in 1878 in an altercation with white settlers in Middle Park.

. . . I came upon wild pine forests (probably Florissant Canyon) *with huge masses of rock from 100 to 700 feet high, cast here and there among them; beyond these pine-sprinkled grass hills, these, in their turn were bounded by interminable ranges, ghastly in the lurid evening, with the Spanish Peaks* (Sangre de Cristos) *quite clear, and the colossal summit of Mount Lincoln, the King of the Rocky Mountains, distinctly visible, though seventy miles away. It seemed awful to be alone on that ghastly ridge, surrounded by interminable mountains in the deep snow knowing that a party of thirty had been lost here a month ago. Just at nightfall the descent of a steep hill took me out of the forest and upon a clean log cabin, where, finding that the proper halting place* (Castello's hotel) *was two miles farther on, I remained. A*

93

truly pleasing, superior-looking woman (probably Lydia Long, Atlanta Long Thompson's mother) *placed me in a rocking-chair; would not let me help her otherwise than by rocking the cradle, and made me "feel at home." The room, though it serves them and their two children for kitchen, parlour, and bedroom is the pattern of brightness, cleanliness, and comfort. At supper there were canned raspberries, rolls, butter, tea, venison, and fried rabbit, and at seven I went to bed in a carpeted log room, with a thick featherbed on a mattress, sheets, ruffled pillow slips, and a pile of warm white blankets.*

Among her harrowing experiences, Bird tells of traveling through snow as high as Birdie's back, and of weather so cold that ice crusted one of her own eyes closed. However, her adventures in Colorado's Rockies seems only to have whetted her appetite, and she followed it with travels to Japan, India, Tibet, China, Korea, and Persia. She finally made a home in Scotland where she died at the ripe old age of seventy-three.

Bird and Dickinson were not the only tourists visiting Pikes Peak's backcountry during the early 1870s. The *Centennial*, a newspaper published out of Georgetown (just west of Denver) reported on the several tourist sites at Florissant in 1876.

FLORISSANT, in El Paso County, 35 miles west of Colorado Springs, is celebrated for the great variety and abundance of geological and mineralogical specimens found in its vicinity; and it has become a noted resort for tourists passing through that portion of the Territory.

An earlier *Centennial* article in February of that year asserted that "many" thousands of pounds of crystals had been removed from the Crystal Mountains (Topaz Butte/Crystal Peak) located about eight miles north of Florissant. This article reported that "last summer and fall there were from twenty-five to thirty miners here constantly, beside some thousands of tourists and excursionists." A large rectangular prism, measuring six inches at the base, and eighteen inches long, was supposedly found in the area. Among these crystals were found Smoky Quartz, Adularia, Green, Purple and White Fleur Spar.

A Lady's Life in the Rocky Mountains
Lady Isabella Bird and her horse, Birdie.

These were the sacred stones of the Ute, their "wotai," that their holy people carried to Pikes Peak for Vision Quest and blessing for use in ceremony and healing. In addition to these minerals, the article also expounded on the fascinating petrified stumps and fossilized remains at the "Petrified Stumps."

Not all of these early travelers came to revel in the fresh air and the scenic wonders, or to haul precious crystals from the Ute's sacred peak. Some came to work. Arthur Lakes, a professor at Golden, came to study the area's geology in 1877. (The journal that he kept of this trip was recently published under the title *Discovering Dinosaurs in the Old West*) In August, 1877, he wrote that he traveled across South Park and arrived at Castello's "well known ranch . . . a combination of a number of little houses which have grown together one after another as they were needed forming a little village . . ." The "big bellied jovial old" judge housed him in a "delightful little cottage . . . papered with illustrated newspapers." He and the eminent Professor Scudder studied the fossils and petrified trees in the Florissant Valley, and returned from each day's labors to a " . . . roaring fire of logs in the bar room . . . The logs were burning in a large open fire place the pillars and mantelpiece of which were quaintly enough formed of big blocks of the petrified stumps of the basin and the walls of Miocene shales entombing abundance of beautiful leaf impressions and fossil insects."

Judge Castello delighted in showing his curious guests the Ute stronghold on the hill above his ranch house. Professor Lake noted that "The side and top of the hill were profusely scattered over with loose fragments of trachyte which the Indians had piled up into rude honey comb rifle pits . . . There were some remarkable funnel like holes in portions of the massive lava regular and smooth and circular as a funnel [the mortises] about a foot in diameter and penetrating in one case five or six feet . . ."

Another of the early and prominent settlers in the Florissant Valley was the Welty family. In 1871 Levi Welty and his three boys rode up Ute Pass and across the hills to Castello's trading post. When they asked about ranch land, the Judge directed them eighteen miles south, toward the Cripple Creek area. Welty took the Judge's advice, and soon had a prosperous ranch in the very valley that would later be platted as the town of Cripple Creek—the world's greatest gold camp. In fact, it was the Weltys who gave the little stream coursing through their ranch lands the name of "Cripple Creek" after two cowboys and a cow were injured there all in the same day.

Judge Castello found it easy to begin a ranching enterprise at his newly established home on Twin Creek. Many of the travelers up the Ute Pass Wagon Road arrived with lame or foot-sore horses and oxen. These were easily traded, usually three or four jaded animals in exchange for one healthy animal. Within a few weeks, the investment paid its dividends as the mineral-rich grasses and pure mountain air quickly restored the vigor of the tired animals. And there was no shortage of the life-giving grass, as "vast acres of waving grass were visible" from the Castello's door.

Judge Castello soon added a second cabin, which was used as country store and trading post. Castello's trading post would have carried the staples common to pioneer life—flour; coarsely ground corn meal; coffee; dried apples, apricots and peaches; dried onions, squash and chili peppers; Mexican *piloncillos* (sugar squares); salted pork and salt. For his trade with the Indians, the Judge would have lined the walls of the trading post with Navajo blankets, bolts of calico, and rifles. Iron cooking pots, strings of red chili, and bundles of crude tallow candles would hang from the rafters, as well as various pieces of harness and tack. Brightly colored glass beads would mingle with boxes of powder and shells along rough-hewn log counters.

Travelers were pressed into service as mail carriers until 1872, when Judge Castello established a post office. He named his post office Florissant after his home town of Florissant, Missouri. The little community of Twin Creek was now officially "Florissant." Fred Smith soon established a much-needed blacksmith shop within a block of the trading post, and thus the seeds were planted for a small town. By 1876, the population of Florissant had increased to approximately seventy residents, living in twenty-two log houses. There was now a small log schoolhouse and three sawmills. However, ranching remained the principal commercial activity in the area.

Samuel Hartsell had set the standard for ranching west of Pikes Peak when he established a 9,000-acre ranch at the fork of the South Platte and Fairplay branch of the Platte in 1863. He gained his place in history by bringing the first pedigreed short-horn cattle (an English breed) into Colorado. Hartsell also built a small community around his ranch, with a hotel at the hot springs, a school house, wagon and blacksmith shops and a sawmill.

To be a really large Colorado cattle baron, however, it seemed that one should be named John Wesley. Colorado's two preeminent cattle growers were John Wesley Iliff, who ran 25,000 head on the plains east of Denver; and John Wesley

Prowers, who ran 10,000 head on the Arkansas east of La Junta.

Iliff began buying longhorns from Texan Charlie Goodnight in 1866 and crossing them with his shorthorn Illinois bulls. He was able to quadruple his investment on each cow, and the two entered a very lucrative partnership. Goodnight, and his Texas partner Oliver Loving, blazed a cattle trail from Texas, up through Denver, to Wyoming (along present-day I-25). Between 1866 and 1884 they moved over five million longhorn cattle over what was called the Goodnight-Loving Trail. Charlie Goodnight finally moved all of his ranching operations to Colorado in 1869. He bought a large parcel—a third of the Nolan Land Grant—just west of Pueblo and became a prominent business man in that town.

Ranching in Colorado was becoming big business. Hungry miners, as well as homesteaders and the new city dwellers, created a thriving market for beef. In 1867, Colorado's ranchers organized the Colorado Stock Growers Association to begin recording brands. Branding was critical in establishing ownership of the cattle herds that mingled on the open range land. Colorado had virtually unlimited open grazing until the advent of barbed wire in the late 1870s. Until then, however, the homesteaders in the Florissant area had to build picket or log fences around their homes and precious kitchen gardens in order to keep the cattle out. The Florissant school had a charming three-rail fence in order to keep the cattle from tramping over the children at play. Area ranchers held cooperative roundups each spring and fall in order to sort their respective stock for branding and shipping.

When the Castellos first settled in Florissant, there were only a handful of other communities in the entire state. The closest, of course, was Colorado City (formerly El Paso), at the base of Ute Pass, which was founded about 1859. About sixty miles south of Colorado City, a handful of Mountain Men had established a small fort, "El Pueblo," in 1841, but were all murdered by angry Utes in 1854. The gold fever of 1859 was key to reviving the settlement, however, as well as to giving birth to Canon City located another fifty miles west.

All of these early settlements were propitiously located along the major roads leading to the gold strikes. In addition to these towns, the gold strikes also gave birth to a number of short-lived communities—Tarryall, Fairplay, Hamilton, and Jefferson, to name a few. With few exceptions, the towns that were established to serve travelers enjoyed longer lives and a more steady prosperity than those playing host to the gold seekers. There was greater stability, and less risk, in supplying food, clothing, transportation and other services than in challenging the stubborn earth to release her precious minerals.

A year after Judge Castello established his trading post on the banks of Twin Creek, General William J. Palmer was struck by the beauty of Pikes Peak and platted his Fountain Colony—now called Colorado Springs. He began construction immediately on his grand vision of an intercontinental, north-south railroad. By 1872, the tracks of his narrow-gauge Denver & Rio Grande Railroad had reached Pueblo from Denver, pausing momentarily before snaking their way down through New Mexico and further up the Arkansas River on a detour to Colorado's gold camps.

Palmer and his young friend, Dr. William Abraham Bell (a homeopathist), diversified their railroad portfolio by buying a 10,000-acre ranch just north of present-day Woodland Park, near Manitou Lake. The twenty-six-year-old Bell, an attractive "very British young Irishman . . . eager, impulsive and pure," was the social leader of Little London (Colorado Springs) society. Marshall Sprague noted that General Palmer's love for his young business associate was akin to the "puzzled love of a father for a precocious son."

Doctor Bell married the genteel Cora Georgina Whitemore Scovell, who became notorious for her absent-mindedness—at one time totally forgetting one of her five children after a visit to a friend's house. Somewhat disconcerted, she returned late that evening, breathlessly running up the stairs, waving her hands, and exclaiming "Can a mother forget her child!" With the slightest provocation, she and her equally gregarious husband hosted frantic, frenzied parties at the Tudor-style Briarhurst manor in Manitou Springs.

Dr. Bell's kindred spirit, the son of Marquis of Cholmondeley, Francis "Chumley" Thornton oversaw their cattle operation up Ute Pass in Bergen's (later called Manitou) Park. And the equally eccentric Homer Foster built his little railroad to haul the lumber to the partner's lumber mill. But Doctor Bell also wanted a resort hotel. His Manitou Park Hotel opened in 1873, boasting a comfortable, two-story log building with a porch on three sides and crowned with a pretentious Mansard roof.

Frances Metcalfe Bass wrote in *Heritage of Years* that a family of "bed-bugs were in possession of the hotel. I carried at all times a blower of Persian Insect Powder which I squirted in every crevice when I was not scrubbing, washing, or reading Matthew Arnold's verses in the black shadow of a stately pine."

Dr. Bell's idyllic hideaway was also plagued by poor management and a series of fires that finally destroyed the hotel in 1886. In spite of its shortcomings, the Manitou Park Hotel had a warm and inviting ambiance. Frances Bass wrote that she:

> . . . loved the ranch house. The cots, tables, curtains made from Turkey red cotton and seats made from barrels half-sawed in the front, and filled with gunny sacking stuffed with hay, invited rest before the wide mouth of the stone fireplace, crowned with antlers, where burned pitch-pine logs that spluttered and blazed. The walls were enlivened with portraits and scenes cut from pictorial magazines; pelts of deer, coyote and buffalo covered the floor, making it a pleasant place to lounge.

Further distraction was offered the hotel's guests at the nearby sawmills. Bass attended the revelries and later reminisced that:

> . . . two fiddlers scraped their bows; standing on a pile of rough boards, the head lumberman called out the dances, while the guests, arriving on horseback, danced on the rough floors, swinging to the strains of the Virginia Reel and quadrille. The head lumberman despised our ignorance as he shouted 'balance to partner,' 'dos a dos,' 'allez main left,' 'all promenade.'

In the midst of the national financial panic of 1873, General Palmer and his business partners became justifiably anxious about their ability to sell the town lots in Fountain Colony. Palmer's financial backer, the Englishman William Blackmore, had formed a fortuitous relationship with the new chief of the U.S. Geological and Geographical Survey, Dr. Ferdinand V. Hayden. Hayden and Blackmore met in Laramie, Wyoming, in 1868 while Hayden was working on his famous survey of the Nebraska Territory and Blackmore was consulting with officials of the Union Pacific Railroad. Blackmore and Palmer were considering the purchase of the vast Sangre de Cristo Land Grant, and enlisted Hayden to do a resource survey of the area. Hayden spent several months traveling through the grant area in Northern New Mexico and Colorado's San Luis Valley, assessing its potential. He then submitted a five-page report to Blackmore. In 1869, Blackmore published Hayden's report in London in a promotional book titled *Colorado: Its Resources, Parks, and Prospects.*

Blackmore later accompanied (and helped finance) Hayden's famous second survey of Yellowstone in 1872. Tragically, however, Blackmore's lovely young wife died of "fatigue" during this survey. Publication of this survey, which included breathtaking photos by William Henry Jackson and ethereal paintings by Thomas Moran, resulted in the creation of Yellowstone Park in 1872.

Blackmore felt that Hayden could generate as much excitement about Colorado as he had for Yellowstone with one of his surveys. He also convinced Hayden to include an assessment of his coal fields near Trinidad and Raton. Hayden agreed to this plan, and convinced Congress to finance a similar survey of Colorado beginning in September 1873, complete with Blackmore's coal fields. Hayden then had his second-in-command, James T. Gardner, publish the results in a *Report Upon the Southern Coal and Iron Fields Of Colorado Territory.* When this report came to light, it caused a small scandal. It solely benefitted Palmer and Blackmore's land holdings in that area, but was financed by the United States Congress. Fortunately,

USGS

Members of Hayden's survey party relax in camp. From left: William H.
Jackson (photographer), Dr. A.C. Peale, G.P. Dixon and Doctor Turnbull.
It was Peale who first recognized the scientific importance of the fossils
he found in the Florissant Valley during the 1873 Hayden survey.

however, the remainder of the Hayden's survey benefitted all of
Colorado.

Hayden was an ex-professor and ex-doctor who found his
calling as a geologist and paleontologist in the far reaches of the
unknown West. He was a slightly-built man with an enormous
dark, bushy beard and mustache. He had a penchant for dressing oddly, usually sporting a weather beaten frock coat and ever
present leather pouch filled with stones. The Sioux Indians had
long before christened him "He Who Picks Up Stones Running"
because of his habit of constantly jumping off his horse and
gathering rocks along the way.

Dr. A.C. Peale—a former student of Hayden's and a noted
mineralogist—accompanied Hayden on his Colorado survey. In
1874, he recognized and documented the scientific importance
of the "Petrified Forest." He presented his specimens to the
famous paleobotanist, Leo Lesquereux, who determined that

Florissant's fossils were approximately forty million years old.

Hayden spent the summers of 1873, 1874, and 1875 directing his highly-trained, youthful parties of about twenty men each in the daunting task of mapping the Colorado Rockies. Hayden's gang also spent a good deal of time at Ben Requa's general store and restaurant in Fountain, Colorado. It was there, in 1873, that the erstwhile cowboy Bob Womack met Hayden. Hayden quizzed Womack about the mountains and meadows on the west slope of Pikes Peak, which was their present objective. Womack directed the survey team up Ute Pass to Florissant, then south down

Colorado Springs Pioneers Museum
Bob Womack, a local cowboy, learned how to find gold while scouting for Hayden's survey west of Pikes Peak. He used that knowledge later to discover gold on Cripple Creek.

the trail to the Welty Ranch. One of Hayden's base camps, about twenty-seven miles west of Colorado Springs on the Ute Pass Wagon Road, was later named Hayden's Divide (now called simply "Divide"). When Hayden's team visited the Cripple Creek area a week later, they discovered a large volcanic formation of "trachorheite."

One of the surveyors, H.T. Wood, returned to the area in 1874, convinced that the trachorheite held gold-bearing ore. He formed a partnership, and dug a 100-foot tunnel, which he named the Lone Tree Prospect Tunnel. Womack watched and listened to all this activity, gaining the knowledge that enabled him to make his famous discovery of Cripple Creek gold in 1890. Wood was not so fortunate, however. He and his partners abandoned their site after finding a worthless "white iron"—

103

which was very probably sylvanite, Cripple Creek's character-
istic gold ore.

Hayden made a practice of meeting with the local settlers in
each region, and strictly adhering to the place names that were
currently in use. Many of these names have, however, changed
in the intervening years. Hayden's maps, for instance, show
"Topaz Butte" rather than Crystal Peak; Witcher Creek is
labeled "West Twin Creek;" Four Mile Creek is "West Oil
Creek;" Hay Creek is "East Oil Creek;" Woodland Park is simply "Junction;" and Lake George is "Links Ranche."

After leaving Judge Castello's on her horseback tour in 1873,
Lady Isabella Bird continued west on the Ute Pass Wagon
Road, to Link's Ranch.

> That afternoon I rode through lawnlike upland parks,
> with the great snow mass of Pike's Peak behind, and in
> front mountains bathed in rich atmospheric coloring of
> blue and violet, all very fine, but threatening to become
> monotonous, when the wagon road turned abruptly to the
> left, and crossed a broad, swift, mountain river, the head-
> waters of the Platte. There I found the ranch to which I
> had been recommended, the quarters of a great hunter
> named Link, which much resembled a good country inn.

At the time of her arrival, Link had yet not returned from his
day's hunting, and so a somewhat annoyed Isabella had to
spend a half hour tending to her horse before supper. Link's stables offered an interesting diversion, however, in the form of a
"partially domesticated" buffalo calf. Isabella told her sister
that this pet was a:

> . . . very ugly thing at seven months old, with a thick
> beard, and a short, thick, dark mane on its heavy shoul-
> ders. It makes a loud grunt like a pig. It can outrun their
> fastest horse, and it sometimes leaps over the high fence of
> the corral, and takes all the milk of five cows.

Isabella was soon joined by a German lady and three gentlemen that she had met in Manitou Springs. Link's wife was a
"pleasant, friendly woman" who prepared a "splendid though

rude supper" for her five guests. Isabella was somewhat uncomfortable during dinner, however, for her hostess mistook her for
a Dane or a Swede and spent the meal "orating on the greedi-
ness of English people." When Link returned later in the
evening, he assured Isabella that he was the oldest hunter and
settler in the district. With that pronouncement, he and his
hunting buddies—a hunter, a miner, and a teamster—entered
into a heated discussion concerning the best trail for Isabella to
follow on the remainder of her journey. In spite of Link's dire
admonition, Isabella chose to follow the Hamilton/Tarryall
Road the next day.

Future travelers in Pikes Peak's backcountry would benefit
from the unequaled success of Hayden's survey. It was so well
done that it paved the way for Congress' decision to make
Colorado a state in 1876. Unfortunately, the selling of Colorado
came too late for Palmer and Blackmore. In 1877, Palmer
defaulted on the Denver & Rio Grande bonds that Blackmore
had so avidly sold to his friends. Sickened by this failure,
Blackmore became a hopeless alcoholic and ended by commit-
ting suicide in England. Palmer, of course, went on to make
other fortunes with his town and his railroad. Pikes Peak's
backcountry, however, received a new lease on life now that the
area had been properly surveyed. The Homestead Act of 1862
stated that:

> . . . any citizen, or person with intention of becoming a cit-
> izen, who was the head of a family and over twenty-one
> years of age, could become possessed of 160 acres of the
> surveyed public domain after five years of continuous res-
> idence on his tract and the payment of a small ($26 to $34)
> registration fee. If the homesteader desired, the title could
> actually pass into his hands after six months residence
> and the payment of the minimum price of $1.25 per acre.

PIKES PEAK BACKCOUNTRY

CHAPTER SIX

Homesteading

W ithin the mysterious circle of life, birth and death closely follow one another in endless succession— much as summer always follows winter. Each cloud threatens a storm and promises a rainbow. In its embryonic state, the little town of Florissant was not immune to these cycles of life.

First, the much beloved old Judge Castello died in the spring of 1878. The *Rocky Mountain News* carried his obituary, noting that "the state (of Colorado), and especially his county, have lost a most worthy and useful citizen, and a wide circle of personal friends will mourn with his stricken family in their great bereavement." Close on the heels of the Judge's death, a terrible drought struck the entire state of Colorado, devastating farmers and ranchers alike. Lightning struck the crisp, lifeless grasses and the dry, brittle trees, sending forest fires blazing all over the state. Smoke from the fires on Pikes Peak obliterated its snow-shrouded summit, and filled the lungs of the mountain settlers as well as those of the wealthy new land owners in Palmer's Fountain City.

As the earth humbled her people with these natural disasters, she also grudgingly yielded more of her riches. Silver had been found in Leadville, and it soon became the world's largest silver camp. Incited by Hayden's survey reports, Leadville's argonauts spilled westward, over the Sawatch Mountains, staked their claims, and established Aspen (originally named Ute City). The ink wasn't even dry on the 1868 Hunt Treaty with the Utes before miners began staking claims in the San

Juan Mountains and demanding a new treaty, the 1873 San Juan Cession. In October 1873, Agent Thompson wrote to the Commissioner of Indian Affairs that the Ute's treaty delegation, including Agent Adams, Chief Ouray, and ninety lodges, had made a side trip, down the Hamilton (Tarryall) Road to Florissant, before proceeding on the train to Washington. Apparently, Ouray wanted to consult with his trusted friend, Judge Castello, before signing another treaty and relinquishing yet more land.

Wave after wave of obsessed prospectors engulfed the Shining Mountains—the sacred Ute hunting grounds, assured as theirs "forever" in treaty after treaty. Treaty after treaty guaranteed the Utes that "The United States now solemnly agrees that no persons . . . shall ever be permitted to pass over, settle upon, or reside in the (Utes') territory . . ." And the government meant to keep its word—unless there was gold or silver to be found.

Silver was the money of the land. Any miner with a pick, a shovel and a will to work could quickly fill his pockets. Silver was now worth $1.29 per ounce. And during this period, wages of $1.00 per day were the standard. With a little sweat, a miner could easily dig the equivalent of a month's wages in one day or less. Once it was removed from the ground, the silver was readily converted to cash at the numerous smelters springing up around the state. There were now smelters at Pueblo, Denver, Leadville, Durango, Salida, Silverton, Telluride and Lake City. Colorado's mountains were "the stuff that dreams were made of"—but the Utes were a problem.

Why should these few Indians own such vast stretches of Colorado's mountains and wealth? They didn't even value the riches beneath their feet and, in fact, felt that the whites were stabbing their Mother Earth in her face with each stroke of a miner's pick. Indeed, they felt that ripping into Mother Earth for her minerals was much the same as ripping open the belly of one's own mother in order to feed oneself. When Colorado's ancient volcanoes erupted, creating vast mineral deposits, they also fomented the later conflict between the two cultures, White and Red.

108

Colorado's Utes were a peaceable people, more inclined to cohabitation than to confrontation, and this posed an ethical dilemma for their covetous white neighbors. The *Denver Tribune* sought to remedy this untenable situation by beginning a "Utes Must Go" campaign. The paper was soon filled with slanted stories of Ute misconduct, even attributing the numerous forest fires to the Ute. The paper neglected to point out that Colorado was in the midst of a drought, and that the United States government documented lightning as the cause of all the fires.

Tensions between the settlers and the Utes began to mount, and finally ignited a fatal conflagration at the White River Ute Agency in northwest Colorado. Senator Henry Teller, one of the staunchest opponents of the Ute presence, appointed reformist Nathan Meeker Indian agent at White River. Meeker's rigid management style, and his overbearing efforts to transform his nomadic charges into sedentary farmers, propelled him along a tragic path. When he finally threatened to shoot all of their ponies, the Utes rebelled, killing Meeker and ten of his men.

The Meeker Massacre was exactly the catalyst that the *Denver Tribune* needed. The "Utes Must Go!" campaign now echoed throughout Colorado, and the United States Congress soon responded to its pressure. The small band of angry White River Utes had succeeded in undoing all that had been gained from over 200 years of treaties and peaceful cohabitation. In 1881, Colonel McKenzie herded thousands of Ute exiles to newly created reservations in southern Colorado and eastern Utah. No longer would Ute warriors seek guidance from the Great Spirit in Vision Quests on the slopes of Pikes Peak, where their people were created. No longer would sick or troubled Utes bathe in the healing mineral waters at Manitou Springs. No longer would Ute medicine men and women gather sacred healing stones on the slopes of the Crystal Mountains. No longer would the Ute hunt the elk and the deer and the antelope in their ancient hunting grounds.

A flood of eager new homesteaders followed close on the heels of the Utes' departure. However, this flood was preceded by a modest first wave of homesteaders in 1877. They came after the publication of Dr. Ferdinand Hayden's *Atlas.* For Hayden had not only delineated the probabilities of Colorado's mineral wealth, but also its suitability for farming and ranching. An added bonus to Hayden's surveys was that the land could now be legally homesteaded. It is interesting that the Act does not discriminate by either gender or race. This lack of discrimination proved to be the lure in attracting another of Florissant's more famous settlers—Adeline Hornbek.

Adeline was born in the Year of the Shooting Stars, 1833— the same year that the Ute Chief Ouray was born. Her brother, Alexander, had become an Indian trader on the Creek Indian land that is now Oklahoma. Adeline met and fell in love with his friend and fellow trader, Simon A. Harker. They married and settled in Oklahoma for a while. However, Simon was seized with bad health shortly thereafter which he attributed to exposing himself to bad weather while out buying cattle. This lingering illness, and the coming Civil War, probably motivated the Harkers to move to Colorado. Adeline, Simon and their two infant children, Frank and Annie, made the trip across the arid plains by ox-drawn wagon. She was only twenty-seven when she and Simon settled on Cherry Creek, just east of Denver. Here they established a cattle ranch in 1861, and began a forty-year ranching odyssey for Adeline.

In addition to ranching, Simon also served as Indian agent for the newly founded Colorado Territory. Raising beef for hungry miners and employing diplomatic skills with Native Americans was a major cultural transition for Harker, who had emigrated from England when he was only thirteen. The family seemed to prosper, however, and engaged in a number of real estate transactions in the area. A second son, George, was born in 1863. Simon became a member of the Masonic Order, and was also active in the Republican Party.

Another of the gold-seekers of 1859, Dr. George M. Willing, provides a rare glimpse of Denver at this time in his diary, published by the *Daily Missouri Republican* on August 9, 1859.

> *Denver City and Auraria together make up but an inconsiderable village, with Cherry Creek—when there's any water in it—running through the middle of it. There*

are here about one hundred and fifty houses, with about forty lodges of the Arrapahoe (sic) Indians—quite a number of negro women, with a pleasant but scanty sprinkling of white ones, and a mixed male population of white, black, red, and yellow.

Dr. Willing's fellow traveler, William Magill, wrote to his sister in Florissant, Missouri, in June of that same year that he had "not seen or heard anything of the Florissant Boys (Castello's?) with the exception of Henry Haner . . . We suppose that they are all in the mountains."

It may have been during this period that the Harkers met another Indian agent, Judge James Castello of Fairplay. Historians have not yet documented when these two families met. However, the Castello's were to become friends and neighbors of Adeline when she later moved to Florissant. Colorado's Indian agents were a small but elite group, and it is very possible that this group provided the connection with Castello that would later draw Adeline into the Florissant Valley. It is also possible that Judge Castello and Simon Harker met through their mutual involvement in Colorado's Republican Party.

Heavy snows in 1864 kept the Utes from a successful winter buffalo hunt, causing them great distress and starvation. When these same high mountain snows melted in the spring, they caused a devastating flood along Cherry Creek. Its roiling waters destroyed the tranquil pastoral life of the Harkers as they washed through their home and over their pastures. The financial losses were too much for Simon and he died shortly thereafter, though he was only thirty-nine. Adeline was left to rebuild her ranch and her life while caring for her three children, aged from one to five. She seems to have managed very well, and was actually able to purchase their eighty-acre Cherry Creek homestead in 1866.

A few months later, the red-haired, thirty-one-year-old Adeline married Elliot D. Hornbek in Denver. Four years later she bore him a son, and also named him Elliot. This marriage was brief and ill-fated, however, and Adeline was abandoned by Hornbek about 1875. She and her three boys, now aged sixteen, twelve, and five, and Annie, now fifteen, continued in the

111

Hornbeck / Stone family photo
Adeline Hornbek was a single mother
with true grit. Widowed by her first hus-
band and abandoned by her second,
Adeline homesteaded in the Florissant
Valley about 1876.

family tradition of ranching. Fortunately for them,
Texans, Charlie Goodnight
and Oliver Loving, had
opened the Goodnight-
Loving cattle trail. The
demand for beef was so
great that over five million
head of cattle were moved
over this trail between
1866 and 1884.

Adeline's second son,
George Harker, recalls that
his mother and brothers
moved to Florissant in
1876. This complements
the oral tradition of Rev.
David Long's family, which
maintains that Rev. Long's
brother-in-law, Frank Sens,
sold their ranch to the
Hornbeks. Frank had been
given custody of the proper-
ty while Rev. Long took his family on an ill-fated sabbatical to
live at the Mormon colony in Utah in 1874. At odds with this
account, however, is the Homestead Proof form filed by Adam
Hill in 1880. In it he claims that he purchased a shell of a house
and some fencing from Frank "Sence" in 1874. Hill's homestead
lies adjacent to Adeline's on the south.

The first documented evidence of the Hornbek presence,
however, is Adeline's homestead application of 1878. Adeline's
homestead site lies about one mile south of present-day
Florissant on Teller County Road #1, within the boundaries of
the Florissant Fossil Beds National Monument.

Nothing remains of the Long ranch, unfortunately. This is
probably because it was built of "round logs." These tend to
crack in the cool, dry mountain air and then to fill with rain and
snow. The alternate filling, freezing, and further cracking soon

Florissant Fossil Beds National Monument
Adeline Hornbek and her four children built this homestead and successfully ranched in the Florissant Valley for over twenty years. The homestead is now listed on the National Register of Historic Places.

reduce the logs to a hollow collection of sawdust and wood pulp. What was left of the Long's modest Petrified Forest cabin was probably recycled into fence posts to keep the cattle from Adeline's garden.

It is truly remarkable that Adeline, a single mother, had the means to build such a lovely log house. Her new home was one and a half stories with a pine shingle roof. There were three bedrooms upstairs and one downstairs, a kitchen with baking nook, and a parlor. Her compound boasted a barn, which stabled nine horses and had an attached wagon shed. Adeline also built a milk house, chicken house and a large corral for her livestock. In the beginning, she cultivated only three acres, producing some hay and potatoes, as well as her garden vegetables. There were about seventy other residents in the area at this time, and they undoubtedly helped the young widow with a traditional "barn raising."

113

In a 1937 interview with the *Gazette Telegraph,* Adeline's son, George Harker, recalled an alarming incident with the notorious Ute Chief Colorow. As a youth (in 1878 George was fifteen years old) he had a fear of Indians and he said,

> *. . . that as some came near the house, and one started to walk to the house, he got the loaded gun and stood at defense at the door. The wily old Indian chief* (Colorow) *upon being asked into the house quickly sensed what had almost happened and remarked: 'White boy very white. Heap scared.'*

There was a small log school house about a mile from Adeline's homestead, and the boys probably joined the other children of the area in walking to school each day. School records show that Adeline was secretary of the school district in 1880. When Judge Castello died in 1878, his son Frank took over the trading post and soon developed it into the Florissant Mercantile. Adeline ran the store in 1883 while Frank spent a year and a half prospecting for gold in the San Juan Mountains north of Durango.

Ute Pass Wagon Road was heavily traveled during this period, as it was the only road to the gold fields that wasn't a toll road, and Frank Castello's Florissant Mercantile prospered. Florissant's population began to grow steadily and in 1876 the Prussian Count Louis Otto de Pourtales also homesteaded just north of Florissant. He was soon joined by his sister Berthe, an international beauty.

Countess Berthe had come to Cambridge to join her father, the Count Louis Frances de Pourtales, a scientist at Harvard. He had emigrated from France in 1847 to join the Geodetic Survey in Washington, D.C., but later moved to Boston. When she was "hardly more than a child," the slender, blonde Countess Berthe entered into a tragic marriage with the very wealthy Sebastian Schlesinger. Berthe and Sebastian had two small daughters before deciding to divorce. She sought to mend her broken heart by accepting her brother's invitation to visit him at his ranch in Florissant in the early 1880s.

Berthe often traveled down the Ute Pass Wagon Road to Colorado Springs, where she was befriended by society matron, Frances Metcalfe Bass. Berthe was tall and gracious, with a knowledge of several languages, and was considered one of the loveliest women of her day.

Frances Bass later described Berthe at this time as appearing in the Springs "closely veiled, wearing a red cloak tightly buttoned about her throat, with a gray fur collar. She came there broken in health and sad of heart, seeking strength. She had gone first to the Adirondacks with her daughters, where of turkey red calico, she made them dresses— cheap dresses—that were the envy of all campers."

Courtesy Leo and Julia Kimmett

Frank Castello, circa 1900

Frank's father, Judge James Castello, founded Florissant in 1870. Frank transformed the Judge's rustic trading post into the prosperous Florrisant Mercantile, which he sold to William C. Allen about 1898.

Berthe's cousin, Count James Pourtales, left his vast estates in Prussia to follow her to Colorado in 1884. He had been smitten by Berthe's beauty, and determined to make her his wife. Count James was a tall and imposing man, well over six feet. He had a large black beard, constantly smoked a pipe, and was followed everywhere he went by a brace of devoted dachshunds. He was considered a "good fellow" on account of his never-failing good humor.

Count James had been an intimate of Chancellor Bismarck, and easily fit in with the society of Colorado Spring's "Little London." His mother had been a German princess, and was the toast of Paris at the Court of Empress Eugenie. In the midst of wooing his cousin Berthe, Count James also was taken by the

115

Pikes Peak Library District
Frank Castello's Mercantile, circa 1886. McLaughlin & Horrigan's
Drug Store shared a wall with Castello's store. The building on
the far right is the McLaughlin home, which still graces the
corner of Highway 24 and Teller County Road #31.

beauty of a failing Colorado Springs dairy farm, the Broadmoor.
The Count bought the 1,600-acre farm and implemented
numerous reforms in an attempt to make it a profitable enterprise.

He steadily increased his land holdings, and is credited with
being one of the earliest settlers to understand the importance
of water rights. He bought 250 acres of nearby ranch land, irri-
gation ditches and water rights from the Rose Brothers. He
then built Cheyenne Lake, and endured a constant feud with
prairie dogs to keep them from burrowing into the dam and
draining the lake. In a further scheme to enhance his profits, he
platted Broadmoor City, then dreamed up a fancy European-
style casino as an added attraction. He and the Countess
Berthe were eventually married and became the cream of
Springs' society.

In the meantime, Berthe's brother, Count Louis Otto de
Pourtales, was also making a reputation for himself. He homesteaded a section of land about four miles north of Florissant
and begin building a credible ranch of his own. Frances Bass
writes that he was a good "horseman and dancer, born lover, he

116

A Sunday afternoon outing, 1880s style. Burros were the
preferred mode of transportation in the mountains. They
were strong and more sure-footed than horses.

carried a guitar on which he picked a few chords, singing a
monotonous tale of unrequited passion as persistently
melancholy as the call of a mourning dove." He became somewhat notorious over his infatuation with Queen Palmer,
General Palmer's young and beautiful wife. He often rode down
to Palmer's palatial home in Glen Eyrie to sing his melancholy
love songs under Queen's window. Frances Bass and her friends
dubbed him the "Mute Seraph"—perhaps for his manner of quietly hovering around any beautiful woman.

Frances Bass writes that her Mute Seraph once threatened
suicide after being rejected by another of his unrequited loves,
"Little Peaches." His heart seems to have staunchly rebounded
at each of these devastating blows, however, for he eventually
married and settled down. In August, 1881, the hopelessly
romantic Count Louis Otto deeded the ownership of his
Florissant ranch to his new bride, Laura Mary Montgomery, for
"one dollar and the consideration of love and affection."

Count Pourtales built a beautiful log home on his 320-acre ranch, and ran fancy imported German cattle on the surrounding open range. His eye for beauty and grace did not fail him in siting his home—it claimed a breathtaking view of Pikes Peak to the southeast as well as an imposing view of Crystal Peak to the west. His bride, Countess Laura, later delighted in regaling her grandchildren with stories of her life at the ranch. It seems that most of Little London's society traveled up the Ute Pass to attend the fancy balls at the ranch house with its Parisian wallpapers and expensive appointments.

Her sister-in-law, the beautiful Countess Berthe, always created a stir with her visits, arriving in a fancy carriage, elegantly dressed and accompanied by an entourage of assorted dogs straining at their leashes.

A favorite family story centers on the fortunes of a hapless young Lord from England. Frances Bass writes of these unfortunate gentlemen in her memoirs *Heritage of Years:*

> (These) *Younger sons* (who did not inherit) *came from England with Anglo-Saxon land-hunger, equipped with the best of saddles, shotguns and rifles, and coin enough to pay their way. Unfortunately, many had a taste of life en route, and arrived penniless, with their belongings in pawn in Kansas City, or some other hard town, having bucked the tiger in gambling houses. The heart's desire of all was to own a large ranch . . .*

It seems that Count Louis Otto had made a friend of one such young Englishman. According to Countess Laura, this unfortunate young man had not only lost his fortune, but had fabricated glowing accounts of his "ranch" in letters to his family. Naturally, his proud parents were eager to visit this remarkable son and see his vast lands and cattle. The young man was in a delicate quandary, but Count Louis Otto came to his rescue. He and Laura planned a timely visit with friends in the Springs, allowing the English Lord to produce a charade for his parents at the Pourtales ranch in Florissant!

Unfortunately, Count Louis Otto also chose to use round-log construction for his beautiful home. Rain and frost have

Walts Collection, Florissant Heritage Foundation
Count Louis Otto De Pourtales, Countess Laura Montgomery
De Pourtales, and their daughter, Louis Berthe, circa 1892.

steadily worked on the logs for the last 100 years until their hollowed cores collapsed, sending the beautiful dormer windows crashing through the roof of the kitchen and the parlor below. Remnants of the elegant cut granite fireplace lie scattered in a meadow of feathery blue flax. Only the extensive, well-built corrals have survived, giving silent testimony to the great care that Count Pourtales extended to his pure-bred cattle.

Another of the Count's neighbors, Thomas Burnham, filed a homestead claim in 1872, about a mile west of Florissant, on the Ute Pass Wagon Road. He found an old trapper's cabin there (perhaps left by Kit Carson's trappers) and lived in it while he built his large log homestead house. Some of the rough hewn beams measure almost two feet thick, and their sturdy presence even to this day gives mute testimony to the wisdom of squaring the logs. Burnham steadily added to his ranch over the next few years as members of his family filed on adjacent homesteads. He eventually accumulated over 500 acres for his

119

Twin Creek Ranch. He added a small shed for saddles and harness, a bunkhouse for about twelve "waddies" or cowboys, and a carriage house.

Adjacent to the western boundary of Twin Creek Ranch, John and Mary Wilson staked a homestead claim in 1874. And adjacent to them on the north, Charles H. Sisler staked a homestead. In the tradition of the "Florissant Boys," the Wilsons and their nine children also came from Missouri in a covered wagon. Twin Creek's clear, meandering waters and grass-filled meadows soon became home to the Wilson's cattle, too.

However, economics compelled them to summer their stock in the cool, high valleys of Breckenridge. Calas, the oldest, inherited the lonely job of moving the lumbering animals north along the Tarryall Creek into Como, and over Boreas Pass into Breckenridge each spring. The long trek was reversed in the fall before the heavy snows fell. Calas' progress was monitored by a herd of wild mustangs, led by an ethereal, prancing roan stallion with flaxen mane and tail. This Strawberry Roan was coveted by all the local ranchmen, but somehow always eluded capture.

In 1881 Calas married seventeen-year-old Berta Van Horn, best friend of his fifteen-year-old sister Betty. Future generations will continue to benefit from the collection of Berta's revealing letters to Betty, written in 1883, and her subsequent letters to her family in Missouri, written in 1885. A little over a year after they were married, Berta, now three months pregnant, joined Calas on his annual cattle drive into Breckenridge.

Breckenridge, Colorado
May 20, 1883

Dear Betty and All,
Well we are here, but it was hard work to make it. I promised to give details of our trip, will begin at the first.
The first night camped about a mile yon side of McGaughlins (on the Tarryall Creek, north of Lake George), we were all pretty good spirits that night. Next morning got up nearly to McL. House, an old cow got into

the ditch and mired down, had to help her out, all along here calves kept falling out of the wagons, too. (Spring is calving time, and these newborns had to be hauled in wagons as they were too weak to walk the entire trail to Breckenridge.) *Second night camped this side of Farnums. I was not feeling so funny that night. Third night got to Charley Dunbars. Drove up near the house, no one showed themselves and we did not go to hunting them up. The wind blew a gale had just got supper over, it began to snow. I crawled into the wagon and went to bed. After a while Charlie came out and said "had better come in" but did not accept the feeble invitation. I will know how to treat her in the future. Next day got to Hamilton at noon and such another breeze as did blow as we crossed the park, I thought it would take wagon and any over sometimes. We fooled around there in the wind the rest of the day. The next morning they drove the cattle up about five miles further, got back and found Charley* (the horse) *gone. Put in the rest of the day hunting him, found him at C. Dunbars. Sunday noon the Bear River outfit came driving in. Sunday after Calas took things to Como and got them on the train we moved camp up where the cattle were, that night snowed about four inches on us. I had the "blues" bad by this time.*

Monday we came across and such another time I Will not try to write. But finally we arrived at our "Mansion" and such another place there never was. There had been an old cow in the house that had bowel complaint and that bad, too, and everything was hanging. Oh! but I was sick and mad and could see not one thing to laugh at. But I soon saw it was of no use to be that way so went to work in getting things to look a little more like a home. Calas seems to be satisfied so I ought to be. He is off today calling on his old customers. As we came through town look which way, you could see an old woman in the door grinning at him and some would yell at him. I tell you I began to get wrathy. Men kept stopping him to buy calves. The Bear R.(River) *folks are all over. They gave $80 for four*

Ute Pass Historical Society

A youngster gets a taste of bawling calves and burning hide during a roundup west of Florissant in 1895.

cars to ship things in. Guess (they) *thought there was too much back bone required to shovel. Calas did not bring his wagon across* (on the railroad). *Cost $7.00 to ship empty wagon. Drove the hack across in R.R. was not smooth riding by any means. Alice B. was crying when I last saw her because she had to wash too many dishes and she was so sick of moving. Last night snowed, there are four more inches again.*

Well guess must close for this time, will try and write a more interesting letter next time. With love to all.

Write us soon, Berta

Still in Breckenridge in July, Berta complained of the weather and the difficulties of living under a sod roof.

It has been raining every little bit all day and part of last night. The wind blew terrible hard in the night. I thought we were all gonners sure, little old cabin shook so

*and the dirt just poured down. Oh! There is nothing like a
dirt roof. . . .*

She noted that the final calf of the season was born on the
trail at Hamilton, and that Calas sold him for $26.75.

*(Calas) Sells most all the milk he gets yet. The cows are
doing real well I guess have heard no complaint. I have
churned but once got real nice 'yaller' butter. We have not
had a smell of greens yet, have been buying rhubarb it is
cheap enough, 5 cts. A bunch, one bunch will make two
pies.*

A mining camp was a lonely place for a young ranch woman,
however, and Berta urged her best friend to come for a visit as,

*. . . there is to be a circus in town 22nd of this month, come
over. Betty, I wish you could come and stay a while for it
is so lonesome here.*

In August, Berta was even more homesick, writing to Betty
that:

*I am getting more anxious every day for the time to start
back to Florissant to come. Calas tries sometimes to get me
to think I had better go on before it gets so cold but I guess
I will <u>freeze to him</u> till he can go too."*

Several weeks later, her husband attempted to alleviate her
loneliness when he got her a:

*. . . little cat in town and it is a tearer, has cleaned the mice
all out and has gone to catching Chipmunks. . . Will bottle
it up and bring it home I think.*

Berta and Calas drove their ninety-some head of cattle back
to Florissant around the end of October. It was a bittersweet
trip, however, for Berta's best friend, Betty, had died on October
4, at age fifteen. Berta gave birth to a little girl, Stella, on
November 8, 1883. Then she was silent during 1884, only
resuming her correspondence in May 1885 as she and Calas
again took their livestock to Breckenridge. She was one month

pregnant as they began their two-week trek which was hampered by deep snows.

> *The men all turned out to shovel a trail to get the cattle over* (the pass into Breckenridge) . . . *Everything promises to be lively in this camp this summer. Calas sells all the milk he gets now. We only have 6 calves he is milking some of his fathers cows and some of another mans he brought up.*

They returned from Breckenridge at the end of October, and Berta began having labor pains at the end of November. Mrs. Long (Atlanta Long Thompson's mother) was called in as midwife at a cost of five dollars per week. Berta complained that she felt "most awful miserable most the time." But she effused over her little Stella (now two), noting that she

> . . . *wants a book first thing in the morning and the last thing at night. She knows several of her letters anywhere she sees them. She learns very quick, talks everything most, not very plain but I can understand easy enough. Will stand at the window and call 'poor papa' calls herself 'my poor baby' whenever she gets hurt . . .*

This last letter was never finished. Berta died in childbirth on December 1, 1885. Her newborn baby died eight months later.

Calas Wilson eventually left the lonely life of cow punching and opened a barber shop and a cafe in the blossoming town of Florissant. As Frank Castello's Mercantile prospered, Calas purchased a half interest and watched his investment steadily grow. In 1887, he married a lovely woman, Eliza Allison, who had come to enjoy the beauty of the Florissant Valley on the Wildflower Train.

When gold was found in Cripple Creek, Calas was struck with gold fever. He fiendishly worked his claims, certain that untold wealth was just a day's work away. Vainly he tried to ignore the bitter cold of Cripple's winters, working his claims and sleeping in a flimsy tent. But he died of complications from pneumonia when he was only thirty-nine, leaving a young wife and four small children.

When Calas left the family ranch, his chores fell to his younger brother, George. He learned early to ride a bronc, rope a calf, brand cattle, build fences and all of the other ranching skills he would need for the rest of his life. George married an aristocratic young Englishwoman, Ada Plaisted, when he turned twenty-nine, and together they built up the family homestead over the next forty-three years.

Hayden's 1873 survey maps labeled current-day Wilkerson Pass "Puma Pass." This scenic overlook (at 9,507 feet) of South Park, lies near the western boundary of Pikes Peak's backcountry, and was one of the key points on the Ute's Trail and on the later Ute Trail Wagon Road. At some point in the intervening years, however, locals began to refer to the pass as "Wilkerson" in memory of John W. Wilkerson who simply visited the area around the 1870s. He was probably accorded this honor because his great-grandfather, James Wilkerson, cast a mantle of celebrity upon him by his outstanding service to George Washington during the Revolutionary War.

Nearby Badger Mountain (part of the Puma Hills chain that escorts the Tarryall Creek to its headwaters above Como) is heir to a more traditional naming process. Former Englishman and retired Union Army officer, John Badger, built a homestead at the base of his namesake mountain around 1872. He was known to regale his friends and neighbors with stories of the Civil War and the Indian wars prior to his death in 1896.

One of Badger's early neighbors was former Rhode Islander, William M. Farnum, for whom Farnum Peak (about five miles north of Puma City) is named. (Berta Wilson noted that she and Calas encamped near Farnum's Ranch while driving their cattle to Breckenridge.) Farnum himself had become a rancher by accident. In 1863, he and his family were drawn to Colorado by the promise of gold. As they journeyed across the Great Plains, they lost one of their oxen. The only replacement available was a large, shorthorn cow with a heifer calf. They yoked her to their remaining ox and resumed their trek. This wonderful cow not only supplied them with milk their entire journey, but was

Photo courtesy Rolland Wilson
Ada and George Wilson lived on the 1874 Wilson Homestead, a mile west of
Florissant, adjacent to Burnham's (later Allen's) Twin Creek Ranch.

eventually bred again upon their arrival at Como's gold fields.
When Farnum relocated his fledgling ranch further south on
Tarryall Creek he boasted a small herd of fine cattle.

The Hamilton, or Tarryall Road as it is now called, was originally also a Ute trail. In these early days, the Ute people still
frequented the area in accordance with their treaties which
assured them access to their ancient hunting grounds. Ute hospitality decreed that any stranger be made welcome by giving
them something to eat and drink immediately upon arrival. Of
course, Ute people assumed that white people were at least as
civilized, and expected to be fed accordingly when they visited
the scattered ranch houses. Grandmother Farnum was
nonetheless caught by surprise one day when she heard a loud
commotion in her root cellar. She had been standing in her
doorway watching a cavalcade of Utes as they headed south,
toward Lake George, when a young warrior sought to avail himself of her unwitting hospitality. As he climbed down through
the air vent in the root cellar to help himself to the wild raspberries and gooseberries that he saw there, the sod roof suddenly gave way. When she opened the cellar door, the frightened
Ute brave tore past her and rejoined his comrades, empty

William C. Allen's Twin Creek Ranch.
The compound includes Thomas Burnham's 1872 log homestead/barn
and outbuildings, and a trapper's cabin dating from the 1850s.
The ranch is on the National Register of Historic Places.

handed. In 1880, Farnum's Mountaindale Ranch was designated a United States Post Office with William Farnum as postmaster. Six years later, the Farnum's sold their ranch and made one final move to Colorado Springs.

Berta Wilson wrote that their first night of the Breckenridge cattle drive they encamped near "McCaughlins"—actually, the correct spelling is McLaughlin. This beautiful log home is one of the most prominent homesteads along the Tarryall Road, and has a colorful history to match. Dan McLaughlin and his family ran a livery stable and freighting company, initially at Como and then around 1878 they relocated to the Tarryall Valley near the point where the Tarryall Creek abruptly turns east and empties its waters into the South Platte River. Dan's son Ray was known to have a bad temper, and shot and killed one of their ranch hands in an altercation over his "short" wages. Ray later had his foot amputated by Doctor McIntire in Florissant

127

Photo courtesy Kathleen Cramer
William P. Allen
William, father of William C. and Silas, homesteaded south of Florissant in 1883.

after one of his hunting buddies accidentally shot him. This "surgery" was performed in the manner typical for these early pioneers. Ray was simply given a shot of whiskey, then his friends held him on the kitchen table while the good doctor sawed off the injured limb. His stump was later fitted with a metal harness, and thereafter he stomped around the ranch on his hand-hewn wooden foot.

Settlers in the Florissant area were provided with farm fresh milk and freshly churned butter when Richard and Mary Houghton homesteaded a dairy just a mile north of town in 1885. Houghton was a Civil War veteran, and took advantage of the special homestead provisions accorded them. "Uncle Dick" became very active in community affairs, serving on the school board for a number of years. Residents of the area were no longer forced to build log homes, as the population was increased by J.F. Frizzell and Robert Berrs, who operated sawmills. They were soon joined by a family of extremely skilled carpenters, the Allens.

William P. Allen, the father, homesteaded about three miles southwest of Florissant at Big Spring Ranch, now home to Sanborn Western Camp. His son, William, chose a homestead site about a mile northwest of his father's, at the base of Blue Mountain, later adding a second section near Burnham's. His brother, Silas, chose a site adjacent to his father's on the south. Carpentry was the Allen family forte—they built the elegant Victorian-style Cliff House Hotel and skating rink in Manitou

128

Springs, and then built the steps to Seven Falls in Cheyenne Canyon.

Young William undoubtedly led the family to the area, for he also worked as a stagecoach driver on the McLaughlin Line, carrying passengers along the Ute Trail Wagon Road to the gold fields. Florissant now had mail service three times each week, as the Concord stages were pressed into service hauling letters and packages.

Passengers were snugly tucked into the coach under buffalo lap robes. Four matched horses snorted in the cold morning air as they plodded along at five or six miles an hour. Fifteen miles up the Ute Pass Wagon Road, at Summit Park (now Woodland Park), the horses were changed and the passengers were offered a light lunch. Back into the stage all would pile, as the fresh horses proceeded to pull their burden to the 9,165 foot crest of Ute Pass at Hayden's Divide. The coach then burned its brake as it rolled down the winding, boulder-lined slopes of Twin Rocks Road, arriving in Florissant in time for supper and an overnight stay. Early next morning, the stage would continue on its way, either due west on the South Park Road to Sam Hartsell's, or north from Links Ranche (Lake George) up the Hamilton Road to Tarryall or Como.

There was no shelter for the driver of the coach during inclement weather, and winters in the Pikes Peak area often range at thirty degrees below zero. An unknown journalist left this colorful description of his stagecoach driver.

It was interesting to notice this man during his run. Whenever he would become cold he would wave his arms vigorously and slap his chest. Clad in a great fur overcoat and wrapped in buffalo robes from his head to the tip of his toes, he was a sight to behold as he peeped out through the opening for his eyes. Whenever his hands and fingers would become cold we passengers sitting in the rear of the coach would observe him winging his lower arms and slapping his hands and fingers upon his thighs or body to stimulate the blood circulation. We in the rear would often imitate his calisthenic movements but as he received squarely in the face the full benefit of the cold wind and as

Colorado Springs Pioneers Museum
A stage prepares to leave Florissant on Piah Street (Highway 24).
Passengers usually arrived in time for supper, then stayed
overnight before proceeding to their destinations.

we were sheltered by a partition of canvas, we escaped considerable of the exposure.

. . . Gulches and ravines are passed as the stage rolls along and steep hills to climb and steep ones to descend are trying times for the horses and spicy periods for the driver and the passengers. Often there is uncertainty whether the bus [stage] will remain right side uppermost and the horses keep from running away. But these are but small incidents of the trip that furnish spice and variety.

Each arrival of the stage was a great social occasion in Florissant, and most of the town crowded around the tired, steaming horses and greeted the dusty, cramped passengers. In the early days of postal service, each parcel had to be signed for as duly received. Florissant's early postal ledgers reflect the eager signatures of residents such as Count Pourtales and Adeline Hornbek and their many neighbors, while Postmaster Frank Castello attested to their identity with his signature. Neighbors stood around on Piah Street (now Highway 24) waiting for the stage as they swapped bits of gossip and news. Stagecoach drivers were pressed for news from Colorado

Springs, and heavy bundles of the *Gazette Telegraph* were burst open and read voraciously.

Daniel Nevitt operated the Florissant House where many of the stage guests stayed overnight. It was probably this business relationship that fostered the friendship between Nevitt and Allen, the stagecoach driver. When young William (Bill) Allen later homesteaded in Florissant, he worked for Dan Nevitt for a while. He later worked for Charles McLaughlin, brother of stage line owner Matthew McLaughlin, who operated a general store with his partner John Horrigan. They bought the Florissant Mercantile from Frank Castello about 1892.

Bill Allen bought and operated the post office and drug store next door.

Denver Public Library

Piah

The Tabeguache chief for whom the main street in Florissant was named. Piah was Chipeta's brother and a great favorite of Denver society.

Bill Allen had an extremely eventful year in 1891. First, a horse fell on him, pinning his leg under a piece of wood lying on the ground. His aunt, who was a doctor, was visiting from California at the time. She recognized the signs of blood poisoning, and urged that Bill be taken to the hospital in Colorado Springs. His father and aunt loaded him in the farm wagon, and started on their way. They arrived at Silas Thompson's ranch in Divide about midnight. Attie and Silas made room for

Silas and Atlanta Long Thompson
Atlanta had to have a leg amputated.
The Thompsons also lost two
infant daughters.

Bill and his family, and Silas sent one of his hired men for the doctor at Manitou.

When the doctor arrived the next morning, he saw that he needed to amputate the injured leg immediately. When this was done, Bill was again loaded in the wagon and taken on down the pass to Manitou. After he had been there a few days, the doctors had to operate a second time, taking a little more of the poisoned flesh and bone. Bill was left with a stub just below the knee.

About five years later, in 1895, Bill Allen rode out to Silas Thompson's ranch to visit Thompson's wife, Atlanta Long Thompson. Ironically, "Attie" had just had her leg amputated, and it was Bill Allen's turn to lend her moral support. A doctor had to come up from Colorado Springs to do the surgery. As there was no hospital, her doctor made an operating table out of some rough boards covered with a comforter. Bill commiserated with Attie over the loss of her leg, warning her of using too much morphine for the pain, and saying, "Well, they could cut all my arms and legs off and I would never take it again."

Allen's second major event of the year was of a more pleasant nature—marriage. He and his brother Silas each married one of the Dodge sisters, Dora and Flora, respectively. The girls had come to Florissant with their parents, Emma and Jonathan E. Dodge, Jr., from Missouri. When Bill Allen later bought the Florissant Mercantile (about 1898), his father-in-law, Jonathan Dodge, operated the drug department for him.

By 1889, there were about 150 residents in the Florissant area. Homesteaders, ranchers and other settlers continued to find their amusement in many of the same simple ways as they had ten years before. Cattle roundups, berry picking, and the arrival of the stagecoach were still major social events. Barn dances were now so large that they were held either at the new schoolhouse or at one of the sawmills.

Photo courtesy Marge & Don Christiansen
Dora Dodge Allen, 1895
Dora and her twin sister, Flora, married brothers William (Bill) and Silas Allen.

Frances Bass writes that there was little social distinction at these affairs. One would probably find the Count and Countess Pourtales swinging to the strains of the Virginia Reel and the quadrille along with Adeline Hornbek, the Allens, Burnhams, McLaughlins, Castellos, Longs, Thompsons, and other families of the area. One of the favorite musicians for these dances was Jesse Cook. He always drove to the dance in a homemade, horse-drawn cart, bringing his faithful dog with him. His price for an evening of his fiddle music was $5 plus a piece of cake for his dog. "If his dog didn't get any cake, Jesse didn't play the fiddle."

Entire families attended these dances, bringing everyone from one to ninety-one to eat and dance and socialize. This included eligible young daughters, who served as magnets for the lonely cow punchers who spent most of their lives tending

Photo courtesy Douglas & Virginia Pearce
William C. Allen, 1895
Allen purchased the Florissant
Mercantile about 1898 and later
acquired the Twin Creek Ranch.

cattle in remote mountain pastures. These young men were chivalrous and held women in high esteem, always treating them with frontier gallantry. They wore the best clothes that they could afford, and took great pride in their appearance. It was not unusual for them to spend a month's wages for a fine pair of custom-made boots. The late historian Granville Stuart wrote a colorful description of the typical cow puncher in the 1927 issue of *The Cascade Courier*.

Their trappings consisted of a fine saddle, silver mounted bridle, pearl-handled six shooter, latest model cartridge belt with silver buckle, silver spurs, a fancy quirt with silver mountings, a fine riata sometimes made of rawhide, a pair of leather chaps, and a fancy hat band often made from the dressed skin of a diamond-backed rattlesnake. They wore expensive stiff-brimmed light felt hats, with brilliantly colored silk handkerchiefs knotted about their necks, light colored shirts and exquisitely fitted, very high heeled riding boots (with trousers tucked into their boots).

A cowboy's first priority on riding into town for a dance was to see that his horse was properly cared for at the livery stable. He next visited Calas Wilson at his barber shop, for a close shave and a much-needed haircut—and perhaps even a bath. Dances were also the occasion for potluck suppers, but the "waddies" and "buckaroos" were seldom asked to pray over the food. Their pithy and humorous graces were a little too outrageous for most of their hosts.

Eat the meat and leave the skin;
Turn up your plate and let's begin.

Another irreverent grace went something like the following:

Yes, we'll come to the table
As long as we're able
And eat every damn thing
That looks sorter stable.

At dawn the next morning, the tired dancers would all pile into their farm wagons to head home, huddled against the cold mountain air under layers of blankets and comforters. The buckaroos would mount their wiry mustangs, and whoop and yell as they bucked their way out of sight.

Crofutt's 1885 *Grip Sack Guide of Colorado* reports that Colorado Springs now boasted over 5,000 residents, and nearby Colorado City another 350. There were still no communities in Pikes Peak's backcountry other than Florissant and Dr. Bell's Manitou Park Hotel. Nonetheless, Little London's society exulted in traveling into the mountains to enjoy their "wild, rugged, romantic and grand scenery . . . There is no hay fever, no asthma, no malaria. The nights are delightfully cool. In the daytime there is a gentle breeze, and the ozone from the pine covered mountains is so invigorating that one quickly forgets sickness and business cares."

One of the freighters along the Ute Pass Wagon Road saw more than beauty in the rich mountain grasses that lined Fountain Creek. In 1881, George Howard sold his ranch near Buena Vista and acquired 160 acres of meadowland in what is now Green Mountain Falls. He and his family set up housekeeping in an abandoned sawmill boarding house, near the present-day site of the Lakeview Terrace Hotel.

Trout Park (now Crystola) also attracted would-be ranchers by the name of Benedict in the 1860s. Without proper legal title, they established and maintained their cattle empire through threats and intimidation. In the early 1870s, three new families—the Sharrocks, Scotts and Talcotts—moved into the area and withstood a barrage of harassment to lay claim to ranch land of their own. In a cowardly, unfriendly gesture, Benedict burned George Sharrock's home. He stubbornly built a second, which Benedict as promptly chopped up and tore

For the cowboy of the 1800s, home was wherever he hung
his hat. Consequently, hat, boots and saddle were of prime
importance—often costing an entire month's pay.

down. He then built a third home, but this time his resolve
proved too much for the unneighborly Benedicts and they left
him alone. Eventually, Sharrock built a fourth home that is listed on Hayden's 1873 survey maps as "Junction House." Atlanta
and Silas Thompson had built a fine ranch at Hayden's Divide.
There were several other ranches in the area, but no town.
Indian Agent Thompson reported that Chief Colorow and his
band were accused of burning fifty acres of grassland in
Hayden's Park in October of 1873. As usual, however, lightning
was the true culprit.

South of the Thompson's Divide Ranch, near a place called
Sheep's Rock, a group of horse thieves set up operations from
about 1876 until 1880. Stealing horses to sell to footsore miners
was a lucrative business around this time, as a second such outfit also set up business on nearby Cabin Creek (in what is now
Mueller Park). This second group of entrepreneurs was known
locally as the White Brothers. These brothers worked from the

Soda Springs and the guard house at Canon City, circa 1880.
In 1868, the Colorado Legislature established a state penitentiary
at Canon City. The first prisoner was incarcerated there in 1871.

neighborly confines of two small cabins in what is now called
Horsethief Gulch. They were astute enough not to steal from
their neighbors, and instead preyed on the hapless citizens of
Pueblo and Canon City. "Liberated" horses were stealthily
herded to their base of operations, where they were rested and
re-branded. They were then taken to the lucrative markets in
Denver. The White Brothers made a comfortable living in this
manner, and didn't retire until around 1918 when the automobile displaced the horse in popularity.

Canon City also benefitted from the increased traffic to the
silver and gold fields, and now had a population of about 2,500.
A state penitentiary was built there, and incarcerated about
200 prisoners—more people than lived in the entire Pikes Peak
backcountry. Hamilton, on the Tarryall Road, still claimed
about 100 people in the area.

Adeline Hornbek's ranch had greatly increased in value.
When she first filed for her homestead, the property was worth
$1,200. She now had twenty-one horses, over 100 cows, three
swine and fifty poultry. She had sown thirty acres in hay and

twenty acres in Irish potatoes. By 1885, her ranch was valued at nearly $6,000. Adeline was a success. She had survived a flood, financial ruin, death of one husband and abandonment by another. She, her daughter and her three boys had made a very good life for themselves.

Adeline was not a pretty woman, but she had a commanding presence with dark eyes gazing resolutely from a square, thickset face supported by square, thickset shoulders, and crowned with a coronet of flaming red hair. The story of her life would end happily when she again married at age sixty-six.

This time the lucky man was a Prussian emigrant named Frederick Sticksel, and the two traveled extensively in the United States and Europe. Adeline died of paralysis in 1905 at age seventy-two. She was laid to rest in the Four Mile Cemetery just south of the Florissant Fossil Beds.

In 1973, the government bought Adeline's old homestead to renovate in time for the 1976 bicentennial celebration. It was incorporated into the boundaries of the Florissant Fossil Beds National Monument. In 1981, her homestead was placed on the National Register of Historic Places. This is a fitting tribute to a truly remarkable woman.

CHAPTER SEVEN

The Colorado Midland
Railroad arrives

Coloradans shared a common ailment in the latter half of the 1800s—gold fever. Residents of the state had become inured to Colorado's unlimited amounts of precious metals, simply waiting to be found. A staccato succession of gold and silver finds throughout the state had made a reality of this perception. Hayden's surveys, published in a series of annual reports, only validated this assumption, as they glowingly detailed the rich geological resources of the state. Thus, when anyone merely breathed the word "gold," most were only too ready and willing to jump up and head for the Rockies with their bedrolls and miner's picks.

An enterprising scoundrel, S.J. Bradley, concocted a devious scheme to capitalize on this gold fever. History books have labeled it the "Mount Pisgah Hoax," which was an exacerbation of the lie itself—Mount Pisgah was actually about fourteen miles east of Bradley's salted McIntyre Mountain. Pisgah was probably named by the renowned Colonel Kittredge whose log homestead still stands near the Fourmile Church. Pisgah's namesake is the biblical mountain in Jordan, at the northern end of the Dead Sea. It was from the "top of the Pisgah" that Moses viewed the promised land.

Bradley had earlier schooled himself on mining hoaxes in a similar swindle in Leadville. In the fall of 1883, Bradley did some prospecting on the Gribble Ranch just north of Canon City, and ten miles southwest of Florissant, near McIntyre Mountain. In the spring of 1884, Bradley returned with a band of eight conspirators from Leadville. Together, they excavated,

139

panned, and constructed placer operations on their respective twenty-acre claims. Bradley and D.G. Miller dug an eighteen-foot trench into Gribble's pasture and labeled it "Teller Placer, 7 April 1884." They then loaded some of the placer's supposed ore samples into a wagon and drove to the nearest assay office, thirty-five miles south in Canon City. Reports from the assay tests were explosive—they ranged from four to 107 ounces of gold per ton. Just one wheelbarrow full of ore could be worth $80 to $200. Announcements of this tremendous gold discovery were headlined in newspapers all over Colorado. The stampede was on!

Gold seekers swarmed to this new El Dorado, first by the hundreds, then by the thousands. Each man staked out a twenty-acre claim, and soon the pasture for miles around McIntrye Mountain was pockmarked with the diggings of frenzied miners. Bradley sat atop his claim with a loaded shotgun, just in case a claim jumper might take a fancy to his Teller Placer. He and his partners had the "foresight" to draw up maps, diagrams, pamphlets, and stock certificates—ready for sale when the first would-be millionaires arrived.

The Rio Grande Railroad ran special trains from Denver to Pueblo and Canon City; the South Park train carried prospectors to Como and Buena Vista; the road through Ute Pass was reminiscent of the Leadville boom days. The Colorado Springs *Daily Gazette* enthused about the quality of the road through Ute Pass, sniffing that the "Denver papers, in the interests of Canon City, satirically or ironically, but certainly untruthfully, refer to as the 'terrors of the Ute Pass road.'" In an attempt to "show the apparently purchased untruthfulness of the assertions of those newspapers which have characterized the Ute Pass road as a dangerous and the longest route to the scene of the late gold excitement" the *Gazette* published (on 4/25/1884) a detailed description of the journey up Ute Pass to the gold strike.

By the route we traversed, which is certainly the best one from any railway point into the exploded mining section, the distance is forty-six miles from Colorado Springs, made up as follows:

From Colorado Springs to Summit Park
(Woodland Park) *Post Office*   *16 mi.*
Thence to South Park house   *3 mi.*
Thence to Copeland's ranch house
(Coplen's Ranch, Florissant)   *9 mi.*
Thence to Four Mile road   *4 mi.*
Thence to Root's ranch house   *2 mi.*
Thence to Kittredge's ranch house   *7 mi.*
Thence to alleged gold mines,
Appropriately termed "Suckerville"   *5 mi.*
                                                  —————
                               Total   *46 mi.*

We divided the route up thus in order to indicate stop-ping places, or places which one must branch off from the main traveled road.

At the Summit Park (Woodland Park) *post office, where is located the old "Junction house," (now closed up temporarily) we left Manitou Park road on our right, and proceeded on the main Leadville or Fairplay road. At the South Park house, kept by Mr. Jas. K. Fical, late of Cheyenne Canon, we found excellent accommodations for man and beast, including clean, warm beds for the former.*

At Copeland's (Coplen's Ranch, Florissant) *one may find good food and clean beds, and a hearty welcome. On top of the first hill beyond Copeland's [Coplen's], and about three-fourths of a mile from his house, the road branches to the right and left. We took the left-hand road. So also at the Four Mile road, four miles beyond Copeland's [Coplen's], we kept to the left.*

At Root's ranch we obtained a nice dinner, with excellent coffee. Just before reaching this point we met Mr. B. Lowe, of the "Times," and Mr. Baird, the mining expert, who gave us the first reliable news of the barrenness of the prospect ahead of us at our journey's end. We reached Colonel Kittredge's early in the afternoon, but as he had been up to the camp and as we could obtain much preliminary and valuable information from him; and as,

141

moreover, we were assured of a generous and acceptable entertainment for ourselves and animals at his hands and under his spacious roof, we concluded to defer our entry into the camp until the following day (Thursday) and remain with him over night.

The main road branches right and left at Kittredge's. We left his house to the left and proceeded by the right-hand road along West Four Mile creek in a direction almost due west (about five miles).

The *Gazette* reported that Bradley's hoax had drawn as many as 5,000 men to McIntyre Mountain in just a few short weeks. It didn't take long for some of the more wizened prospectors to sense that there was something very wrong as they dug around in the non-auriferous granite, trachite, loam and sandstone. A number of these men dug a shaft next to Bradley's to test the genuineness of the assays. As suspected, the "Teller" had been salted! The *Gazette* published a report by the Committee Sent to "Suckerville," concluding that "the latter covering assays made at Colorado College of samples of stuff brought from the Alleged mines . . . will speak for themselves, and show why this mining boom, the greatest and quickest that Colorado had ever known, was so speedily exploded."

Two of Colorado's greatest gold discoveries were designated as being near Mount Pisgah. Ironically, the first discovery—the Pisgah Hoax of 1884—was immediately accepted as being authentic. The second discovery, which was the authentic multi-million dollar Cripple Creek bonanza of 1891, was rejected at first as a hoax.

In addition to exposing the Pisgah Hoax, the stories of the *Gazette* also brought to light the problems of declining use of the Ute Pass Wagon Road. The *Gazette* intimated that this lack of use was the result of a clever propaganda campaign waged by the cities of Denver and Canon City. These two cities hoped to cut into the lucrative business of outfitting prospectors on their way to the gold fields. As a result, the merchants of Colorado City and Colorado Springs were feeling the impact.

The true culprits, instead, were the railroads. In 1879, the Denver South Park & Pacific line was laid into South Park all the way to Weston Pass Road, and soon reached all the way to Buena Vista. By July, 1880, Palmer's Rio Grande ran to Pueblo and then wound along the Arkansas until it reached all the way to Leadville itself. Morris Cafky writes that as a result, "The Ute Pass wagon road sank back to a placid existence, serving the needs of ranchers in the country west of Pikes Peak and providing an outlet to market for several lumbering firms in the region."

In fact, it was the lumbering activities at Summit Park that ultimately led to the rebirth of the Ute Pass Wagon Road as a parallel path for the Colorado Midland Railroad.

About two miles north of Summit (Woodland) Park, an enterprising logger named Homer D. Fisher cast about for a way to make his operation more efficient. His outfit produced telephone and telegraph poles, railroad ties, and mining and bridge timbers for customers in Colorado Springs. In 1881, he sought to cut the costs of hauling these timber products by constructing an eight-mile, narrow gauge railroad from the timber-cutting area down to his sawmill. Fisher leased the locomotive, named *Ouray*, from his friend General Palmer for the next eight years. Ironically, the engine had to be dragged up Ute Pass by mule team in order to reach his logging site.

Ouray was a great success in cutting Fisher's costs. It didn't take long before Fisher sought to apply this same solution to the transportation of his finished lumber down Ute Pass to Colorado Springs. Merchants in Colorado City and Colorado Springs often shared their pipe dream of a railroad up Ute Pass and westward into Colorado's gold mining towns. Fisher seized upon this idea as also solving his transportation needs. It was cumbersome and expensive to haul his products down Ute Pass using wagons drawn by oxen and mules. He had already proved to himself the efficiency and economy of railroads with the short *Ouray* line at his lumber camp. Doggedly, Fisher set about making his vision a reality.

Fisher arranged to have a noted railroad engineer, Thomas Wigglesworth of the Denver & Rio Grande, make a preliminary survey through Ute Pass. With this expert opinion supporting his concept, Fisher then went about organizing a railroad company, and in November 1883, the Articles of Incorporation for the Colorado Midland Railway were filed with the state of Colorado. Inertia then set in as sufficient funding to build the railroad eluded its visionaries. At last, in 1885, their idea sparked the interest of a newcomer to the area, James John Hagerman.

Hagerman had arrived in Colorado Springs the year before, hoping to vanquish the tuberculosis which threatened his life. He had previously amassed a fortune in Milwaukee with his iron smelters. When he arrived in Colorado, his health rapidly improved and he was soon casting about for something to relieve his boredom. His energies quickly vented themselves in the mining industry, as he took possession of Aspen's Mollie Gibson silver mine, and several coal mines near Glenwood Springs. Hagerman was quick to see how the proposed Colorado Midland Railroad (CMRR) would facilitate shipping both his silver ore and his coal to the markets in Colorado Springs and beyond. Hagerman joined the corporation, and was soon applying all of his business acumen in raising the construction funds.

Building a standard gauge railroad through the Colorado Rockies, as the CMRR proposed, was considered a radical idea in 1884. Narrow gauge railroads were better able to navigate the steep mountain passes and narrow winding canyons of the Rockies than were standard gauge. So while almost all of America's trains sang along standard gauge tracks, they hit a virtual "iron curtain" when they reached the base of the Rocky Mountains. The railroad tracks from Denver south to Colorado Springs reflected this conundrum—for they were laid with three rails in order to accommodate both standard and narrow gauge.

At this point, however, cargo destined for points west had to be off-loaded from the standard gauge and then re-loaded onto the narrow gauge—a time consuming and costly undertaking.

Construction contracts were let by the CMRR in April 1886. Hagerman and his new chief engineer, Wigglesworth—or "Wig" as Hagerman called him—began a frenzy of activity in charting the path for their history-making standard gauge. By March, 1887, the CMRR's rails had been spiked down all the way to

Florissant, and by June they had reached Buena Vista. Ute Pass had been conquered by the CMRR *standard* gauge!

On each side of Hayden's Divide, the grades of the track were laid for a three percent climb—a three-foot climb for every hundred feet of track. This engineering glitch—standard gauge performance was intended for no more than a two percent grade—insured Florissant's future for the next forty years. Helper engines were needed to assist each train over Hayden's Divide, and Florissant became their home.

Within a year, the CMRR erected an elaborate passenger and freight depot in Florissant (where the Thunderbird Inn now sits), and began construction on a large roundhouse for sheltering the six helper engines to be stationed there. There were also a telegraph office, a bunk house, and a large assemblage of corrals and stock pens. A large wooden water tank, across from the station (where the Fossil Inn now sits), supplied water pumped from Twin Creek with a steam pump. When the first train rolled through Florissant on July 13, 1887, the residents were jubilant, and met its arrival with all the pomp and circumstance the little town could muster.

Construction of the railroad provided a boom for the sawmills up and down the line, as the railbed was built using mostly native pine for the trestles. Atlanta Long Thompson and her husband Silas benefitted from this demand and also from boarding many of the men working on the tracks near their ranch in Divide. Nevitt's and Coplen's both benefitted by increased occupancy at their hotels, as did Gill's, Bean's, and Allen's sawmills. Florissant's population jumped from about seventy in 1885 to well over 150 by 1887, as about twenty-two railroad men and their families moved into town to work for the CMRR.

Florissant's one-room log school house could not accommodate all of the new students. A building fund was begun in 1886, and Frank Castello sold an acre of land to School District Number 13 for one dollar. Coldwell and Spoon received the $884 contract to build the school, and began construction in the summer of 1887. In October, they were awarded an additional $66

Photo courtesy Marge & Don Christiansen
A Colorado Midland train prepares to depart the Florissant
station in 1887. The station was moved to the nearby
fossil bed in 1922, where it served as a hotel.

to build two privies, artfully screened with Victorian lattice-work.

Florissant's little log school was sold to the high bidder for seventeen dollars. No records have been found on the exact location of this original log school, but it was probably located near the Florissant Cemetery on Upper Twin Rocks Road.

Florissant's merchants were no longer the ruling class in the little community. Veterinarian Dr. H. A. Burton, whose father was an engineer for the Colorado Midland, wrote vividly of the ensuing conflict in Cafky's *Colorado Midland.*

In its heyday, Florissant had several general stores and other business houses. These did a good business catering to the railroad employees and to the ranchers and farmers in that part of the west Pikes Peak country. Naturally, the merchants tried to run the town, and often did so, much to the annoyance of many of the railroaders and ranchers.

The railroaders and the ranchers became aware of the fact that they constituted quite a voting bloc in a town as small as Florissant. There were six locomotive engineers stationed there, nine firemen, two water service men operating the pumphouse on day and night shifts, a couple of

Photo courtesy Hal Quist
Colorado Midland Engine No. 17 and Engineer Frank Smith.
The engines were gaily colored,with gun-metal blue smokestacks
and bright green tenders. The engineer worked in a redwood cabin.

men who shoveled coal from gondolas to the locomotives—
there was no coal chute—Mr. Banner, the station agent, a
night telegraph operator and my father, the road foreman.
The farm and ranch population was larger, of course.

Finally, when a school election was approaching, Dad
tossed his hat in the ring as a candidate for Teller County
School Board. Opposing him was a Florissant merchant.
After a vigorous campaign, Dad was elected. There was a
great celebration on the railroad when the votes were tal-
lied—whistles blew and bells rang on all the helper
engines present in town at the moment the results were
known, and cheers floated into the air from the Midland
tracks. All was quiet around the "business district" as the
merchants were very unhappy.

Florissant continued to grow and prosper, and in 1889 the
school board voted unanimously to build an addition on the east
side of the white frame building. This time the contract, for

147

Students pose with their "school bus" outside the Bethel School. The one-room log school was probably similar to the one Florissant replaced in 1887. Students include, from left: Dorothy Feizel, Oscar Mascick, Merrill Daw, Vora Mace, Wesley Daw and Alice Haggerty Jeffryes.

$1,310, was awarded to the Allen family—original homesteaders and noted carpenters.

Standardization of school construction had been established in the early 1800s, and Florissant's new school proudly conformed. White, framed, one-room schools within walking distance of the family ranch or farm were duplicated within most townships of the state. These little schools were generally modest, with windows along both sides, and an entrance at one end. Ornamentation consisted of a potbellied stove and a blackboard.

Students sat on wooden benches and committed their lessons to small, square slates.

Each student usually carried a small jar of water and a rag with which they cleaned their slate in between lessons. Older and more capricious children would dispense with the bottle and rag, substituting a bit of spittle and the sleeve of a shirt.

Florissant replaced its log school with this white frame
building in 1887. A rail fence surrounded the building to
protect students from wandering livestock.

Florissant's little white school was built with its entryway
facing south, toward the Ute Pass Wagon Road and West Twin
Creek. This little room was lined with brass coat hooks on one
wall and wooden shelves on the opposite wall. These shelves
were used by students to store their lunch buckets, made from
a half-gallon size lard or syrup pail. Most lunches consisted of a
jelly sandwich, or perhaps a fried egg sandwich, placed on thick
slices of homemade bread or biscuits. It wasn't unusual to find
that the bread had frozen while sitting in the anteroom, and
had to be toasted on the top of the pot-bellied stove. These sand-
wiches were washed down by cold spring water, brought up
from the Creek and shared from a common dipper.

With the addition to the school in 1889, Florissant loosened
its purse strings for an embellishment—a large bell tower with
a Queen Ann-style turret. This school bell was essential to the
life of the Florissant community. It not only called the children
to school, but also rang in case of any emergency, especially fire.

Ute Pass Historical Society
Frontier schools usually were within a five-mile walk or ride from the homestead. Nate Snare later wrote, "we kids tried riding to school in the winter on burros, which wasn't so good, so we walked most of the time, two and a half miles each way."

Somewhere around this same time, the school district also added a shack for storing coal out behind the schoolhouse. This shack was later used in the early 1900s as a cook shack when hot meals were served to the children. A teacher's residence was also added in the early 1900s. All of these buildings, including the school, were placed on the National Register of Historic Places in 1991.

Florissant was primarily a ranching community in the 1800s, and so the school year usually commenced in October after the fall roundup. Classes were held for only six months, and the children were sent home at the end of April in order to help with calving and the spring roundup.

As in most rural communities, Florissant's schoolhouse became the focus of all the local activities. In addition to being used for the education of the community's children, Florissant's schoolhouse was also used for weddings, church services, funerals, and as the polling place on election day. As one pioneer wrote, "There were many gatherings at the schoolhouse during the years. At Christmas and at the end of the year there were programs, parties, and dinners. The favorite gatherings were

Ute Chief Severo's children, 1875. Ute children didn't receive
formal education until they moved to the reservations where
boarding school attendance was required.

dances." Florissant's school was the "heart of the community.
People liked to go there and visit friends from up and down the
valley."

One of the more unusual "students" at the Florissant school
was fondly remembered by Dr. H.A. Burton.

Dad was an engineer for the Colorado Midland and would have four helper engines pulling the train up the four (three) percent grade to Divide. One day they hauled a load of sheep to Divide and dad returned to Florissant with one of the helper engines. He saw this small lamb beside the track, apparently it was born and fell out of the freight car, so he stopped the engine and brought the lamb back with him to Florissant. Mother bottle-fed this lamb, which got to be a real pet to us kids and would follow us to school. It would sit out on the school steps and follow us around during recess, then tag us home. On the hill back of our home, (the first house on the right side as you now come into Florissant), there was nothing but a prairie dog village—thousands of these prairie dogs. The government had a drive to get rid of them, having poison grain put out to kill them. The sacks of poison were down by the depot and some of it spilled out on the ground. Our lamb, who walked all over Florissant, ate some of the poison and died. My brother brought her home in a wheelbarrow and we had a regular funeral out in our back yard for that lamb we all loved; mother even read some verse from the bible.

Frank Castello's Mercantile encountered its first full-fledged competitor in 1890. Partners J.S. Lentz and J.E. Handbury began operation of the Handbury & Lentz General Store. They hired William (Bill) Spell as their head bookkeeper; for the store, for their two sawmills, and for their lumber yard. Spell had recently moved from Hugoton, Kansas, in order to escape a bloody feud with the rival town of Woodsdale over which town should become the county seat. He had followed several of his other Kansas friends to the Florissant area, notably George Carr and Alec King.

In the summer of 1890, the rivalry between the two general stores took on a more sinister dimension. Three bandits attempted to hold up Castello's post office and store shortly after the monthly payday. Castello had been warned, probably by George Carr, and was prepared. He had his watchman and several others waiting to ambush the would-be bandits. Shots were fired and one of the robbers was injured. However, they all were able to mount their horses and race into the timbered hills.

Early the next morning, Florissant's Marshal Ed Bell deputized a posse and set off after the robbers. (One of the posse members was none other than the lackadaisical cowboy Bob Womack.) They followed the trail all that day and through the night. Early on the second morning they surprised the outlaws, camped in a small valley near Sedalia, casually preparing their breakfast. Bell gave no chance for surrender, but instead opened fire on the three men. One of the trio, a young man of about twenty, was killed instantly. His two companions dashed for the woods, and eluded the posse. Marshall Bell gathered their horses, throwing the body of the young man across one, and brought them back to Florissant.

Feelings ran high in Florissant, and most of the townspeople pressed simply to bury the young man in a hole in the ground. Bill Spell argued that youth deserved a coffin and a decent burial, and prevailed upon the citizens. When the deceased was identified, and his relatives came to bury him, it was learned that he came from a very good family of modest wealth.

Spell's sons were able to identify the horses of the other two outlaws as belonging to former neighbors from Kansas. Castello questioned Spell's previous acquaintance with the two holdup men, Noble and Robinson, and his seemingly unwarranted interest in the proper burial of the young outlaw. Even though it was later found that it was Alec King who had masterminded the attempted robbery, Castello still viewed Spell with a jaundiced eye. As a result of this incident, distrust and friction smoldered between the rival stores of Castello and Handbury & Lentz (Spell's employers) for years afterward.

Ranching remained the primary source of Florissant's economy even after the advent of the Colorado Midland Railroad. Actually, the railroad provided a boost to the ranching community. It was now possible for area ranchers to herd their cattle into nearby Florissant to the CMRR stockyards. There they awaited one of the freight trains which then hauled them to the markets in Colorado Springs or to the gold camps in the central

Roundup west of Lake George, August 1895. Virtually all of the
area west of Pikes Peak was open range and fences were nonexistent.

mountains. This saved the ranchers the trouble and expense of
driving their cattle to market over long, dusty trails. It also
allowed the cattle to be sold at a much higher weight, for the
long foot-trek to market inevitably caused a material loss of
valuable pounds on each cow.

Most of the country and Pikes Peak's western slope was still
open range available to everyone. Area ranchers simply branded their stock, and then turned them out onto the lush mountain pastures to graze where they might. Early each spring, the
ranchers would get together and designate representatives or
"reps" for the roundup, lay out the roundup area on certain
creeks, and set a date.

At the designated time and place, the reps and cowboys from
the different outfits gathered. A roundup boss was elected, and
then they all began to comb the hills and valleys and to bunch
the cattle they collected into pole corrals or box canyons. Pole
corrals were portable and were easily constructed, as they
required only a hatchet to chop down the tall, slender aspen or
pine trees. These trees were then laid atop one another, parallel to the ground in a zig-zag pattern.

Once the cattle were gathered into the corrals, the cows and their calves were sorted and the calf was given the same brand as his mother. Bawling calves and their bellowing mothers filled the pure mountain air with a cacophony of fear-filled voices. Acrid smoke from the branding fire and calves' singed hide mingled with the sickly smell of blood from the de-horning saw and the castration knife.

Anne Hawkins wrote of watching her older brother at spring roundup one year in the 1927 *Independent*.

> . . . *I remember hearing my cowpuncher brother describe a very "busy" time he had with an irate cow critter. They were branding inside a pole corral and he was just ready to put the iron on the calf when the old cow charged him. He didn't have time to do a thing but roll over on his back and begin kicking dust in that cow's eyes and while she was shaking it out and wiping her eyes, brother made the top of the fence. "Fly for the fence, boys. She's on the prod." was a familiar slogan in those days— as familiar as "Railroad crossing, look out for the cars" is in these days, and much more effective. I have vivid memories of the burning hair when the hot iron was put on the poor little bawling calf calling for his ma-ma, and I presume that is one reason I am not more partial to a marcel. I am sure it must have been every little calf's ambition to be a maverick.*

Mavericks were orphaned calves whose ownership was doubtful. It was up to the Roundup Boss to come up with an equitable method of allocating these unbranded cattle. On at least one occasion, ownership was determined during the nightly rounds of poker among the cowboys. One old timer recalled such a poker game where "They played for unbranded cattle, yearlings at fifty cents a head and the top price for any class was five dollars a head."

Once the spring calf crop had been branded, castrated, dehorned, and ears cropped, the animals were turned loose again. They then spent the intervening summer months grazing on the rich mountain grasses. In the fall, the entire roundup

155

Cattle roundup and branding, 1895. Local ranchers helped each other
gather, sort and brand cattle in the spring after the calves were born.

process was repeated. This time, however, the herd was culled
of the calves, any non-producing cows, and any other animal
deemed ready for market. These beef were handled with great
care, as each pound of their flesh meant more profit at the market. Once the cattle were gathered, they were carefully herded
to the nearest railroad siding with its attendant corrals. When
these cattle were loaded on the Colorado Midland, the stock
trains were given the right-of-way. Passenger trains would be
sidetracked in order to let the stock trains through with their
precious cargo.

Ranching on the west slope of Pikes Peak was not always
easy. Sometimes the winters were extremely harsh, as they
were the year that George Frost lost his entire herd when their
flanks froze. In a cold wind or blizzard, cattle will generally
stand with their backsides to the gale. It was probably for this
reason that only their flanks froze. In that tragic winter of
1886-1887, nearly half of all Colorado's open-range stock perished in the blizzards and deep snow.

By far, the advent of barbed wire onto the open range had
the most dramatic impact on ranching. Barbed wire, consisting
of two wires twisted together with barbs twisted into the wire
in varying designs, was first invented around the 1860s.
Between 1868 and 1873, there were a total of eleven patents
filed with different barbed wire designs. Joseph Glidden

became the most famous manufacturer of these thorny fences after he began production in the mid-1870s. Ranchers began to use the stuff to keep their cattle from drifting all over the open ranges. Unfortunately, however, it was very often instrumental in the deaths of cattle when they were unable to seek shelter from blizzards and predators.

Fred Howarth, an English immigrant who arrived in Florissant about 1889, recalled the days before barbed wire:

> *You could get on a horse and ride all day in most any direction without having to open gates. The only fences were along Halthusen Lane south of Florissant* (now part of the Fossil Beds), *the Burnham Lane west of Florissant* (along the eastern edge of Twin Creek Ranch), *and the Silas Thompson Lane west of Divide."*

Most of these homesteaders found the barbed wire invaluable in protecting their tracts of cultivated land from the invasion of open-range cattle. Even the ranchers found that they needed to protect their hay fields in order to harvest enough of a crop to prevent another winter kill such as that of 1886-1887.

Cattlemen also forced the railroad to fence its right-of-way. They effectively lobbied for laws that made the railroads liable for cattle struck by their trains. Fencing these rights of way was cheaper than paying ranchers for cattle stricken by the trains.

The Pikes Peak cattle industry went into a slump in the early 1890s as a result of several severe winters, the encroachment of the railroad, and the increased presence of barbed-wire fences. It was this volatile environment that awaited the first sheep introduced to the area. Sheep found the rich mountain grasses as nourishing and tasty as the range cattle did. But cattlemen generally shared a pathological hatred of sheep growers, contending that sheep, unlike cattle, cropped the grass too closely and killed off valuable pasture lands.

Most notable of the sheep ranchers was fifty-four-year-old Herman Halthusen. Halthusen first filed on his homestead claim near the present-day Florissant Fossil Beds Visitor's Center in February 1888. (His red barn still sits opposite the

Colorado Springs Pioneers Museum
A CMRR locomotive belches smoke at Florissant about 1888. The new
school is just visible beyond the hill ar far right. Engineer Duffy
Malone's two-story house marks the left edge of the photo.

gate to the visitor center.) He already had sheep ranches in
Colorado Springs and in Leadville.

Halthusen flooded the remaining open range of Florissant
and Four Mile valleys with over 9,000 head of sheep!
Understandably, the cattle ranchers were outraged. At most,
these same grasslands were capable of supporting only about
1,000 head of cattle. Furthermore, cattlemen were still struggling from the earlier depredations to their herds. Racial over-
tones were added to the conflict when Halthusen hired Mexican
herders for his sheep. The *Denver Times* reported the conflict on
October 31, 1900.

> *Three days ago the first outbreak occurred, when set-*
> *tlers tore down the herders' tents and posted a notice on a*
> *post giving the Mexicans ten days to withdraw from the*
> *district under pain of severe punishment. Halthusen was*
> *away at the time. He returned to his herd yesterday and*
> *was shown the notice. He said nothing, but one of the*
> *herders remarked: "We'll be ready for anything that*

comes." A week of the ten days' grace has passed. Within three more days it is probable there will be a fight or Halthusen's sheep will be withdrawn from the open range.

The situation seems to have smoldered for a while, and then erupted in a second conflict. A follow-up story by the *Denver Times* on December 18, 1900, sheds further light on the situation.

The sheep and cattle war at Florissant after slumbering for about six or eight weeks seems likely to break forth again. Last Thursday night two lots of dynamite were exploded near Halthusen's house, one blowing the fence around the house into the road, the other wrecking the corral fence where there were 3000 fat sheep, but doing no other damages. The next morning fifteen sticks of powder were discovered in a gunny sack right among the sheep. It is supposed the sheep had cut the fuse by trampling on it. Examination showed the tracks of two men from the corral to where their horses had been tied. Both men had work overshoes.

Halthusen no doubt drew the further ire of area residents by flaunting his material well being. At one time, he was considered a millionaire. In addition to his lovely home and barns, he turned an excellent profit from his sheep growing. One invoice from a Denver hide dealer discloses that in 1895 alone, Halthusen received over $3,000 for his wool. This was at a time when the average annual income for most families in the Florissant area was just $300.

Sally Halthusen, Herman's daughter, further blighted the family name as she searched for a wealthy husband among the new millionaires in Cripple Creek. Marshall Sprague describes Sally in his posthumous book, *The King of Cripple Creek.*

. . . Charlie (MacNeill) was accompanied by a spectacular, big-bosomed, big-hipped girl almost 6 feet tall, named Sally Halthusen, a daughter of a . . . sheep-and-grain man. Sally had the outside structure of a Gibson girl. But inside she was packed with fierce desire instead of sweet

159

gentility. She was said to have collected $10,000 from a Denver father to remove her outside structure from the vicinity of his son. Sally liked men as big and husky as herself and she always had a lot of big fellows around. But what she liked most was horses. She could mount the wildest bronc in Colorado and tame him. One of Cripple's finest sights was Sally astride her white thoroughbred moving along Bennett Avenue. Sally, like Georgia Hayden, was on the prowl for a rich man. But, whereas Georgia wanted luxury and social position, Sally just wanted to get going on a horse farm.

In the midst of Florissant's range wars, its lush meadows of wild flowers continued to bloom. Fragile, blue wild iris contrasted with the deeper blues of flax and columbine. Sparks of bright red-orange Indian paintbrush danced in the mountain breezes against a backdrop of deep blue-purple Pikes Peak penstemon. Lush meadows of pastel-hued loco weed added to the ethereal beauty of these high mountain valleys. It wasn't long before the new Colorado Midland Railroad came up with a way to capitalize on the area's beauty.

Morris Cafky included several interviews about the "Wildflower Express" in his book *Colorado Midland*. Jack Hickman, an engineer on the CMRR, wrote of his experience on these excursion trains:

> *The Colorado Midland, like other railroads of its era, handled a great deal of summertime excursion business. The most famous, of course, were the Wildflower Excursions which ran from Colorado Springs to Spinney and return[ed]. They were very well patronized and there are many old-timers who, to this day, still remember them with pleasure.*
>
> *Around the turn of the century, the Midland operated still another summer excursion train, this one between Colorado Springs and Leadville. This train would leave Colorado Springs at 8 A.M., lay over at Leadville for 1 1/2 hours, and return to Colorado Springs at 8 P.M. It was always a three-car train, as I recall. The first car was a*

Florissant Fossil Beds National Museum
Sheep rancher Herman Halthusen moved to the Florissant Valley
about 1895. He started a local range war when he flooded the area
with 9,000 sheep. His barn still can be seen opposite the entrance
to the Florissant Fossil Beds National Monument.

combo with a lunch counter in the baggage section—an
arrangement later adopted on the Wildflower trains—a
coach and a chair car.

W.A. Coffin, whose father was a crew member on the CMRR,
also shared his memories of these colorful expeditions:

*Dad was often a crew member on the famous
Wildflower Excursion trains which rolled daily, each summer, between Colorado Springs and Spinney at the eastern
edge of South Park. Those were gala trains. The crew generally took responsibility for choosing stops to pick wild
flowers, and looked for spots where flowers were plentiful
and in non-hazardous locations. Flower stops were made
in the west-bound direction. After stopping for passengers
to picnic, usually at Spinney, we turned the entire train on
the wye for the trip back to Colorado Springs. Near
Florissant there were some fossil beds, and a stop was
made here to allow passengers to search for fossils.*

*The official train photographer was Lloyd Shaw, who
later became famous for his Cheyenne Mountain High
School dancers. Lloyd would take pictures of people*

161

The Wildflower was one of the Colorado Midland's popular excursion trains that began running in the 1890s. This scenic one-day trip left Colorado Springs at 8:45 a.m., turned around at the west end of ElevenMile Canyon, and stopped in the Florissant Valley for flower and fossil gathering. It returned to Colorado Springs about 5 p.m.

gathered around, and all over the engine, or grouped at the rear of the train.

Dr. H.A. Burton, whose father was a Colorado Midland engineer, also told Cafky of his memories of these famous excursion trains.

> *The Midland's famous Wildflower Excursions proved to be a source of summertime spending money for the children of Florissant. We boys looked forward eagerly to the summer tourist season and the daily operation of the flower train.*
>
> *Near Florissant, and just a short distance from the Midland right-of-way was a large fossil bed. It was the practice of the railroad to stop the excursion train there, and let the passengers who desired to do so hunt for fossils. We kids were always present when the train stopped,*

Colorado Historical Society
The Wildflower Express stops so tourists can pick up fossils.
Some riders preferred to hire local children to find their fossils.

and would sell fossils to those tourists who were too lazy to find their own, or who were unable to locate any.

We also sold crystals and attractive stones. These were obtained in occasional hikes to Crystal Peak, north of Florissant.

Another Florissant resident, Jessie Juanita Patten Barr, shared her early memories of the Wildflower excursion trains:

During the summer, the Midland Railroad ran a special every week through August. It was known as the flower excursion, with four open cars and always loaded with people. My two brothers and I sold wild columbines at fifty cents a dozen to these tourists. We would get on the train at Florissant, catch a ride up to the fossil beds, and dig fossils to sell. Some brought two dollars. Everyone was interested in them. When the train went on its merry way

163

Built in 1888, the elegant Hotel Ramona dominates this view of Cascade.

*back to Colorado Springs, we would start our five mile
walk home and do our chores after we got there.*

Florissant's prosperity gained momentum during these early
years after the Colorado Midland Railroad arrived. Other small
towns along the Ute Pass Wagon Road also sprang to life with
the advent of the railroad. Developers were quick to realize the
potential of town sites located along the railway, and made
haste to ensure their profits.

At the mouth of Ute Pass, the Cascade Town Company was
incorporated in 1886. D.N. Heizer, the mayor of Colorado
Springs, became president of the Cascade Town Company,
which listed over 100 residents as members. Within the year,
the town was surveyed and platted. A few years later, a lake
was built and stocked with trout. By 1889, the stately Ramona
Hotel was completed and towered over the town for thirty-five
years with her elegant Victorian turrets.

Cascade's charm captured the hearts of two 1895 honey-
mooners, Thomas and Mary Cusack. Cusack was a poor Irish
immigrant who made himself a millionaire when he created the

164

Ute Pass Historical Society
Marigreen Pines, Thomas Cusack's baronial summer home
in Cascade. In 1978, the Cusack family donated the
property to the Congregation of the Holy Cross.

outdoor advertising business. He became known as the
Billboard King, but ironically prized Cascade for its pristine
beauty. Cusack began systematically to purchase property in
the town, and in 1920 he purchased the Cascade Town &
Improvement Company. In 1923, Cusack built the baronial
Marigreen Pines mansion for his beloved Mary. He also purchased a sizeable ranch just south of Florissant, which is now
part of the Florissant Fossil Beds National Monument.

Just a few miles up Ute Pass from Cascade, the fertile mountain valley called Ute Pass Park provided the embryo for another small mountain town—Chipita Park. Most of the valley had
been the property of General Palmer's friend William
Blackmore. After his tragic suicide, however, the land was sold
to several ranchers and farmers. With the advent of the
Colorado Midland Railroad, developers saw the area as having
more potential as a town than as fodder for cows. In 1890, the
Ute Pass Land and Water Company was incorporated with an
eye to transforming the verdant pastures into a lucrative

165

resort. The elegant Ute Hotel opened in the fall of 1890, over-looking the new Colorado Midland depot and the five-acre Chipita Lake.

Several more miles up Ute Pass, in 1881, former teamster George Howard paid $600 for some promising ranch land that would later become Green Mountain Falls. This transition came about through the efforts of an English real estate devel-oper named W.J. Foster, who gained title to Howard's ranch in 1887. He envisioned a high-class summer resort town. And so Green Mountain Falls Town and Improvement Co. was incor-porated in 1887. By the summer of 1888, there were an esti-mated 500 people living in tents at the new townsite.

The small town was further enhanced in 1888 when its lake was excavated. This required the combined efforts of over twen-ty teams of horses pulling plows. A small island was left in the center of the lake, and it soon sported a charming Victorian gazebo. Green Mountain Falls, the town, was formally incorpo-rated in July 1890.

As the Colorado Midland wound its way up the Ute Pass, it continued to spawn new towns every few miles. Crystola, the next stop up the line, also began as a ranching community, called Trout Park, when several ranching families moved into the area in 1870. They received only threats and harassment from earlier squatters, however, until they proved their resilience. One of these tenacious ranchers was George Sharrock who named his place Junction House.

Henry Clay Childs, Speaker of the U.S. House of Representatives, moved to Trout Park in the late 1870s. Childs and his wife were spiritualists, and entertained a number of psychics and mediums at their small ranch. Childs and other spiritualists organized the Brotherhood Gold Mining and Milling Company in 1897. This unique company proposed to save aspiring miners from the drudgery of locating a mine by utilizing psychic powers instead. Their brochure boasted that:

> . . . the prospector is saved the trouble of locating a mine by an accommodating wizard who, instead of locating the future bonanza for himself will locate it for anybody who will put up a sufficiency of cash in advance.

166

Ute Pass Historical Society
A Colorado Midland train stops briefly at Green Mountain Falls.
The site was formerly George Howard's cattle pasture.

Crystola, the town, germinated from this psychic quest for gold. In 1899, the company was renamed the Crystola Brotherhood Town, Mine and Milling Company. Still undaunted, the company built a gold processing mill in Crystola Canyon. Nearby, a large stone building was designated as the site for storing the yet un-found gold. Gold never was found, so the widowed Childs drowned his hopes in the amber fluid of Duffy's Malt Whiskey. When he died, he left his 2,000-acre estate to be used as a school for spiritualism. All that is left of his dream is the Crystola Inn, which once served as the town's grocery.

Woodland Park emerged as a fully incorporated town on January 21, 1891. Unlike Crystola, the roots of the new little community were based on something a little more solid than a spiritualist's advice. Daniel Steffa, an area rancher, saw the potential for a tidy profit with the advent of the Colorado Midland Railroad in 1887. He quickly worked to have his pasture land along the railway platted and named his proposed

town "Manitou Park." The Colorado Midland Railroad responded by naming its station there "Manitou Park Station."
Legitimacy was fully granted, however, when the United States
Postal Service opened its Manitou Park Post Office in March
1888.

Although the area was previously known to travelers along
the Ute Pass Wagon Road as Summit Park, Steffa's new name
held fast until the town incorporated in 1891. Steffa, no doubt,
wished to capitalize on the popularity of Dr. Bell's elegant
resort with the same name, located just a few miles north.
Water in the west has always been more precious than gold,
and Manitou Park was not immune to its importance. The
Woodland Park Town Improvement Company was organized in
1890 in order to provide water for the area, and a pipeline and
reservoir were built. When the town incorporated in 1891, the
name was officially changed to Woodland Park.

In addition to obtaining a water system, it seems that the
122 residents were also greatly concerned about the character
of their community. Their first order of business after incorporation was to pass a morals and decency ordinance three
months later. One can only wonder at what event prompted this
ordinance to assess a $100 fine for nude or lewd dress on the
streets. Bawdy houses and gambling were banned within the
town's limits. Drunks were to be both fined and sent to jail. And
anyone who beat an animal was to be assessed a fifty dollar
fine. With its moral environment now firmly secured,
Woodland Park began to plot a course of steady growth. Noted
Colorado historian Frank Hall described the new little town as
it appeared in 1891 in his *History of Colorado*:

> *Woodland Park is situated on a high broad plateau,
> 8,484 feet above sea level, and has a protected and shel-
> tered situation. It affords a fine view of Pike's Peak, and
> near by are Iron and Sulphur Springs, almost hidden by
> native shrubbery and wild flowers. During the past year a
> hotel and several cottages and stores have been erected as
> well as a church and school. Here is also a good-sized lake.*

Woodland Park, 1887. Main Street (Midland Avenue), now Highway 24, was busy even then. The building in the upper left corner is the Woodland Hotel.

Beyond Woodland Park, the frequency of new towns began to wane. Seven miles west of Woodland, on the Ute Pass Wagon Road—and now along the Midland's railbed—lay a small ranching community called Hayden's Divide. South of the settlement a plateau had provided a temporary camp for F.V. Hayden's survey team in 1873. Ute Pass also reached its summit at Hayden's Divide, with an elevation of 9,198 feet. Ranchers had always referred to the area as a "divide," for its elevation sorted the rains and melting snows into creeks that flowed east into Fountain Creek and ultimately to the Arkansas River, or west into Twin Creek and on to the South Platte River.

Hayden's Divide was primarily a ranching community. Atlanta Long Thompson and her husband, Silas, were among the first area ranchers to profit from the advent of the Colorado Midland Railroad. Silas opened a sawmill and provided the Midland with railroad ties and telegraph poles. Atlanta converted their ranch house into a boarding house, providing food and beds for the railroad workers.

Five miles west of Florissant, an astute ex-Bostonian, George Washington Frost, also saw a way to make money from the Colorado Midland Railroad. Frost made a small fortune on the sale of his Boston box factory and bought Toll Witcher's

169

ranch south of Florissant about 1886. As recounted in the previous chapter, Frost lost most of his cattle in the blizzard of
1886-87, however.

In an irony befitting a true westerner, Frost saw a way to
make "lemonade from his lemon." The same raw cold that cost
him his cattle herd could also make him rich. He saw the
Midland as the means to effecting this turnaround and recoup-
ing his losses. He prevailed upon his former business associates
back East to buy $95,000 worth of stock in his proposed dam on
the South Platte River. Frost waited for his newly-built lake to
freeze, and then began business in earnest. He constructed several large ice storage houses, and then proceeded to sell his "liquid assets" to the Midland for use in their refrigerated box cars.
Frost's ice was instrumental in ensuring the safe shipment of
fruits and vegetables from the western slope all across
Colorado. Perhaps even more importantly, his ice also cooled
the beer that quenched the thirst of Colorado's miners.

D.A. Cuthbert related his memories of these shipments in
Morris Cafky's *Colorado Midland*:

> *In late August and early September of each year, the
> Grand Valley fruit crop—peaches, principally, although
> some apples also moved in the Colorado Midland's day—
> was shipped to Midwestern and eastern markets, as well
> as to large Colorado communities. Both the C.M.
> (Colorado Midland) and the D.&R.G. (Denver & Rio
> Grande) were kept busy moving in empty reefers (refriger-
> ated cars), and hauling the fruit out in solid trainloads of
> perishables . . . The fruit blocks were really "given the
> road" on the Midland, and often came close to making pas-
> senger train time. Because of the nature of the perishable
> freight, refrigerator loads were light as compared with
> loads handled in freight cars of equal capacity . . .*
>
> *Speaking of icing cars, the Midland had an ice cutting
> operation at Lake George, including a large ice house. Ice
> trains operated each winter, making round trips between
> Colorado City and Lake George. Some of the ice was stored
> at the C.M. ice house at Colorado City for reefer cooling the*

Courtesy Mel McFarland
Divide, 1887. Silas Thompson and other area ranchers supplied
the Colorado Midland Railroad with ties and telegraph poles.
The Little Chapel on the Hill is at the upper left.

*following summer; the rest was sold to the Santa Fe for the
same purpose.*

Frost's lake was first called Lidderdale Reservoir, but later
came to be called George's Lake. When the community merited
its own post office in April, 1891, it was named Lake George.
Though Frost's business prospered, his little town did not keep
pace. It soon boasted several saloons, a small CMRR depot,
blacksmith shop, school and general store, but remained unin-
corporated.

Northwest of Lake George, about seventeen miles up
Tarryall Creek, homesteader G.N. Ohler added the claims of
neighbors Andrew Glenn and Isaac Brown to his ranch, then
sold it all to Frederick Wicks. Wicks continued adding adjacent
homesteads to his ranch, and then sold his Tarryall River
Ranch to the brothers, Karl, John, and Joseph Strickner. The
ranch changed hands several more times, finally resting in the
hands of Alice Bemis Taylor in 1932. The Bemis family owned
the Bemis Box and Bag factory in St. Louis, Missouri, and were
quite well to do. Finally, in 1961 Cotton and Joan Gordon purchased the ranch and have turned it into one of the most successful dude ranches in Colorado.

One of the most intriguing stories from the Tarryall Valley
concerns a displaced Swiss adventurer, Gottlieb Fluhmann.

171

Colorado's gold fields lured him from his homeland, and when he failed to find his El Dorado, he instead homesteaded near Platte Springs in the Tarryall River Valley, about five miles north of Lake George. His neighbors are said to have ridiculed this small (five-foot, four-inch) foreigner with the strange accent, causing him to declare that he "could never love these no good fellow homesteaders."

Instead, he kept to himself and looked to his cattle for the friendship and acceptance he needed, calling each one by a pet name. On one of his infrequent trips into town in 1890, he drew the taunts of a neighboring rancher, Ben Ratcliff, who declared that the juicy steak he was eating was none other than one of Fluhmann's pet cows that had disappeared. This only confirmed Fluhmann's contention that he was "an angel living amongst the devils," and he sadly returned to the safety of his homestead. This pastoral peace was shattered, however, when Ratcliff's sons trespassed on Fluhmann's land. He lost his temper when they rode up to him and spit tobacco juice into his horse's face, and so fired his musket over their heads with a warning to leave him alone.

Ratcliff was furious when he learned of the incident, and sent his daughter to warn the little Swiss man that he intended to kill him in the fall. Ratcliff's reputation insured the danger of his threat, so Fluhmann developed an emergency plan. He would relocate to a cave he had found in a rocky cliff about a mile from his home. He secretly made a new home within this five- by fifteen-foot cavity, installing a strong door at the entrance for added protection and a glass window for surveillance. He ran a wire rigging from the roof that he attached to a dishpan. Into this mouse-proof container he placed all of his valuables—his 1860s Swiss passport, letters from his family, carved pipes, surveying instruments, a telescope, and his firearms (a .45 caliber pistol and two double barreled, gold inlaid flintlocks).

He made one final trip into town in 1892 for supplies, and along the way adopted a stray dog. He carefully placed these goods on the wooden shelves he had built along the sides of his cave, and made a pet of the dog. Soon his new home was cozy with a slight trickle of fresh water running down the back wall, an efficient cook stove vented out the roof, and shelves lined with canned goods, cooking utensils, lamps and kerosene, and jugs of gooseberry and choke cherry wine. He only lit his cookstove at night, and was careful to slip down to care for his livestock under cover of darkness. In spite of all his precautions, however, Ratcliff found him.

When Fluhmann first disappeared, everyone, including the local sheriff, assumed that he had returned to Switzerland. But not Ratcliff. He knew his prey would never leave his beloved animals unattended. When they still appeared well-cared for after several months, he began a systematic search for the little foreigner. Finally, it was the smell of wood smoke and the reflection of the setting sun from the cave's window that betrayed Fluhmann. Ratcliff waited on the ledge above the cave until early the next morning. As Fluhmann cautiously opened the heavy door to greet the new day, Ratcliff fired, sending a fatal bullet through the stock of Fluhmann's gun and into his chest. He then climbed down to his victim and dragged him back into the cave. The Swiss man's faithful mongrel dog laid down beside his master as Ratcliff closed the door and attempted to hide the scene of his crime with tree limbs and underbrush.

On November 1, 1944, the *Gazette Telegraph* reported that "A mystery which has puzzled the old timers of the Lake George section for more than 50 years" was solved by a deer hunter.

Master Sargent Francis Brahler of Peterson Field discovered the old cave while he was hunting. He spotted the old window frame on a ledge and upon investigating found the cave entrance. The big dishpan was still suspended with the letters, pipes and other items including the two gold inlaid flintlocks. He took many of the items back to his campsite and returned the next day. This time, he found a human skull and bones and what appeared to be the skull of a dog. He notified the Pike National Forest Ranger who, in turn, notified the Park County Sheriff. Accompanied by Dan Denny, who had known Gotttlieb Fluhmann, they cleared out the old cave. They discovered *it had had a wooden floor and they found the old kerosene would still burn after 50 years. Dan Denny had seen Fluhmann on his last day in town gathering his supplies. He also reported that sometime after Fluhmann's disappearance his cattle were auctioned to Sam Hartsel, Sol Thompson and John Beyer. His land was auctioned to Will Evans, and a Mr. Kribble, executor of Fluhmann's estate, received $900 from the proceeds of the auction to satisfy a debt owed to him by Fluhmann.*

Although Ratcliff never paid his debt for killing Fluhmann, fate did collect from him for killing three school board members on May 6, 1895. His children were again the catalyst for his dangerous temper, and he unleashed his fury when he learned they were having a special meeting to discuss them. He rode up to the school house, dismounted, and walked in, shooting Samuel Taylor, Lincoln McCurdy, and George Wyatt. He later turned himself in to the sheriff at Como, was tried, convicted, and later hanged at the Colorado State Penitentiary in Canon City.

Unfortunately, the Ratcliff murders were not an isolated incident, for the new growth up and down the path of the Colorado Midland Railroad was bound to bring trouble as well as prosperity. Claude Harris, a fireman for Midland Railroad, left an account of one of the more interesting troubles that beset the Railroad. This story is vividly recounted in Morris Cafky's *Colorado Midland*:

One evening in 1910, engineer "Four-Spot" Frank Stewart and fireman Paul Bochman were called to handle Train 3 from Colorado Springs to Leadville. No. 3 was the night passenger run, usually consisting of a baggage car, open platform coach, open platform chair car, a Leadville sleeper and a Denver to Grand Junction sleeper. Frank and Paul's engine was one of the passenger 4-6-0's with 60-inch drivers.

Between Divide and Florissant, where westbound trains descended a 3% grade, it was the custom for the fireman to clean his fire into the ash pan. Then, the ash pan

174

would be emptied during the stop at Florissant. Paul Bochman began this chore just after No. 3 departed from Divide. He happened to look up and noticed that Frank Stewart was looking back intently at the tender. Frank motioned with his thumb at Paul, and the fireman turned around to see a man coming over the coal gate with a rifle.

The intruder forced Frank to stop the train near Pisgah siding, then ordered both enginemen off the locomotive. In climbing down, Frank slipped and fell. He scrambled to his feet unhurt; unknown to the bandit, he now clutched a large stone in his hand.

The two enginemen were marched back to the baggage car by the thug, who then ordered the fireman to pound on the door and arouse the Wells Fargo express messenger. Instead of obeying, Paul ducked under the car and scrambled to the other side of the train; he intended to run back to the coaches and give the alarm. The bandit leaned over and fired under the car at Paul, wounding him. Just as he fired, Frank Stewart brought his stone down on the bandit's head with such force that the man was killed instantly. A moment later, another shot could be heard down Twin Creek Canon (Florissant Canyon). This second shot led authorities and railroaders to believe that more than one person was involved in the robbery attempt. It seems likely that the dead bandit had ordered the train stopped in the wrong place.

Paul was carried back and placed in a Pullman berth, and the bandit's corpse was placed in the baggage car. At Florissant, a helper engine station, services of another fireman were secured and No. 3 went on to Leadville. Paul Bochman was hospitalized there, recovered from his wound, and was soon back at work. Frank Stewart was presented with a gold watch by the Colorado Midland Railway; details of the incident were engraved thereon. Frank died many years ago, but his descendants still possess the watch.

There is a second, slightly different, variation on this story as recounted by Chester Allen in an unpublished letter to his niece, Marge Christiansen.

Yes, there was a train hold up and it was described pretty good only the names were wrong. Sam Millward was the engineer who knocked the guy out with a rock then he got the guys gun and killed him with it. I was just a curious kid at the time and was there when they brought the holdup man to town and watched the Sheriff probe the bullett [sic] hole, a picture that always stayed with me, he was shot between the right cheek bone and nose just below the eye.

Millwards were our neighbors lived in Uncle Silas (Allen) house across the road at the time and he was allowed to keep the gun and he displayed it a lot of times, was a 38 Colt automatic. Posses rode the hills for a week but came up empty, so 2 got away.

Fortunately, this attempted robbery seems to be the extent of depredations along the new railroad. Florissant townfolk watched the frenzy of growth up and down the old Ute Pass Wagon Road as the Midland Railroad spread its promise of wealth. Finally, the community jumped on the band wagon and its 242 residents petitioned for incorporation. Their petition was granted, and Florissant celebrated as a fully incorporated town on the 7th of July, 1891.

CHAPTER EIGHT
"Yellow Fever"

W ho can say why a man would dedicate his life to the search for tiny scraps of yellow metal buried in the earth's bosom. Hardship, back-breaking labor, cold, starvation—these were the intimate friends of Colorado's gold seekers. Robert Service, the premiere poet of America's westward expansion, perhaps touched at the heart of the matter when he wrote the following lines:

> *There's gold, and it's haunting and haunting;*
> *It's luring me on as of old;*
> *Yet it isn't the gold that I'm wanting*
> *So much as just finding the gold.*
> *It's the great, big, broad land 'way up yonder,*
> *It's the forests where silence has lease;*
> *It's the beauty that thrills me with wonder,*
> *It's the stillness that fills me with peace.*

Colorado's "Yellow Fever" epidemic continued from 1858 well into the 1900s, as gold-crazed men swarmed over the Rockies. This sickness of the heart forced the Utes from their ancient and sacred hunting grounds in the Shining Mountains. These hunting grounds carried a heavy price tag, however. They cost the integrity of a fledgling nation, as treaty after treaty was broken when fevered citizens demanded yet more land.

Until 1890, Pikes Peak's backcountry had been only on the periphery of this frenzy. Soon, however, a grizzled old prospector set in motion the events that forever changed the Pikes

Peak region, the state of Colorado, and the fortunes of the United States.

Marion C. Lankford was an unlikely catalyst for the Cripple Creek boom. Lankford was a veteran of the Civil War, having served under Confederate General Robert E. Lee. He fled the horrors of the war and its aftermath, building a cabin on the slope of Jones Mountain, near Mount Shavano. A great black mustache ranged across his sunburnt face. Unkempt, ragged clothing on his tall, lanky frame proclaimed the hours he spent swinging a pick at the granite face of the mountain. When the winter snows became too deep, he loaded his few possessions on his burro and sought the comfort of his friends in Florissant—the Spell's.

Snowflakes swirled around the Spell's two-story home, as Lankford and his friend, Bob Womack, traded dreams before the fire in the winter of 1889. Womack boasted of some promising "float"—light weight rock that indicates gold—that he had found while working on the Broken Box Ranch near Mount Pisgah. He was inclined to imbibe a little too freely, but he and Lankford were firmly bound to one another by their passion for gold. Lankford shared his knowledge of prospecting with the younger Womack, and offered suggestions and encouragement. Late the following year, 1890, as the aspens teasingly flaunted their golden leaves, Lankford's protege hit pay dirt when he re-examined an earlier claim.

Womack renamed this earlier, 1886 Grand View Claim, calling it the El Paso instead. When the ore samples were later assayed by Professor Henry Lamb of Colorado College, they revealed an amazing value of $250 a ton! "Crazy Bob" had at last found his gold mine. He had been infected with the Yellow Fever seventeen years earlier, when Hayden's survey geologist had predicted that Cripple Creek's volcanic crater most likely held gold. Womack was, at best, a desultory cowboy, using his time on the range to pick at Cripple's crater under the pretext of searching for strays.

George Harker, Adeline Hornbek's son, also worked his family's cattle in the Cripple Creek area. Harker later told C.S. Dudley of the *Gazette Telegraph* that he and other stockmen would tell Womack that "he was wasting his time; that nothing would come of it for him." Harker said that Womack would invariably answer, "Just wait. You'll see. I'll find gold. Just wait and see."

In spite of the high assay value of Womack's ore, he had difficulty in raising the $15,000 to $20,000 required to remove the ore from his mine. Potential investors in Colorado Springs were still smarting from the Pisgah Hoax, and weren't about to be "suckered" again. However, Womack's friend and mentor, Marion Lankford, did believe in the erstwhile cowboy.

Late in February of 1891, Lankford convinced his friends from Florissant—William Spell, the justice of the peace, and Handbury and Lentz, who owned the general store—to grubstake and outfit him. This group included George Carr, foreman of the Broken Box Ranch, as their fourth partner. As soon as the February weather permitted, Lankford explored the area around the Carr Ranch. Just as Womack had reported, Lankford soon found gold-bearing ore in a gulch about a mile and a half from the ranchhouse. When he returned to Florissant with ore samples, the partners decided that Spell should return with him to Cripple Creek to stake their claims.

Spell and Lankford wasted no time in staking out five claims on February 20, 1891: the Robert E. Lee, the Blanche, the Hobo, the Panhandle, and the Blue Bell. Later, when George Carr was working on the Hobo claim in a gulch near the top of Guyot Hill he unearthed the grave of an Indian woman. This gulch was thereafter known as Squaw Gulch.

As the partners continued to work their mines, Spell purchased an ore wagon and four horses. Dick Dickerson was hired to haul the ore from Cripple Creek to Florissant, where it was then transferred to an ore car on the Colorado Midland Railroad and hauled to the smelter in Colorado City. Although the assays had promised about $175 a ton, this thirty-ton shipment only yielded a total of $1,930—about $64 a ton. It was the first and only ore shipment from Cripple Creek in 1891.

Ironically, Florissant carries the dubious honor of delaying the Cripple Creek bonanza—eventually one of the greatest in the world. It all started when Hiram Rogers, a reporter for the

179

Gazette, wrote a story of a "very rich strike of gold" made near Florissant on February 12, 1891. Captain J.H. Hensley found this "strike" on his ranch, about a mile southeast of Florissant, just across the wagon road from the Florissant cemetery.

Atlanta Long Thompson worked for Mrs. Hensley during the previous year, 1890, while Captain Hensley was busy freighting to Leadville. Atlanta wrote that Mrs. Hensley was a woman about sixty years old, "overflowing with good nature and a pleasant word for everyone." She had fallen and broken her ankle, and needed help in managing her long, rambling log house. Captain and Mrs. Hensley also boarded many travelers, as their ranch was located along the Ute Pass Wagon Road, and Atlanta was expected to cook for them. Silas Thompson, Atlanta's future husband, and his sister Becca Nevitt together with her husband, Dan, also became boarders at the Hensley's in the early part of 1891.

When the Midland deposited Rogers, the *Gazette* reporter, in Florissant that February morning in 1891, he noted that the townsfolk were "not early risers. It was not until after 8 o'clock that the streets became at all inhabited, though they are not very lively at any stage of the game." Rogers finally found a group of ranchers, lumbermen and tie choppers gathered around the wood stove at Handbury & Lentz'. He noted that though they all talked of the mine at Hensley's, they were mostly inclined to be skeptical. Newcomers were dubiously questioned as to when and where they intended to stake their claims.

Rogers at last succeeded in finding a guide, and was escorted to the site by none other than "M.C. Langford (sic)" (our Marion Lankford) "who claimed to have had considerable mining experience, and who carried an old battered gold pan."

Rogers continued the story of his fact-finding trip to the "gold strike" in Florissant:

> . . . *After traveling on this road* (Upper Twin Rock) *per-haps half a mile* (east), *a thinly tenanted graveyard came into view on the south side of the road and directly opposite was a long, low log house, one story high, chinked up with mud in regulation style. At one side was a well and*

in front were two or three corrals, through the lowered bars of which two cows are aimlessly meandering about. The mine, the natives said, was behind the house, so the three (of us) went through the yard and up about 200 yards from the house, where, on a hill-side a windlass and the top of a ladder could be seen above a pile of grayish broken stone. As the three (of us) came up a tall, very erect man, seemingly about 55 years old, with a long white beard, climbed the ladder bearing a basin full of a greenish gray stone. This was Captain J. H. Hensley, the discoverer of the vein . . .

The *Gazette* accorded Rogers a full three columns of details on Hensley's "strike." Rogers noted that about 150 claims had already been located in and around Florissant, the majority being in Hensley's potato patch. Rogers collected a sack of ore samples from Hensley's mine, and took it to Professor W.E. Strieby in Colorado Springs for a final analysis. Unfortunately, these tests showed that the metal "was beyond all doubt copper." In a final understatement, Rogers offers the insight that "the very decided opinion given by Prof. Strieby regarding the ore (from Hensley's) will put something of a damper on the boom . . ."

Ironically, Rogers concluded his story on the boom/bust at Florissant with the following paragraphs:

The talk about the find at Florissant brought to light a matter that the Gazette had promised to keep quiet until better developments gave it a foundation. This is the fact that a vein of gold ore has been found in the mountains and not a great way from Florissant. The story as told is as follows: About one month ago a young ranchman, (forty-six year old Bob Womack) *rather well known in the city, came here with the statement that he had found a vein of rich ore. Very little attention was paid to it, but one citizen* (Lankford) *determined to look into the case.*

. . . A Gazette representative was yesterday shown rock that it is claimed was taken from the vein and that it is alleged assays over $220 to the ton . . . This find is about

Courtesy Carl Quist

Dr. Thomas A McIntyre and CMRR Engineer Frank "Duffy" Malone,
stand next to the observation platform built on top of Fortification Hill.
McIntyre gained brief notoriety in 1915 when he wrote a prize-winning
rebuttal to Julian Street's scathing *Collier's Weekly* article on Cripple Creek.

*thirteen miles south of Florissant and not far from Mt.
Pisgah, but is not in the red salted district. Developments
will be awaited with interest.*

This was the first that the public would know about the
great gold strike that would change a nation. It was, however,
overshadowed and undervalued because of the false excitement
generated by Hensley's Florissant potato patch!

Florissant more than atoned for this slight derailment of
Cripple's gold boom. This contribution came because the area
attracted and held one of the most beautiful women of the period, Berthe De Pourtales.

Count Louis Otto's homestead north of Florissant provided a
health-giving refuge for his recently-divorced sister, Countess
Berthe. Berthe, in turn, was the lovely magnet who compelled
cousin Count James De Pourtales from his Prussian estates to

Colorado Springs in 1884. By the fall of 1886, Count James and Countess Berthe had entered wedded bliss, and traveled to his estates in Glumbowitz, in Silesia—a region within what is now southwestern Poland. Count James' grandfather made a fortune in the 1700s, and dedicated this money and his allegiance to the Prussian King, who returned the favor by making Jacques Louis De Pourtales and his progeny counts and countesses.

Count James was an engaging, energetic man, with a creative, analytical mind. He determined that he could benefit from the boom he was sure would come to Palmer's fledgling Colorado Springs. When a friend gave him a tour of his struggling dairy farm, The Broadmoor, Count James was hooked. He bought half interest, and then began a series of failed attempts to turn a profit on his $25,000 investment. Count James was a "big, cheery, positive, stubborn man who ate and drank and played and worked with gusto. He loved to think up bold schemes and to gamble his shirt on them." The Broadmoor proved a challenge worthy of such a man.

Broadmoor, as a dairy farm, met one catastrophe after another, and none of Count James' brilliant ideas nor thousands of dollars made a difference. Meanwhile, Colorado Springs was growing by leaps and bounds—from a mere 2,000 residents to over 8,000 in a little over five years. Count James therefore decided on a different course of action. From 1889 to 1890, he mortgaged the farm for $250,000 in order to develop it as Broadmoor City, boasting its own electric plant and water system. He planned and built the fabulous Broadmoor Casino as the crown jewel of his little town.

It was of no use. It seemed that a large black cloud of bad luck had stalled over the Broadmoor area and would not budge. With his Broadmoor investment at risk, and daily losing money, Count James was becoming desperate. And then came the rumors of gold at Cripple Creek. This news engendered thoughts for a different source of income. Everyone knew that Colorado's Rockies were full of gold and silver. In September of 1891, the Count boarded a Colorado Midland train for Florissant. He then traveled the eighteen miles south to

183

Cripple Creek in a rented buckboard, probably from Hundley's Florissant Livery.

What Count James found there could hardly have raised his hopes. "The Greatest Gold Camp on Earth" still consisted of Welty's log ranchhouse, a log store and a modest log hotel. Most of the would-be miners were simple cowboys from Florissant— William Spell, Marion Lankford, Sheriff Ed Bell, and Bob Womack—to name just a few. Nonetheless, Count James bought a few shares in a placer mine on Mineral Hill. He then returned to Colorado Springs after only two days of inspection.

In November, however, Count James returned to Cripple Creek with his friend Tom Parrish. They stayed with George and Emma Carr who now leased the Welty ranch. Emma was thoroughly charmed by the Count, and gave him the "bed of honor"—on the kitchen table. Making breakfast the next morning proved a challenge worthy of Emma, who simply moved the snoring Count's feet apart in order to roll out her biscuit dough. In return for their hospitality, the Count regaled his hosts with lusty renditions of arias from *Fidelio*.

Pourtales and Parrish remained in Cripple Creek a little over a week this time. They inspected Stratton's Independence Mine and several others. Count James hired an Aspen mining engineer, Wolcott Newberry, as his technical adviser. Ironically, Newberry, the expert, advised him to steer clear of the Independence, and instead invest in the Buena Vista Mine on Bull Hill. But Newberry failed to understand that mining at Cripple Creek differed from other gold mines. In most mines, gold veins boldly emblazon their milky-white quartz-rock hosts, virtually screaming "look, I'm GOLD." But not Cripple's gold. It coyly hides in Cripple's volcanic rock, an andesite breccia commonly known as porphyry because of its deep purple color. The ores from this breccia are the tellurides, calaverite and sylvanite, and they reveal their gold content only when heated.

But Newberry wasn't alone. Cripple's ores befuddled most experts, and it was one of the main reasons that the boom at Cripple was off to such a slow start. Fortunately, however, Count Pourtales had seen these very same tellurides in his Transylvania mountains. Extracting the gold from this ore was an expensive process, and required a substantial investment, but Pourtales knew the value of that risk and took it.

News of Count Pourtales' investment in Cripple Creek was splashed across the *Gazette* on November 10, 1891. This proved to be the seminal event in the history of the gold camp. Count James was one of the more glamorous members of Little London's social set, due, no doubt, to his title, his estates in Prussia, and his engaging manner. Whatever Count James did, the rest of Springs society tried to emulate. Suddenly Cripple Creek exploded with rich bankers and playboys from Denver and Colorado Springs.

Unfortunately for Count James, the Pikes Peak area still held that large, black financial cloud. In 1896, the count had to liquidate all of his mining interests and the Broadmoor City. He realized a net loss of over $200,000.

Spencer Penrose ultimately bought the Broadmoor, where he and Julie built their man-

Colorado Springs Pioneer Museum
Countess Berthe De Pourtales
Without her, Count James Pourtales might never have come to Colorado and there might never have been an investor willing to risk money in the new Cripple Creek Mining District.

sion. Under Penrose's guidance, lots sold like proverbial hotcakes, and the Broadmoor Hotel became one of the world's premiere luxury resorts. Stratton's spurned Independence Mine sold for eleven million dollars. James J. Hagerman, who had bought controlling interest in the Count's Buena Vista Mine,

185

became one of the wealthiest men in Colorado Springs. Count James had the Midas touch. Unfortunately, however, it seemed to have a delayed reaction and benefitted only those who came after him. Nonetheless, without his involvement, Cripple Creek may very well have died on the vine for want of investors.

Happily, Count James was willing to gamble again—this time on the Commonwealth Mine in Pearce, Arizona. His share of the thirty million dollars produced by this mine allowed him and his beautiful Berthe to return to his estates in Prussia in grand style, where they then remained.

When Count James became involved in Cripple Creek, the groundwork had already been laid for the boom by those "erstwhile" Florissant cowboys lounging around Welty's ranch house. Most miners vividly recalled the debacle at the original Tarryall some thirty years before. In 1859, a few greedy miners staked out every claim available in the Tarryall region, precluding latecomers from participating in the strike. These unfortunate men derisively called the strike "Grab-all," and were careful to fairly organize the next strike which they thoughtfully named Fairplay. Similarly, Florissant's cowboys wanted to ensure a fair playing field for all miners in Cripple Creek.

Appropriate and fair organization of a new mining district was vital to Cripple Creek's development. United States laws were very liberal in allowing miners to establish their special districts themselves. When Bob Womack rode the Colorado Midland from the Springs to Florissant in late February 1891, he met Ed De La Vergne and his partner who had just returned from staking claims adjacent to his in Cripple Creek. Womack seemed overwhelmed that his prophecies of gold in Cripple Creek were at last validated by others. He remained in Florissant for another three days, sleeping on the sugar sacks in Frank Castello's Florissant Mercantile.

Captain Hensley's Florissant potato patch had temporarily overshadowed Womack's gold strike, so poor old Bob was met with derision and skepticism while in Colorado Springs. Florissant was a different matter, however. Some dozen or so Florissant residents had already staked their claims, led by

Womack's old mentor, Lankford. Womack now luxuriated around the pot bellied stove in Castello's Mercantile, as his entourage of future millionaires talked excitedly of Cripple. It was decided that a proper mining district must be organized as soon as practicable. Frank Castello assumed command, and announced a meeting date of April 5 at the Carr's Broken Box Ranch.

George and Emma Carr were always delighted at the prospect of having visitors. Emma was one of those most remarkable ranch women who seemed capable of doing anything, and doing it well. She spent the three days prior to the miner's meeting cleaning house and baking pies for her guests. Leslie and Oakley Doyle (Doy) Spell, Bill Spell's children, recalled their admiration for Mrs. Carr in their book *Forgotten Men of Cripple Creek:*

> . . . *We especially enjoyed watching Mrs. Carr gracefully riding sidesaddle, weaving in and out among the cattle, cutting them out as wanted. We admired the dexterity with which she handled her horse, for she was an accomplished horsewoman and made a striking appearance with the flowing skirt of her riding habit, her auburn hair tucked neatly under the mannish hat she wore. Mrs. Carr keenly enjoyed her part in helping with the roundup, but didn't neglect her obligations as hostess and made our visit a most pleasant one. No matter how busy, she was always gracious and hospitable—the true gentle-woman.*

Cripple's first miner's meeting was held on Sunday, April 5, 1891, as scheduled. Castello arrived early from Florissant, leading three mules laden with refreshments from his store. Bill Spell served as temporary chairman, and opened the meeting held around a bonfire on the hillside next to the Carr's ranch. Fifteen of Florissant's cowboys were present, outnumbering the other prospective millionaires. George Carr was elected chairman, and a committee was formed to write camp rules and regulations. The name "Cripple Creek Mining District" beat the name "Womack Mining District" by only a few votes.

Cripple Creek was named by Levi Welty who had ranched in the area since 1871. Welty built a house and corrals near a little stream that ran down the valley, below the current town site. (Welty's homestead later became the Broken Box Ranch, leased by George Carr from the owners, Horace Bennett and Julius Myers.) Early on, one of the Welty boys fell off the roof and broke his arm. Another of the boys cut his foot while chopping wood. Their hired man, Ben Roberts, set out to pack some bear meat to one of the roundup camps when his horse got a whiff, began to buck and then stepped in a prairie dog hole, breaking both his leg and his rider's leg. All of these misfortunes caused the Welty's to proclaim that "that sure was one cripple creek!" The name stuck, and has been used since that day, in spite of several attempts at other names.

This new mining district, Cripple Creek, was six miles square, or about 23,000 acres. Its rules were markedly liberal. Anyone could file a lode claim, 1,500 feet long and 300 feet wide—about ten acres. All that was required was to set six location stakes, tell the El Paso County clerk about it and perform $100 of labor on the claim each year. Prospect holes were designated by placing a pick and a shovel at the entrance as evidence of possession.

Bill Spell was appointed Camp Marshal, mainly because he already held the office of El Paso County deputy sheriff. Marshall Spell was also pressed into service as the recorder of mining claims, and spent many long nights laboriously making entries in the district's leather-bound ledger while seated at the kitchen table of his Florissant home.

By 1893, the fledgling mining district had grown sufficiently that the records were kept in an office on Bennett Avenue. However, Cripple's disastrous fires of 1896 destroyed all of these carefully kept records. Cripple's miners were therefore required to make affidavits as to the date and location of their claims. To this day, there are numerous duplications and errors in the mines, which were recorded in the fire's aftermath.

Most of the real money in a gold mining camp is made by anyone astute enough to understand a miner's basic need for sustenance. This is easily reflected in the use of the term "grub stake." And Cripple Creek was not exempt from this rule. Cripple's population grew exponentially as word of the gold strike spread. Shortly after the first district meeting at the Carr Ranch in April, 1891, there were about 450 prospectors in the district. By the next year, their ranks had swollen to a hefty 2,500. By 1893, there were easily 12,500! By the turn of the century, the bowl of Cripple's ancient volcano resembled a beehive of activity as 50,000 people searched for the golden needles in her granite haystack.

Frank Castello was easily poised for profit with his tidy little mercantile store in Florissant. Until 1894, Florissant was the main route for gold seekers, tourists, and ore haulers from and to Cripple Creek. Colorado Spring's *Gazette* reported on Florissant's newly found prosperity in a story on February 2nd, 1892:

> *Florissant, one of the prettiest and best located little towns in El Paso county had several booms, but none of them have ever succeeded in raising the town much above the level of a lumberman's center. Since the Cripple Creek excitement Florissant has been the chief railroad point for the new camp and the majority of the travel has gone that way. Many people are of the opinion that the metropolis of Twin Creek will continue to be the main supply point for the gold mines. Be this as it may, its beautiful location and the fact that it may some day be a county seat give Florissant a strong claim on the future.*

John Hundley operated the first stage line from Florissant to Cripple Creek. Fifteen six-horse stages met the daily demand for transportation to the gold camps. Miners, supplies, and U.S. Mail were all hauled up Ute Pass aboard the Colorado Midland Railroad, where they were unloaded at Florissant. Miners who had not yet outfitted themselves wandered into Castello's store or Handbury & Lentz' Mercantile, bought picks, shovels, tents, coffee, beans and flour. Those that could afford Hundley's ten dollar fare then climbed aboard the Concord for a rollicking ride to the gold camp.

Mrs. Nellie S. Pyles of Florissant was a passenger on the first stage to Cripple Creek. She later told C.S. Dudley of the *Gazette Telegraph* that "there was fear the stage might slide off the road, so at places all the men but the driver got out and pushed on it to keep it from going sideways, and she was the only passenger in it." (Nellie and her husband, Thomas Benton Pyles, published the first newspaper on the west slope of the Peak. Unfortunately, no copies of the *Crystal Peak Beacon* have ever been located. Their paper was printed in Florissant from 1889 until 1894.)

Hundley's Concord stages were usually packed with those seeking their fortune in the new-found gold fields. Many of the Concords were equipped with an additional center row of seats which folded down when not in use. Needless to say, packing six to nine adults into this cramped space sometimes proved an overly interesting experience. One of these early travelers noted his experience on just such a packed stage coach.

This gentleman was already aboard when a rather heavy-set woman, in voluminous skirts, boarded. After a prolonged, uncomfortable silence the gentleman finally asked the new passenger if she would kindly consent to "dovetail" with him. Dovetailing was a common means of affording everyone comfort. This was done by interlacing the facing passenger's legs from the two opposing seats. This very proper lady had obviously never encountered the term before, however, and soundly slapped her facing partner, the offending gentleman. She also demanded that the driver discharge her at the next stop, where she fled the coach in an indignant huff!

Most passengers vied for the very best seat on the stage. This was up front, in the open air, next to the driver. The scenery from this vantage point was usually spectacular. It was considered a great honor when the driver allowed one onto the coveted seat next to him.

Demand for stagecoaches and freight hauling made the entire venture a lucrative one. By the close of 1892, there were three stage lines into Cripple Creek—Hundley's, Montgomery's, and Welty's. By the winter of 1893, three more stage lines offered their services. In the spring of 1893, a toll road was opened from Hayden's Divide into Cripple Creek. Hundley then expanded his operations to include a coach which met the Colorado Midland at Divide, and carried its passengers down the new toll road on an even more perilous ride to the gold camp.

Over 8,000 pounds of express were tugged daily up the 2,000-foot climb from Florissant to Cripple. Ore wagons were pressed into service in hauling food stuffs and equipment to the miners, returning with loads of gold ore for the Colorado Midland Railroad to haul to Manitou Springs for processing.

Remarkably, there were few thefts of this precious gold ore. Adeline Hornbek's son, Elliot, was one of the first stage drivers. He reported to C.S. Dudley of the *Gazette Telegraph* that it "was usually kept a secret just when the most valuable ore was to be brought down and that, strange as it may seem, he cannot remember that there were any holdups or robberies."

Dudley goes on to describe (in the *Gazette Telegraph*) the boom that came to Florissant in those early days of Cripple Creek madness:

> . . . *Florissant was the jumping-off place for the Cripple Creek district before a railroad was built to Cripple Creek (in 1894). Gold seekers went to Florissant by rail and then made their way, first on foot, then by stage, to the land of prospects. Up the Florissant-Cripple Creek road toiled six and eight-horse teams with wagons loaded with provisions and vast amounts of machinery and other mining equipment. Down the road came these same wagons filled with ore, sometimes a single load valued at thousands of dollars. This ore was shipped over the Midland railroad to Colorado City, now west of Colorado Springs, for treatment. Things happened so fast, and there was so much activity, in Florissant in the 1890's that it is difficult to imagine the picture of the town, now an agricultural and stock-raising center, as the mining town of those romantic days described by old residents.*
>
> *Gold was not found at Florissant, but for several years Florissant was the door out of which Cripple Creek's golden stream poured, and the stories of fortunes made almost*

overnight, and of the telling, as something of new interest loomed up ahead.

Castello's Florissant Mercantile not only proved a virtual gold mine for its owner, but it also paved the way in making Frank Castello one of Cripple's first millionaires.

Richard Houghton, a kindly man with a fondness for liquor, homesteaded about three-quarters of a mile north of Florissant on the East Oil Creek Trail (now Wildhorn Road) about 1884. Houghton, like many other veterans, used his Civil War experience to take advantage of the special homestead provisions accorded them. Although plagued with a permanent limp from his war duty, he developed his homestead into a small dairy with about a dozen milk cows. Florissant's growing populace relished "Uncle" Dick's supply of sweet, fresh milk, cream and cheeses. This income, coupled with his small government pension, provided a modest living for him, his wife and four children.

Dairy farming is a severe taskmaster, however, and is especially so in Colorado's Rockies. It is not unusual for frigid winter nights to dip to thirty and forty below zero. Uncle Dick's hands became cracked, red and rough, as did those of his beautiful Mary. Cows had to be milked twice daily no matter what the temperature. William Spell's children, Leslie Doyle (Doy) and Hazel, later fondly recalled Mary McKinney Houghton in their book *Forgotten Men of Cripple Creek:*

> *. . . Mrs. Houghton, nee Mary McKinney, was a woman beloved of the entire community. Doubtless when younger, she was a beautiful woman. However, at the time I, as a lad of six or seven, knew her first, her beauty had faded in a physical way with the years of toil and responsibility of rearing a family, as well as caring for a husband who sometimes drifted home in a drunken stupor. She never lost patience with Uncle Dick for his faults, often undressing and putting him to bed with no words of recrimination. To my childish eyes, she was still beautiful. I have pleasant memories of the many times she would lift me onto her homemade kitchen stool and offer a glass of milk*

*and cookies from her well-filled cookie jar when I
appeared at her door with a pail for our family's supply of
milk . . . It was Mrs. Houghton's task to milk the cows and
care for the milk. Her hands were calloused, the knuckles
misshapen from hard work, but gentle as a fairy's when
lifting me to the stool.*

Uncle Dick was a valued member of the community, and
served as chairman for Florissant's school district. It was mainly through his efforts that the new well-constructed, two-room
school was built in Florissant in 1887. Nonetheless, Houghton
hoped for a better life for his family, and assuaged the pain of
his wounded ambitions in cheap whiskey.

Houghton and his sons, John and Haddon, had acquired a
smattering of knowledge about mining and had half-heartedly
picked at the rose-colored granite around Florissant. They, too,
were skeptical of most claims—having first-hand experience of
the hoaxes at Mount Pisgah and at Hensley's potato patch.
However, two separate events worked to change Uncle Dick's
mind.

First, his friend Frank Castello filed two separate claims in
Cripple with Houghton's brother, Tom, in early May. Then, he
actually saw Dick Dickerson hauling wagon after wagon of ore
from Spell & Carr's Blue Bell Mine into Florissant. In late
spring of 1891, he could restrain himself no longer. He and his
boys loaded their wagon with a camping outfit and headed for
Cripple Creek.

On the north end of Guyot Hill, Uncle Dick found a small
ravine where the ravages of nature had revealed a well-defined
vein of blue fluorine quartz. Uncle Dick knew enough of mining
to understand that this quartz was a pretty sure indicator of
gold. Excitedly, he panned some of the gravel, and as suspected,
found tiny flecks of gold. He wasted no time in locating his
claim on that fateful day in late May 1891, barely seven months
after Womack's momentous find in nearby Poverty Gulch. At
last he would be able to give his wife the life that she so
deserved. In her honor, then, he named his claim the Mary
McKinney.

Uncle Dick and his sons worked their placer for over a year while Mary ran their Florissant dairy. Finally, he became discouraged. Only three mines were able to produce ore throughout 1891. Even after Count Pourtales validated the strike in Cripple Creek with his investment, there were only about fifty mines shipping ore up to the Colorado Midland Railroad in Florissant by the fall of 1892. Unfortunately, Uncle Dick did not have the wherewithal to continue working his claim and support his family. Also, Mary's health was failing, and he was needed back at his farm. He abandoned his work on the mine and returned to Florissant.

There still was the matter of his grub stake at Castello's mercantile, however. During the year he spent searching for his fortune in Cripple's crater, he had run up a $30 grocery bill at Castello's—equivalent to about one month's wages. Castello felt sorry for his old friend, and agreed to accept title to the Mary McKinney in exchange for Uncle Dick's indebtedness.

Later, Castello was commiserating with his friend, J.P. Ryan, about having accepted the "worthless" mining claim in lieu of cash. Ryan, a telegraph agent for the Colorado Midland Railroad, was smitten. He offered Castello his life savings—$30—for a half interest in the claim. Neither Castello nor Ryan had the several thousand dollars needed to develop the Mary McKinney, so they decided to lease the claim. After several years and as many different lessees, Castello and Ryan finally formed their own mining company in 1895. The Mary McKinney soon became one of Cripple's top producers, cashing in on over $11 million in gold! Frank Castello became a multimillionaire at the age of 44.

William Spell's son, Doy, worked at the Mary McKinney and noted with pride that the "setup and the management was the acme of efficiency. There was a saying around the camp at one time if a man wanted a job at the Mary McKinney mine he would need wait for someone to die, as workman turnover was unusual."

Atlanta Long Thompson recalled in her book *Daughter of a Pioneer* that Houghton did not end up penniless from his mining venture. Her version of Castello's grub stake differs slightly from that of Spell:

> . . . A man by the name of Houghton stumbled over there and staked the Mary McKiney (sic) mine, naming it for his wife's maiden name. He was a man who was seldom sober, but drunk or sober he was always talking about Mary. Poor Mary had a large family and if it hadn't been for Frank Castillo (sic), merchant in Florissant who let them have groceries, they would have starved to death. Houghton came home from Cripple Creek the first winter there had been any prospecting done there, and went to Frank Castillo and asked him how much he owed him. When Frank told him fifteen hundred dollars, Houghton replied, "I haven't any money Frank, but I am sure I have a mine, and I will give you an interest in it." This interest afterward made Frank a wealthy man. Houghton later sold his share for fifty thousand dollars. He then took poor Mary, who was hardly able to walk around, to Denver and put her under the care of the best doctor, while he took the Keeley cure. Mary had a cancer and lived only a year. Houghton stopped at our house on his way home from Colorado Springs, soon after he discovered his mine, to show me a gorgeous hat he had bought for Mary. It was an elaborate affair with quantities of red roses on the crown and when he asked me if I didn't think Mary would like it, I could hardly keep from smiling. I assured him that I knew she would, but I couldn't picture poor, plain, Mary wearing it.

Fifteen years later, Doy Spell chanced to travel to the Old Soldier's Home in Monte Vista, south of Florissant in the San Luis Valley. Doy recalled his poignant encounter with Uncle Dick in *Forgotten Men of Cripple Creek:*

> red: "Of course, Doy, I remember you, Doy Spell." He asked about father, mother, and our family, and then told of his. His daughters had married, his boys were working as foremen of the ore sorting crew at the Mary McKinney. We talked long of Cripple Creek, Florissant, and of the

schoolhouse he had built. After reminiscing for about two hours it was time for me to leave. Uncle Dick's lower lip began to quiver and tears spilled over. I walked along the street for a short distance, then looked back to wave. He was still watching me.

Initially, Cripple Creek's unique type of gold ore was very easily, and quite frequently, found near the surface. For this reason, it became known as the "poor man's gold camp." Many of the mines were worked with a simple farmer's plow, which churned up rich volcanic float laden with gold. A young carpenter from Florissant was one of these fortunate "gold farmers." Matthew Sterrett had joined Castello, Spell, and Carr in the early excitement and in organizing the Cripple Creek District. He then located his "Pride of the Rockies" in April of 1891, and then the more lucrative "Deer Horn Lode" in May of 1891. Atlanta Thompson recalled that Sterrett harvested over "twelve thousand dollars worth of ore at grass roots" from his Deer Horn Lode.

Miss Sarah Elizabeth (Sally) Halthusen, Herman's daughter, found her own unique way of mining for Cripple's gold. She moved from her father's Florissant ranch down to a house on Bennett Avenue, in Cripple Creek. She took most of her rogue horses with her so that she could continue with her hobby of breaking them. Somehow, Sally had managed to capture the attention of Spencer Penrose. And Spencer was enamored with this big-busted, high-spirited horsewoman. He even ignored the fact that she had collected ransom from a Denver family in exchange for breaking her engagement to their son. Spencer's blue-blooded father was much alarmed at this romance, however. So Dr. Penrose sent Dick Penrose to Cripple to talk some sense into his brother.

This approach seems to have been successful, and prevented the smitten Spencer from making Miss Sally Mrs. Penrose. Sally, however, was a mite touchy about the entire episode. She severely beat a young chambermaid whose loose tongue detailed the affair in Sally's hearing. Sally was hauled into court where she was found guilty of assault and fined $10 plus

The brick structure on the left is the Bell Brothers Building, now
home of the Cripple Creek Police Department. Bell was sheriff
of Florissant before moving to Criple Creek in the 1890s.

costs. In 1895, Sally healed her broken heart by marrying
Thomas Gough, Jr., a hotel owner. When her father died in
1903, Sally and her siblings waged a legal battle against his
widow—their stepmother—for possession of the estate.

A few miles south of the Halthusen Ranch, Reverend David
Long (Atlanta Thompson's father) established a homestead on
the road to Cripple Creek when he returned to the area in 1877.
Reverend Long regularly corresponded with his favorite niece,
Julia Snare. Julia and her husband Charles had settled on a
sod farm in southwestern Kansas where the "land was as level
as a floor." Their farm never raised a thing but large clods of
dirt, and so Reverend Long encouraged them to come to
Colorado.

Long's optimism about the prospects of Pikes Peak backcountry was no doubt based on the boom in nearby Cripple
Creek. Farmers and ranchers in the area faced more demand
for their goods than they could possibly supply. Julia and
Charles sold their Kansas sod farm for $5, packed their few
belongings in a covered wagon with a four-horse team, then

headed for Pikes Peak on April 10, 1895. Julia's first two infant daughters had died within their first year of life, and she was anxious about her thirteen-month-old son Claude Maxwell. She fretted over the wind and rain and snow that plagued them as they followed the old Santa Fe Trail into Colorado. When they arrived in Pueblo twelve days later, the baby was quite sick.

Julia's (unpublished) journal reflects her anxiety as they turned north from Pueblo on April 23:

Started out in good time, bad roads and horses hard to get along. Did not get quite to Fountain, we stopped several places to get bread, as we are out, finally got a small loaf. Baby still sick.

When they arrived in Fountain the next day, the horses had to be re-shod and the wagon break fixed. Julia traded her rug-making machine to the blacksmith and his wife in return for their services, and then she, Charles and the baby resumed their journey to the mountains. As they began their ascent of Ute Pass, Julia wrote that the area afforded "grand scenery and narrow roads"—perfectly reflecting her gift for understatement.

They arrived at "Uncle Dave's" at dusk on April 26, sixteen grueling days after leaving their home in Mead, Kansas. Reverend Long helped them settle into their new ranch near Sheep Rock, on what is now Mueller State Park. Charles wasted no time in planting potatoes and seed oats, while Julia made furniture for their new home, cooked, sewed, and tended the baby.

In these early days of ranching, the government allowed an individual to fence as much land as he cared to, provided he didn't enclose it. Most ranchers took advantage of this practice, running the open end of their fenced ranch up against a mountain, a gulch or any other handy obstacle that would effectively "close" the required opening. In this manner, anyone with a small patch of farm land or a homestead could easily expand into ranching without having to purchase the required acreage.

The Snares' new neighbors to the east were the notorious horse rustlers, the White Brothers. Julia notes in her journal on May 24 that "a man (was) here hunting for his horses." But that was life in the West. It was usually best to mind your own business, and just "let the other fellow be." The financial opportunities afforded by the geography of the region were not always legal.

Over fifty years later, Julia's son Walter Nathan, "Nate," wrote about his mother.

> *My mother really liked the mountains, they were doing real good. Had their homestead, built a two-room log cabin and later got enough lumber to build a nice addition. This frame part was painted which was rare in those days, here in this part of Colorado. Of course the gold mines were booming in Cripple Creek, which made a ready market for things they might have to sell. Also sawmills were numberous (sic), and my Dad worked at them when times were slack.*

Nate had an older sister, Alice Ione, who died in 1901 from scarlet fever, two years before he was born. His parents were distraught over the death of their beautiful five-year-old daughter. They were especially grieved that they had been unable to find a doctor in the area to attend to her, and who could perhaps have prevented her death. So Charles and Julia loaded their two surviving children, Max and Wayne, into the wagon and headed to Kirksville, Missouri where Charles studied to become a doctor. He received his Doctor of Osteopathy in 1905.

Pikes Peak backcountry had taken hold of their hearts, however, and they longed to return. The opportunity finally presented itself in 1914, and Max, now nineteen years old, and his seventeen-year-old brother Wayne were sent back to their Pikes Peak ranch to prepare it for the rest of the family. Tragically, their father died the day before Christmas. Their mother wired them from Kansas to dig a grave for their father, that she was bringing him home to bury him. The two teenagers then spent Christmas day digging a hole six feet deep in the frozen ground. Julia returned on December 27, 1914 and buried her husband. In the tradition of Adeline Hornbek, she and the two older boys successfully ranched, raising her three youngest children, aged eleven, eight and six in the shadow of Sheep Rock.

Courtesy Rose White, Dorothy Snare's daughter
Dr. Charles Snare's widow, Julia, and four of her five children, shortly after
her husband's death. The photo was taken at their homestead near Sheep
Rock (now Mueller State Park). From left: Wayne Snare, Julia Snare,
Dorothy Snare, Nate Snare, Hanna Long (Julia's sister), Charles Snare,
Hazel Long (Julia's sister-in-law) and little Julia Long (Hazel's daughter).

Dr. Charles Snare never lived to see his beloved homestead
again, but his sons established a virtual ranching dynasty on
the west slope of Pikes Peak. Max, the oldest son, built the family ranch into a prosperous outfit along the banks of Hay Creek
(originally called East Oil Creek) which he later sold for $4 an
acre to a man named Dwain Werley (or Worley). His ranch is
now part of Mueller State Park. The youngest son, Charles
Julian, took advantage of the revised Homestead Act of 1916
and filed on thousands of acres of ranchland south of the
entrance to what is now Mueller Park and several sections
surrounding Dome Rock. His ranch is also now part of Mueller
State Park.

One of the middle sons, Walter Nathan or "Nate," ranched
along the southern border of what is now the Florissant Fossil
Beds National Monument. In private correspondence, Nate
noted that nearly all the ranchers in the area "were thin-hipped

and broad shouldered and their faces were sunburned." He also noted that many of them ran "old Texas long-horned cattle. They were just hides stretched over the bones, and horns three feet long."

In 1904, a prominent Cripple Creek banker, John Delano Husted, incorporated the Crescent Cattle Company. The company was organized as a ranching enterprise, and sold its stock primarily to religious ministers in the Boston area. Crescent Cattle Company purchased large sections of grazing land from Divide down to the Four Mile area. Headquarters for the ranch was established just west of Divide, but the real business of the ranch was conducted by the stockholders during the summer at an elaborate "cabin" called Jack Rabbit Lodge. It is even rumored that Teddy Roosevelt was a guest here during a hunting trip to the Pikes Peak area.

In the early 1950s, W.E. Mueller began purchasing the fragments of what had been Crescent Cattle Company land (it went bankrupt in 1924). After a twenty-year stint of ranching the area, Mueller approached The Nature Conservancy in the early 1970s. He hoped to sell his property in a way that would protect its beauty and wildlife from the press of development.

The Conservancy purchased the ranch in 1978, and then sold it to the State of Colorado in 1980. Mueller State Park was officially opened to the public in August of 1991. Today, visitors can hike along the park's ninety miles of trail, enjoying glimpses of elk, big horn sheep, mule deer, eagles, hawks and song birds. The park also affords breathtaking views of Pikes Peak, the Sangre de Cristos, and some of the collegiate Peaks.

"Always a bride's maid, never a bride!" might well be applied to the fate of little Florissant. Cripple Creek promised prosperity for the little town, but it came with a whimper rather than a shout. At the peak of the gold strike in the late 1800s, Florissant boasted no more than 300 residents. Eventually, however, three sets of rails were laid into Cripple, which all but negated ore shipments on the Colorado Midland from Florissant. Most of the ore was instead routed through Hayden's Divide, via the Midland Terminal Line, built into Cripple in 1895. The breathtakingly beautiful Short Line

Railroad was built from the Broadmoor area, south around Pikes Peak and into Victor and Cripple in April, 1901. This became the preferred route for sightseers and businessmen traveling to the gold camps. Some sightseers still came through Florissant on the Midland, but only to harvest her still abundant wild flowers and fossils.

Unfortunately, Florissant's new millionaires were not bound to her by her beauty. Frank Castello sold his mercantile to William Allen, and moved to a fancy house in Colorado Springs in 1898. Marshall Ed Bell moved to Cripple in 1896, where he and his brother built their Bennett Avenue-First Street Building. They became real estate brokers as well as stock brokers. Ed Bell later became Teller County sheriff in 1899 when the county was carved out of El Paso County. Fittingly, his old offices now house the Cripple Creek Police Department.

Frank Burnham, Thomas' father, sold their Twin Creek Ranch to Charles Sisler in 1899. Allen then continued the tradition of Castello's Mercantile by grubstaking Sisler as he searched for his fortune in Cripple Creek. Two years later, Sisler defaulted on his grub stake, turning over the title of his beautiful Twin Creek Ranch to Allen for "One dollar and other good & valuable consideration." Allen and his family then plied their excellent carpentry skills and built the lovely Victorian ranch house at the Twin Creek Ranch in 1904.

Adding insult to injury, Florissant even lost her favorite fiddle player, Kale Wilson. Kale had courted Atlanta Long some time before she married Silas Thompson. Atlanta described him as "a lazy sort of fellow but really good company." Others weren't so kind, describing him as a fellow that was "too lazy to live." Nonetheless, Kale found his way down to Cripple where he staked a claim. When a friend of his happened to pass by, he asked him "Why, Kale, what are you digging there for? There is no vein or float there." Kale replied that the spot was chosen because "this big tree makes it shady." Atlanta wrote that her phlegmatic old beau actually did strike gold there in the grass roots, and made a nice tidy fortune. Florissant's barn dances were never the same, however.

As the new-found gold began to drain the life from Florissant, it also infused life into Cripple Creek, which then gave birth to its neighbor, Victor. Locals deridingly called the gold seekers "coffee coolers" in reference to their habit of digging a little bit, then sitting and waiting for their coffee to cool enough to drink it. Cowboys in the area complained about one particular "coffee cooler" who had dug a hole right in the middle of one of their cattle trails at the base of Bull Hill. They kept him supplied in fresh meat, however, in hopes that he would cover up his hole when he was done. This inconvenient hole turned out the be the fourteen million dollar Independence Mine, and the prospector was none other than Winfield Scott Stratton.

Four hundred feet west of Stratton's Independence Mine, an ex-teamster named J.R. McKinnie staked out the Black Diamond Mine and the Mount Rosa Placer. In fact, it was McKinnie—a "jolly, pink-cheeked Santa Claus of a man"—who had befriended Stratton on his first visit into the Cripple Creek District in May of 1891. In 1893, McKinnie sold his 136-acre Mount Rosa Placer to two "quiet, mousy, ardent Baptists," Frank and Harry Woods, for $1,000.

The Woods brothers shrewdly laid out a townsite on their new mine, and called it Victor. They chose the name in honor of the original homesteader of the adjacent Lawrence townsite, Victor C. Adams. In a burst of Cripple Creek fever, the Woods boys sold their town lots by telling prospective buyers that every lot was a potential gold mine. Lots sold so well that the brothers next decided to build the Victor Hotel. However, while Frank Woods was grading the lot for the hotel, he struck a twenty-inch vein of gold. He traced the vein to its source, the Gold Coin Mine, which he quietly and quickly purchased for a few thousand dollars. In a very short time, the Gold Coin was earning $50,000 a month for its new owners.

Of course, Victor grew by leaps and bounds as owners of the town lots saw the promise of gold in their midst. Subterranean Victor kept pace with the township above. Vast timbered tunnels soon connected the Gold Coin, the Strong and dozens of other mines. It was possible to walk, underground, the entire

Ute Pass Historical Society
Victor, Colorado in the late 1800s.
Nestled at the base of Bull Hill, Victor was officially born in 1893.

distance from Victor to Cripple Creek. Since these shafts lay underneath the town itself, they soon became a haven for criminals. These cunning men came to know this labyrinth of underground streets and put them to good use. Victor became the capital of crime, although when it incorporated in 1894, it billed itself as The City of Mines.

When labor disputes erupted in Cripple Creek and Victor in the mid-1890s, hundreds of miners left for greener pastures. Many of these men traveled thirty miles west, past McIntyre Mountain (made notorious by the Mount Pisgah hoax of 1884). They sunk their picks and shovels into the surface of an extinct volcano in the Freshwater Mining District. This district earned its name by virtue of two gulches; one carved by a soda water spring, or Soda Water Gulch, and the other by—of course—a fresh water spring. In January of 1896, the town of Freshwater was incorporated based on a townsite survey by Will C. Teller.

"Idaville" was the name originally given to the post office in April, 1895. It was named in honor of Ida McClavey Wagner who owned the mining claims on Gold Hill, which towers above the town site on the north. However, when street improvements

Guffey, Colorado in the early 1900s. George West drives the
team while Amos Hardy plows the snow off the main street.
The building at left is Guffey City Hall.

were needed in town the following year, James McClurg Guffey
provided the funding. In gratitude, the 500 citizens of the town
voted to rename the town "Guffey" in May 1896, in honor of
their benefactor. There were no great gold strikes to ensure
Guffey's place in history. Many miners, however, still contend
that the mother lode of Cripple Creek lies hidden under
Guffey's Gold Hill. Guffey remains notorious in recent times,
nonetheless, for her penchant for electing four-footed mayors.
After a series of cats, the most recent mayor is a lovely and love-
able golden retriever.

Travel to Cripple's rich gold fields proved a boon to the
newly-born towns clinging to the Colorado Midland's railbed on
its twenty-mile climb up Ute Pass. Gingerbread, gables, and
fishscale shingles began to appear on charming Victorian
homes in Green Mountain Falls, Cascade, and Woodland Park.
Cascade soon boasted a number of elegant resort hotels, including the Eastholme Hotel (1885); the Cascade House Hotel
(1887); and, the crown jewel, the Ramona Hotel (1888).

Ramona was the best selling novel by Colorado Springs
author, Helen Hunt Jackson, and the hotel claimed the name

with honor. The Ramona's distinctive "champagne bottle" tower graced the three-story building and commanded the skyline of Cascade. This aristocratic edifice included ninety-three guest rooms, a ladies parlor, dining rooms, smoking rooms, and a spacious ballroom. Guests were encouraged to bask in the brisk mountain air on the attractive verandas which encircled each floor. Wicker hampers packed with exotic foods lured picnickers to the majestic front lawn while children fished and played in Cascade Lake, located behind the railroad depot. More adventurous guests reserved seats on the Concord carriages for a six hour ride to the summit of Pikes Peak on the newly-opened toll road (1888), or hiked up the canyon to the Winnemucca Falls. Evening diversions included gourmet meals in the hotel's dining room, productions by the in-house orchestra, or Saturday night dances. Unfortunately, Ramona felt the impact of the war and the declining fortunes of the Colorado Midland Railroad, and so was torn down about 1924.

In the vernacular of the time, most folks referred to the "founding fathers" of their town. Cascade, however, was indebted to three wealthy, highly cultured sisters: Eliza Hewlett, and Ellen and Caroline Marriot. Soon after arriving in Cascade on the Colorado Midland Railroad, they each homesteaded their favorite area of Cascade Canon. Eliza set up housekeeping in a small log cabin on the Ute Indian trail leading up the mountain. Sister Caroline also took up residence in a log cabin that she soon established as the Cascade Canon Post Office. It was later used as a dining hall and then as a school. Around 1895, the Cascade Town Company answered the demand of its many new residents and donated land where a new, one-room, school was built (it was torn down in 1927).

Eliza's sister, Ellen Marriott, kept her housekeeping on a much simpler scale—she erected a tent with wood floors across the trail at the head of the canyon. Later, sister Caroline married George Hinkle, an Episcopal theological student for whom Eliza built Saint Michael's Episcopal Mission in 1888.

Gunn's Livery (est. 1890), in nearby Green Mountain Falls, prospered as well from the increase in traffic up Ute Pass. He began by renting wagons and carriages, and that Colorado

Courtesy Helen Cahill
Frontier justice, Guffey style. This two-cell jail was built
about 1900 after a local rancher was murdered.

"institution," the burro for "without him no mountain resort could maintain its integrity." These sure-footed little burros were ideal for the steep mountain climbs and thin mountain air, and with their steady dispositions and compact strength they were able to travel further and carry heavier loads than their more attractive cousin, the horse. William Gunn mounted sight-seers on his big-eared tour guides, and strung them out in long lines to climb to Devil's Head, Bald Mountain and Pikes Peak. As the press of gold seekers increased in 1893, he added more horses to his stable and became a change station for the Cripple Creek and Pikes Peak Stage Line.

Gunn's Livery, Feed and Sale Stable suffered as the Colorado Midland Railroad declined, and in 1930 the barn was sold to neighboring homesteader, Henry Brockhurst, who moved it to his Brockhurst Dude Ranch. In 1962, Brockhurst gave his family's old homestead to be used "as a home for children forever." The town of Green Mountain Falls later purchased the now-vacant land and used it to develop the present park and swimming pool.

By 1888, the town had sprouted its own newspaper, *The Mountain Falls Echo*, which sang the praises of its new 100-tent city built by developer W.G. Riddock. By July, there were over 500 people living in the "Cloth Castle Camp," and Riddock began building a resort, the Green Mountain Falls Hotel. The hotel's brochure claimed that its seventy guest rooms, dining room and parlor featured a ". . . good cook, few dishes but well selected, and a sideboard to get his toddy. You don't see the continual changing of dresses here that is so tiresome to many ladies; they sit on the broad veranda with their sewing or book, while the husband reads, plays cards, smokes his pipe and enjoys the same comfort as if at home. The children are as little care as if they were at school, roaming over the hills as free as birds."

Green Mountain Fall's town fathers foresaw a great future, and built a beautiful two-story brick school for the "anticipated" children in 1890. The throngs of little ones never materialized, however, so the second story was never completed. By 1900, its empty halls echoed to empty seats, for the new school teacher found it too difficult to heft her great weight up the hill each day and convinced the school board that classes should be held in the town hall instead.

Nearby developers in Woodland Park knew a good thing when they saw it, and raced to build the wooden floors for a colony of "Cloth Castles" to house the thousands of summer tourists and prospectors that poured off the Colorado Midland's daily trains. In 1890, the town fathers excavated a handsome lake and then placed a wooden pavilion nearby for concerts, dancing and picnics. As the new town grew, it added a two-story schoolhouse which replaced a number of small log school buildings in the area. One of these schools, from nearby Edlow, was recycled when its logs were used to build the Free Methodist Church. The chinking was covered with siding from one of the five saw mills in the area, and two rather pretentious Gothic peaks were placed over the separate entry doors for men and women.

Just below the hill, commanded by the Woodland Park pavilion, Elfonza Dickinson and Harry Marble built the fifteen-room

Crest Hotel in 1889—the first in town. John Anisfield soon followed with his picturesque forty-two bedroom Woodland Hotel, encircled by the requisite verandas and crowned with a cone-shaped Victorian turret. On a more modest scale, Andrew Hackman operated the Midland Hotel after immigrating from Holland with his three brothers in 1887. At one point, demand for lodging became so intense that even his private home became a hotel. The Hackman House still boasts handsome cherry wood fireplaces framed by imprinted Dutch tiles from Hackman's homeland. His son, Andrew D., operated a "first class" livery just behind Terrill's General Merchandise (now home to the Cowhand), the biggest store in Woodland Park.

In November 1895, the *Gazette Telegraph* reported that a "very large number of claims have been staked" sixteen miles north of Woodland Park, in a new mining camp called West Creek. A miner named Pemberton was the first to lay claim to what he believed was a continuation of the Cripple Creek gold belt on the banks of West Creek. He was soon joined by 500 to 600 eager prospectors who named their new town and its post office "Pemberton" in honor of its founder. A few years later, however, Pemberton had fallen from grace and his newly-found town bore the name of its water source, West Creek. Terrill's Mercantile (in Woodland Park) made more than most of West Creek's would-be millionaires as it offered the hungry miners "apples, oranges, lemons, nuts, fine candies, fresh and salt meats, hay and grain" and ready made clothes.

Gold Fever infected virtually every rock, every crevice, every valley and every mountain in Pikes Peak's backcountry, including the Tarryall Valley. Long after the original Tarryall mining camp disappeared from just above Como, a glassy-eyed prospector, J.V. Malone (known as the "other" Rocky Mountain Jim) stumbled upon an outcropping of porphyritic quartz about seven miles northwest of Lake George. Eighteen ninety-six had not been a good year in Cripple Creek, and Malone's two partners, Sam Swingley and W.H. Preston, were more than willingly to pick up stakes and move to the Tarryall Valley. This new mining camp lay on the old Hamilton Road, nestled between the Puma Hills and the Tarryall Mountains, and so appropriated the name "Puma City." Within a year, there were 1,000 other prospectors staking claims around the 40-acre town platted by Denverite C.W. Gilman.

The new town's first priority was to quench the thirst of its hard-working miners, so several saloons from Cripple Creek and Victor were dismantled and rebuilt on the banks of Tarryall Creek. A full complement of watering holes was required, however, and soon there were a total of five saloons. These were followed by three hotels and several boarding houses. Residents were kept abreast of the latest gossip and production from nearby mines by the town's newspaper, the *Puma Ledger*. Not so original, however, was the ultimate naming of the town. As the residents petitioned and won a post office, someone returned from upstream with the nicely-painted town sign from the ghostly Tarryall. It seemed logical to simply use this old sign and the abandoned name rather than take the time away from digging for gold to paint a new sign, and so the second Tarryall was born. This economy of labor seems justified in retrospect, for the boom was short-lived, and by 1905 there were only twenty-five people left in the town. To avoid further confusion, however, both the name Tarryall and Puma City were and still are used.

None of Cripple's gold seemed to stick in Pikes Peak's backcountry. Her total production has been estimated at about $450 million dollars—placing her in fifth place worldwide. But by the early 1900s, Florissant was once again a sleepy little cow town, Cripple fell into a similar fate, and the once-proud resort towns lining Ute Pass barely kept alive. Prosperity had been shipped out by the trainload, and like the Colorado Midland, the Florence and Cripple Creek, and the Short Line Railroads—it soon disappeared.

A different, and perhaps more stable economy, has now come to Pikes Peak backcountry in the form of the Florissant Fossil Beds National Monument, Mueller State Park and the Garden Park Fossil Area. Limited gaming has been introduced into Cripple Creek, and Woodland Park and Divide have become bedroom communities for Colorado Springs. The Gold Belt Tour

Scenic Byway now links all of these treasures to mine their scenic beauty and rich history.

There had been an exciting moment, however, once upon a time in their past. As Robert Service wrote, ". . . it isn't the gold that I'm wanting, so much as just finding the gold."

P<small>IKES</small> P<small>EAK</small> B<small>ACKCOUNTRY</small>

CHAPTER NINE

The Petrified Forest

Fortunately, gold of a more lasting, and perhaps, more enriching nature was buried in the hills surrounding Florissant. Ute Indians, marveling at the dark outlines of fossilized images in the pale-gold shale allegedly named Florissant the "Valley of the Shadows."

Early trappers, returning to Taos from the beaver rich streams surrounding Florissant, reported on the area in typical mountain man hyperbole. "Pa'dners, I seed a pewtrified forest of pewtrified trees with their pewtrified limbs chockfull of pewtrified birds a-singin' of pewtrified songs."

Petrified trees choked the valley south of Twin Creek. So much so that early travelers had a difficult time winding their buggies between the sun-bleached stone trunks and branches. When Reverend David Long homesteaded in the area about 1871, he spent a great deal of time digging in the shale and collecting fossils. Atlanta Long Thompson wrote that

Professors from Colorado College came to see us once in a while and Father gave them any specimen of petrified wood, or choice of pieces of shale that they wanted. They hauled away many wagon loads of these specimens.

Hayden's 1873 survey of the area brought the geologist, A.C. Peale, to the Florissant valley. Peale documented the scientific importance of the area when he later issued his report:

About five miles from the mouth (of Beaver Creek, west of Florissant), *around the settlement of Florissant, is an irregular basin filled with modern lake deposits. The*

entire basin is not more than five miles in diameter . . .
About one mile south of Florissant, at the base of a small
hill of sandstone, capped with conglomerate, are twenty or
thirty stumps of silicified wood.

Paleontologist Samuel Hubbard Scudder followed Peale to
the Florissant Valley in 1877. He, too, was struck with the rich
scientific material shallowly buried under the granite. He
reported his findings in the 1882 Bulletin of the United States
Geological and Geographical Survey:

The very shales of the lake itself in which the myriad
plants and insects are entombed, are wholly composed of
volcanic sand and ash, fifteen meters (over forty-five feet)
or more thick they lie, in alternating layers of coarser and
finer material . . . The insects preserved in the Florissant
basin are wonderfully numerous, this single locality hav-
ing yielded in a single summer more than double the num-
ber of specimens which the famous localities in Oeningen,
in Bavaria, furnished Heer in thirty years. Having visited
both places I can testify to the grater prolificness of the
Florissant beds . . . and the quarries are fifty times as
extensive and far more easily worked.
. . . Our examination of the deposits of this lacustrine
basin was principally made in a small hill, from which
perhaps the largest number of fossils have been taken,
lying just south of the house of Mr. Adam Hill, and upon
his ranch . . . Around its eastern base are the famous pet-
rified trees, huge, upright trunks, standing as they grew,
which are reported to have been five or six meters high
(over eighteen feet) *at the advent of the present residents*
of the region. Piecemeal they have been destroyed by van-
dal tourists, until now not one of them rises more than a
meter (about three feet) *above the surface of the ground,*
but their huge size is attested by the relics, the largest of
which can be seen to have been four meters (about twelve
feet) *in diameter. The gigantic trees appear to be sequoias.*

In addition to the interest expressed by Colorado College,
various museums, universities, and prominent scientists

Courtesy Marge & Don Christiansen
The famous Big Stump at Florissant Fossil Bed, is a 500-year-old petrified sequoia tree. These three gentlemen had this postcard made about 1917.

continued to visit the site. In 1877, a geologist from the mining school in Golden, Colorado, Professor Arthur Lakes, wrote a journal of his travels through the Florissant area, recently published as *Discovering Dinosaurs in the Old West*. In August (1877), he noted that his party had collected ". . . boxes upon boxes full of fine paper like shales covered with the impressions of most perfect insects of various descriptions . . ."

In 1883, Florissant's Calas Wilson wrote to his brother John from Breckenridge, where he had gone to summer his cattle:

If you have any good bugs and leaves (fossils) you can sell them up here. Couldn't you send up a few for a sample. A man wants to see some of them, said (he) would pay 5 cents a piece or more. Send a little paper box full by mail

215

day pouch, of nice ones and if they suit you can bring up a wagon bed full."

Several weeks later, when John had complied with this request, Calas jokingly wrote to tell him that he:

. . . got the bugs today, they was all dead but I sold them anyway."

Pillage of the fossils and petrified wood was a cause for concern even as early as 1883. A number of local citizens organized and incorporated the Colorado Museum Association. M. Keith Singer later recalled that one of the incorporators was John D. Coplen. Of the $30,000 in capital stock which was raised, $8,000 was allocated for the purchase of Adam Hill's "Petrified Forest Ranch."

Coplen had made a fortune in copper mining in both Utah and Arizona. His interest in the Petrified Forest, however, was seen as more of a hobby than as a serious business venture. Nonetheless, the later actions of his Colorado Museum Association proved to be a source of alarm for the future of the fossil beds.

On August 16, 1883, the *Fairplay Flume* reported on the proposed plunder of the petrified stumps:

. . . a company has purchased for the sum of $7,000 the ranch upon which these great natural curiosities rest, and is about to remove one or more of them. As the fossilized stump which they are now operating on is altogether too large to admit of handling entire, being fifteen feet across the top and about the same depth to the bottom of the roots, it will be entirely cut up into sections of about two feet square, by means of steam saws, pure silica sand being placed in the cuts and serving the purpose of saw teeth. The stumps can be easily handled in this manner and will be shipped to some city museum and set up for admiration of thousands who might never see them in their native fastness. This is the only excuse that can be offered for marring the works of nature, and perhaps that excuse is ample.

Seven years later, in 1890, the "Colorado Petrified Forest" was still being operated as a tourist attraction. It was probably still owned by Coplen, as the 1884 article in Colorado Springs' *Daily Gazette* indicated that:

> . . . *good food and clean beds at "Copeland's (sic)" were standard fare offered travelers. Admission to the Petrified Forest was seventy-five cents for adults and thirty-five cents for children, and "entitled each person to as many fossils as he has the patience to dig."*

Exploitation of the stumps and fossils seemed a constant threat in the late 1800s. A reporter for the *Creede Candle* again sounded the alarm in a story on February 10, 1893:

> *The last remnant of the so-called petrified forest one and one-half miles south of Florissant is about to be taken to Chicago.*
>
> *The oldest settlers thereabouts remember that twenty years ago there were twenty of these petrified trunks standing erect besides numerous petrified logs lying over the ground. All have been removed by tourists and relic hunters until now one of the greatest and rarest natural curiosities of the world has been despoiled. The trunks and logs have been sawed up and broken to pieces and taken East, some intact to museums where they are regarded with great interest.*
>
> *The remaining trunk would have been removed long ago but for the great expense of the project. About twelve years ago parties from Denver undertook to remove the stump to the city as a museum curiosity. They worked a long time with horse-power and improved machinery, but finally had to abandon the undertaking. The Rocky Mountain Museum company has now undertaken to accomplish what the Denver people failed to do. Already the work has been begun by making excavations several feet about the roots so as to get as much of the roots as possible. This trunk is over forty feet in circumference and stands eight feet high. It will have to be removed in sections by sawing it lengthwise. The cost of its removal will*

be heavy and the company expects to reimburse themselves and make something by placing it on exhibition at Chicago.

There is no evidence, however, that the Big Stump was actually removed or exhibited at the Chicago Worlds Fair in 1893. The Big Stump prevailed, and ironically claimed the steel saw used to cut into its petrified wood, where it remains embedded to this day.

Unfortunately, some portions of these 500-year-old petrified trees were successfully removed and were shown in museums in London, Chicago, and Washington, D.C. Fortunately, fate intervened before the fossils and stumps were completely obliterated from the Florissant area.

Professors Farnsworth and Strieby of Colorado College in Colorado Springs arrived in Florissant in 1911 with a party from the British Museum. Farnsworth was overawed by what he found. Farnsworth was quoted by the *Denver Post* as he effusively and eloquently reported on what he had found.

. . . This is the greatest fossil field in the world and I am afraid the people of Colorado do not realize what it means to the state and nation. We have come all the way from London to investigate these marvels, and if the fields were 5,000 miles away from here, Colorado Springs and Denver people would be paying their good money to visit them and wishing ardently that they were within the borders of this state. The fields are beyond justification the most remarkable in the way of fossil deposits in the world.

It wasn't until an article appeared in the *Denver Times* in 1915 that anyone suggested that the federal government act to protect the "greatest fossil field in the world." The *Times* article focused on a report that the federal government had just established the Dinosaur National Monument in Utah. Seizing upon the precedent which was established with this Monument, the *Times* urged that the Florissant Fossil Beds also be made a national monument.

. . . Colorado possesses one of the most unique and best known fossil fields in the world, near Florissant. Fossils are discovered here in such numbers that a railroad runs special trains to this field during the tourist season. One is afforded the novel spectacle of hundreds of men, women and children diligently hunting the earth's surface and even digging in the ground, for the fossilized remains of antediluvian creatures . . . Setting aside these fields of fossil richness is in accord with the government's policy of protecting anything which is likely to prove of great public interest . . . Setting them aside prevents their location by individuals and their possible exploitation for gain.

Unfortunately, like the prophet Casandra, the *Times* prediction of exploitation for personal gain was both historically and futuristically correct.

In 1920, David and his son Ira Henderson began a commercial venture that they called a number of different names, among them Colorado Petrified Forest, New Petrified Forest, and Henderson Petrified Forest. Parts of the Halthusen ranchhouse were moved to the west side of the old Cripple Creek wagon road, and a pavilion and ticket office were constructed where the park's visitor center is located today. A museum building was added in 1924, and was operated until 1961. The Hendersons blasted out numerous stump formations, unearthing the formation known as the "Trio" in their efforts. The principal exhibits of the Henderson Petrified Forest were the petrified sequoia stumps.

Adjacent to this commercial venture, and slightly to the north, a second commercial operation was begun in 1922. John D. Coplen—who had ranched on the fossil beds since about 1884—moved the abandoned Colorado Midland Railroad Station onto his ranch in July 1922. At first, he used the old station as a ranch building. Later, he converted it into a hotel, then sold it to Palmer John Singer on March 27, 1927, along with 160 acres of land. Singer then acquired the adjoining property, known as the Chapman Place, just northeast of the Big Stump. Singer labeled his new ranch the Colorado Petrified Forest Ranch.

A bitter rivalry ensued with the neighboring, but unneigh-borly, Pike Petrified Forest when it was sold to H.D. Miller in 1950. His manager, John Baker, proved an eccentric and irasci-ble operator. Agnes Singer recalled that:

> . . . *Baker came over and tried to keep the tourists from coming into our place . . . he was spreading nails on the road and this* (Singer tour guide) *brought his gun and shot him.*

Baker soon recovered from his leg wound, but the rivalry had a new edge to it. He remained bitter, and availed himself of every opportunity to harass the Singers until the Pike Petrified Forest ceased operations in 1961.

Singer was a "born promoter," however, and soon had his dude ranch filled with guests from all over the country. On Sundays, Singer conducted rodeos with many of the days famous rodeo stars. Saturday night dances featured big-name entertainers. Guests who were adverse to the clean mountain air and brilliant blue skies were given the option of filling their days, and emptying their pockets, in front of numerous slot machines in the hotel. Or visitors could instead fill their pock-ets with fossils for the princely sum of fifty cents. In 1943, Singer added more land to the Colorado Petrified Forest Ranch. This time it was Adeline Hornbek's old homestead, located along the northern boundary of the Colorado Petrified Forest Ranch.

Singer's ranch now encompassed what was reputed to be the world's largest petrified sequoia stump, measuring seventy-four feet in circumference at its base, and standing a full fourteen feet tall. Ranch guides escorted guests on a tour of the wonders of the ranch, including four other petrified stumps, a large pet-rified log, and Scudder's 1877-1879 fossil quarry site.

Singer continued to operate the ranch until his death in 1954. His widow, Agnes Ryan Singer and their son Robert then assumed control of the operation until 1973. Agnes had her troubles however, as "Tourists began sneaking in and taking all they could carry." The Singers were concerned with preserving the fossil beds, fearing that "There'd soon be nothing left."

Courtesy Marge & Don Christiansen
Coplen Petrified Forest Resort in 1924. Coplen moved the CMRR station
from Florissant to his land in 1922 and converted it into a hotel.

In 1920, the National Park Service first took note of value of
the fossil beds. Director Stephen Mather wrote that the fossil
beds seemed worthy of national monument status, but that an
examination needed to be made. However, it wasn't until twelve
years later that such an examination occurred, and it resulted
in an adverse report. Unfortunately, this negative valuation of
the area as a national treasure continued until the middle of
the century.

It continued into 1952, when Secretary of the Interior
Chapman sent Yellowstone Superintendent, Edmund B.
Rogers, to the fossil beds for an evaluation. Rogers culminated
his visit by writing "Florissant Fossil Shale Beds, Colorado," in
1953. In spite of recognizing the "national significance of the
Florissant lake beds to scientists," Rogers recommended
against national monument status for the fossil beds.

A large part of this inertia was the perception that there was
"no clear and present danger of loss of these interesting scientific features to the public." These early investigators felt that
the Hendersons' and the Singers' commercial operations were
doing an adequate job of protecting the fossils and petrified

trees while still making them available to students and scientists and tourists.

It wasn't until 1962, however, that the National Park Service addressed the need to protect and preserve the fossil beds, finally acknowledging that they were endangered. A report by the National Park Service that year noted that "Even under the protection of the existing private developments, vandalism and promiscuous collecting of fossils continues . . ."

A report issued by Alberts and Knowles in 1962 (at the request of the Park Service Advisory Board) recommended that the area be preserved as a National Monument "as soon as possible." Their seminal report, "Florissant Fossil Beds National Monument—A Proposal" finally gave voice to the value of the area:

> *The rare quality of the Florissant site lies not in dramatic exposures of big-boned creatures, but rather in the delicacy with which thousands of insects, tree foliage, and other forms of life—completely absent or extremely rare in most paleontological sites of this period—have been preserved. The fossils at Florissant are individually quite small, but in the aggregate are tremendous. Few fossil sites in the world have yielded some 60,000 specimens of over 1000 different species of life. In addition to this vast number of individual fossil specimens, is the remarkable way in which the fine-grained ash has preserved, in minute detail, delicate features of the innumerable specimens sealed within the layers of shale.*

Dr. Estella Leopold, a United States Geological Survey paleontologist, wrote shortly after a visit in 1965:

> *If a single layer of paper shale in the Florissant beds could be uncovered simultaneously over its entire surface, we would have a detailed picture—a photograph in rock— of Florissant as it was some thirty-eight million years ago. As a volcanic tomb, Florissant is a kind of Dead Sea Scroll of evolution. There is simply nothing like it.*

In 1969, Dr. Leopold played a vital role in ensuring that Florissant's "Dead Sea Scrolls" would be preserved for posterity when she joined forces with the Defenders of Florissant.

Bureaucracies are lethargic, cumbersome animals, and the United States Congress is a prime example. Although a bill was introduced in Congress in 1963 to make the area a National Park, the legislation was not voted on. A similar bill was introduced in 1965, but it also failed. In 1967, a third Florissant bill was introduced with an amendment to decrease the acreage from 6,000 to 1,000 acres. This attempt at making the bill palatable by reducing the costs almost worked—the House passed the measure, but it again died in the Senate.

It wasn't until 1969 that a final, successful, bill seeking to establish the Florissant Fossil Beds National Monument was introduced to Congress. In the meantime, however, a real estate development company had purchased 1,800 acres of fossil lands with plans for an A-frame housing development. Concerned conservationists from Florissant and other parts of Colorado banded together, organizing the Defenders of Florissant (DOF).

As the developer's army of bulldozers rumbled toward the endangered fossil beds, the DOF sought an injunction. Led by Vim Crane Wright, a group of women drove up from Denver, prepared to lie down in the path of the bulldozers. Wright recalls dressing in a stylish outfit for the confrontation, certain that no bulldozer driver would run over a woman who was wearing pearls! Unfortunately, a federal judge ruled against the injunction, stating that it was a violation of the constitutional rights of the involved property owners.

Within hours of the federal ruling, however, the 10th Circuit Court of Appeals reinstated a temporary injunction against any further development of the fossil beds. Stalling for more time proved vital.

Three weeks later, Congress passed Public Law 91-60, creating the Florissant Fossil Beds National Monument. This final, successful bill was sponsored by Colorado Senators Gordon Allott and Peter Dominick, and the acreage was increased to the original 6,000. President Nixon signed the bill into law on August 20, 1969.

Public Law 91-60
91st Congress, S. 912
August 20, 1969

To provide for the establishment of the Florissant Fossil Beds National Monument in the state of Colorado.

Be it enacted by the Senate and House of Representatives of the United States of America in Congress assembled, that, in order to preserve and interpret for the benefit and enjoyment of present and future generations the excellently preserved insect and leaf fossils and related geologic sites and objects at the Florissant lakebeds, the Secretary of the Interior may acquire by donation, purchase with donated or appropriated funds, or exchange such land and interests in land in Teller County, Colorado, as he may designate from the lands shown on the map entitled "Proposed Florissant Fossil Beds National Monument," numbered NM-FEB-7100, and dated March 1967, and more particularly described by metes and bounds in an attachment to the map, not exceeding, however, six thousand acres thereof, for the purpose of establishing the Florissant Fossil Beds National Monument.

SEC.2. The Secretary of the Interior shall administer the property acquired pursuant to section 1 of this Act as the Florissant Fossil Beds National Monument in accordance with the Act entitled "An Act to establish a National Park Service, and for other purposes," approved August 25, 1916 (39 Stat. 535; 16 U.S.C. 1 et seq.), as amended and supplemented.

SEC.3. There are authorized to be appropriated such sums, but not more than $3,727,000, as may be necessary for the acquisition of lands and interests in land for the Florissant Fossil Beds National Monument and for necessary development expenses in connection therewith.

Approved August 20, 1969.

Acknowledgements

Writing this book has been a wonderful journey, and I am a bit sad now that it is ended. I could never have made this journey, however, without my best friend and companion, Harold, my husband. Of course, the writing would have been futile if I had not been able to coax the words from the computer, into the laser printer, and onto paper. Thank goodness my computer had a guardian angel, Chuck Mann, who made this all possible. I must also thank my children, who teach me something new every day—Melinda Gallop guided me through the intricacies of word processing and Jessica Hickman graciously allowed me the use of her computer.

My dear friend and advisor, Ed McGaa (Eagle Man), helped direct me through the labyrinth of publishing, and I am deeply indebted. My wonderful friend and amateur historian Kent Borgess gave invaluable advice. It then took the mind of a brilliant (but irreverent) college physics professor, Stephanie Di Cenzo, to ensure that there was logic and order in this book. And it required the analytical mind of a murder-mystery writer, Kari Wainwright, to keep me from murdering the English language too badly. All of these dear and dedicated friends have been vital to the successful completion of this book. I am also indebted to all of my friends in Western Writers of America, especially Chet Cunningham, for their encouragement and support.

Florissant artist Richard Thomas captures the spirit of the American West better than any other artist that I know, and Buck Venman integrated that art into one of the most attractive book covers possible. I am deeply indebted to them both for their impressive talent, and for lending it to this book.

Finally, this entire project was only possible through the generosity and kindness of the families of Pikes Peak backcountry pioneers. It has been an honor and a privilege to work with Judge Castello's grandson, Leo Kimmett and his wife Julia. I am also indebted to the great grandchildren of Count Louis Otto De Pourtales, Laura De Pourtales Clark and Chuck Walts. Also great-great grandson, Dan Pyzel. Virginia Pearce, Atlanta Long Thompson's granddaughter, and her husband, Douglas, have been extremely generous in sharing Atlanta's scrapbooks and photographs. Dr. Charles Snare's grandchildren have been exceedingly gracious and helpful, especially Rose White who copied numerous old family photos and her grandmother, Julia's, diary. Max Snare shared family history and genealogy, and helped me through the maze of Snare family land holdings until it became comprehensible, as did Al Snare. And, finally, I am indeed indebted to the family of Calas Wilson for sharing the letters of Berta Wilson. Janelle Cobb brought her story to my attention, and Shirley Smith Hauser transcribed and annotated the letters for easy reference.

I really began this journey in researching Twin Creek Ranch. Thank goodness that two strangers, Marge and Don Christiansen, stopped at the ranch one day, and shared the Allen family history. They generously and patiently loaned me invaluable photos of old Florissant, the Fossil Beds, the Allens, and Twin Creek Ranch.

I would also like to thank Sandy Sanborn, Helen Cahill, Mel McFarland, Midge Harbour, and Don Nichols for being so generous with their time and photos. Hugo and Elizabeth Lackman of the Ute Pass Historical Society were wonderful for taking the time and effort to help me locate the many vintage photos of Pikes Peak backcountry.

Maggie Johnston, Herb Myers, and Superintendent Jean Rodeck of the Florissant Fossil Beds National Monument provided invaluable corrections and comments. Doris Kneuer and volunteer, Wally Stark, were extremely helpful in research. Jim McChristal's comments and research documents were vital in providing accurate information on the history of the Fossil Beds.

Staff at Teller County Clerk and Recorder, assessor, and treasurer's offices were invaluable in providing assistance for researching original records of the area. The staffs at Colorado Springs Pioneers Museum, Colorado College, Colorado State Historical Society, and Denver Public Library were efficient, pleasant, patient and helpful. I would also like to especially thank Alan T. Knight at Penrose Library for his very competent efforts.

Before I close, I also would like to thank my editor, Wayne Cornell. His enthusiasm, expertise, and his wonderful sense of humor made bringing this book to life a rewarding and enjoyable project.

Acknowledgments usually seem to be tedious things to read. However, nothing worthwhile is ever accomplished by one person. It is only because of the generosity of all of the people listed that this book has come to life. Thank you all so very much. Ten percent of the profits from *Pikes Peak Backcountry* have been designated for the Florissant Heritage Foundation for their excellent work in preserving the history and memories of the area.

PIKES PEAK BACKCOUNTRY

Bibliography

Books

Adams, Maynard Cornett, *Citadel Mountain*, Johnson City, Tennessee: Sabre Printers, 1993.

Atherarn, Robert G., *The Coloradans*, Albuquerque, New Mexico: University of New Mexico Press, 1978.

Bird, Isabella L., *A Lady's Life in the Rocky Mountains*, Norman, Oklahoma: University of Oklahoma Press, 1988.

Cafkey, Morris, *Colorado Midland Railroad*, Denver, Colorado: World Press, 1956.

Carter, Harvey L., Editor, *The Pikes Peak Region*, Colorado Springs, Colorado: The Historical Society of the Pikes Peak Region, 1956.

Cassells, E. Steve, *The Archaeology of Colorado*, Boulder, Colorado: Johnson Books, 1990.

Conard, Howard Louis, *Uncle Dick Wootton*, Lincoln, Nebraska: University of Nebraska Press, 1980.

Conte, William R., *The Old Cripple Creek Stage Road*, Colorado Springs, Colorado: Little London Press, 1984.

Cragin, Francis, *Early Far West Notebooks*, Pioneer Museum, Colorado Springs.

Crofutt, George A., *Crofutt's Grip-Sack Guide of Colorado*, Omaha, Nebraska: The Overland Publishing Co., 1885.

Culpin, Mary S., *Historic Resource Study and Historic Furnishing Study — Florissant Fossil Beds National Monument*, Denver, Colorado: U.S. Dept. of the Interior, 1979.

Cunningham, Chet, *Cripple Creek Bonanza*, Plano, Texas: Republic of Texas Press, 1996.

Dawson, Thomas R., F.J.V. Skiff, *The Ute War*, Boulder, Colorado: Johnson Publishing, 1980.

Dickinson, Anna E., *A Ragged Register (Of People Places and Opinions)*, New York, New York: Harper & Brothers, 1879.

Drannan, Capt. William F., *Thirty-One Years on the Plains and in the Mountains*, Chicago, Illinois: Rhodes & McClure Publishing, 1900.

Egan, Ferol, *Fremont—Explorer for a Restless Nation*, Reno, Nevada: University of Nevada Press, 1985.

Fetler, John, *The Pikes Peak People*, Caldwell, Idaho: The Caxton Printers, 1966.

Foster, Mike, *Strange Genius; The Life of Ferdinand Vandeveer Hayden*, Niwot, Colorado: Roberts Rinehart, 1994.

Grand County Historical Association, *Grand County Historical Association Journal*, Vol. VII, No. 1, June, 1987.

Hafen, Leroy R., Editor, *Mountain Men and Fur Traders of the Far West*, Lincoln, Nebraska: University of Nebraska Press, 1982.

Hafen, Leroy R. and Ann W., Editors, *Reports From Colorado, The Wildman Letters 1859-1865*, Glendale, California: The Arthur H. Clark Company, 1961.

Harbour, Midge, *The Tarryall Mountains and the Puma Hills*, Colorado Springs, Colorado: Century One Press, 1982.

Howbert, Irving, *Memories of a Lifetime in the Pike's Peak Region*, Glorieta, New Mexico: The Rio Grande Press, 1970.

Jefferson, J., R. Delaney and G. Thompson, *The Southern Utes*, Ignacio, Colorado: Southern Ute Tribe, 1972.

Kessler, Ronald E., *Anza'a 1779 Comanche Campaign*, Monte Vista, Colorado: Ronald E. Kesler, 1994.

Kimmett, Leo, *Florissant, Colorado*, Canon City, Colorado: Leo Kimmett, 1980, 1986.

Kohl, Michael F. and McIntosh, John S., editors, *Discovering Dinosaurs in the Old West: The Field Journals of Arthur Lakes*, Washington, D.C.: Smithsonian Institution Press, 1997.

Lecompte, Janet, *Pueblo, Hardscrabble, Greenhorn*, Norman, Oklahoma: University of Oklahoma Press, 1978.

Lee, Mabel Barbee, *Cripple Creek Days*, Garden City, New York: Doubleday & Company, 1958.

Madsen, David B., *Exploring the Fremont*, University of Utah: University Printing Services, 1989.

Marsh, Charles S., *People of the Shining Mountains*, Boulder, Colorado: Pruett Publishing Company, 1982.

McChristal, Jim, *A History of Florissant Fossil Beds National Monument*, unpublished manuscript in Florissant Fossil Beds National Monument possession, 1994.

McConnell, Virginia, *Bayou Salado*, Chicago, Illinois: Sage Books, 1966.

McConnell, Virginia, *The Upper Arkansas, A Mountain River Valley*, Boulder, Colorado: Pruett Publishing Company, 1990.

Noblett, Jeffrey B., *A Guide To The Geological History of the Pikes Peak Region*, Colorado Springs, Colorado: Colorado College, 1994

Olson, A.P., R.O. Roland, T.G. Bridge, *An Archaeological Assessment of Florissant Fossil Beds National Monument*, 1974.

Onis, Jose de, Editor, *The Hispanic Contribution to the State of Colorado*, Boulder, Colorado: Westview Press, 1976.

Pettit, Jan, *Utes, The Mountain People*, Boulder, Colorado: Johnson Books, 1990.

Rockwell, Wilson, *The Utes, A Forgotten People*, Denver, Colorado: Sage Books, 1956.

Roe, Frank Gilbert, *The Indian and the Horse*, Norman, Oklahoma: University of Oklahoma Press, 1974.

Ruxton, George Frederick, *Life In The Far West*, Norman, Oklahoma: University of Oklahoma Press, 1985.

Ruxton, George Frederick, *Adventures in Mexico and the Rocky Mountains, 1846-1847*, Glorieta, New Mexico: The Rio Grande Press, 1973.

Semple, Ellen Churchill, *Influences of Geographic Environment*, New York: Henry Hold and Company, 1911.

Smith, P. David, *Ouray—Chief of the Utes*, Ridgway, Colorado: Wayfinder Press, 1992.

Spell, Leslie Doyle & Hazel M., *Forgotten Men of Cripple Creek*, Denver: Big Mountain Press, 1959.

Sprague, Marshall, *Massacre*, Boston, Mass: Little Brown and Company, 1957.

Sprague, Marshall, *Money Mountain*, Lincoln, Nebraska: University of Nebraska Press, 1979.

Sprague, Marshall, *Colorado, A Bicentennial History*, New York, New York: W.W. Norton & Company, Inc., 1976.

Stewart, Alan J., Editor, *The Denver Westerners Brand Book - Vol. XXX & XXXI*, Boulder, Colorado: Johnson Publishing, 1977.

Thompson, Atlanta Georgia, *Daughter of a Pioneer*, Portland Oregon: Wayne Steward, 1982.

Utley, Robert M., *The Indian Frontier of the American West 1846-1890*, Albuquerque, New Mexico: University of New Mexico Press, 1984.

Whittemore, Loren R., *An Illustrated History of Ranching in the Pikes Peak Region*, Colorado Springs, Colorado: Gowdy Printcraft Press, 1990.

Wislizenus, Frederick A., *A Journey to the Rocky Mountains 1839*, Glorieta, New Mexico: The Rio Grande Press, Inc., 1969.

Winternitz, Barbara L., *The Mueller Ranch: A Unique Mountain Park*, Colorado: The Nature Conservancy, 1981.

Wood, Frances and Dorothy, *"I Hauled These Mountains In Here!"*, Caldwell, Idaho: The Caxton Printers, Ltd., 1977.

Newspapers

Centennial (Georgetown, CO.)	1876
Colorado Springs Gazette	1884-1923
Creede Candle	1893
Denver Times	1900
Fairplay Flume	1883
Gazette Telegraph	1923-1937
New York Times	1874
Rocky Mountain Herald	1860
Rocky Mountain News	1875-1878
The Cascade Courier	1927
The Independent	1927 (?)

INDEX

234

Anatole, the resident ghost of her Victorian house at Twin Creek Ranch, first inspired Celinda Kaelin Reynolds in her quest for the history of Pikes Peak backcountry. Celinda and her husband, Harold, retired to their cow-calf operation in Colorado in 1989. Hoping to rid herself of this other-worldly guest, Celinda began a search for his identity and the cause of his death. This research unearthed a wealth of fascinating stories that had never been told, culminating in this book.

Celinda's love of the West began with her early life on a ranch in New Mexico. She is the granddaughter of New Mexico pioneer and homesteader John Allen Reynolds. Before retiring, Celinda was an auditor on the Inspector General's staff at the Central Intelligence Agency. This work instilled the discipline needed to write history—demanding, thorough research; attention to detail and facts; and the ability to translate the facts into a readable narrative. Celinda has written numerous magazine and newspaper articles, and is a popular lecturer throughout the Pikes Peak region. Her idiom is the American Indian, and her latest book is a study of their spirituality.

Celinda has served as president of the regional historical society for seven years, and is a member of the Western Writers of America and Women Writing the West.

The Colorado Collection
From CAXTON PRESS

From the Grave:
A Roadside Guide to Colorado's Pioneer Cemeteries
Linda Wommack
ISBN 0-87004-386-2 500 pages paper $24.95
ISBN 0-87004-390-0 cloth $34.95

Pioneers of the Colorado Parks
Richard Barth
ISBN 0-87004-381-1 276 pages paper $17.95

Colorado Ghost Towns Past and Present
Robert L. Brown
ISBN 0-87004-218-1 322 pages paper $14.95

Central City and Gilpin County: Then and Now
Robert L. Brown
ISBN 0-87004-363-3 200 pages paper $8.95

Jeep Trails to Colorado Ghost Towns
Robert L. Brown
ISBN 0-87004-021-9 245 pages paper $10.95

Colorado on Foot
Robert L. Brown
ISBN 0-87004-336-6 309 pages paper $10.95

Ghost Towns of the Colorado Rockies
Robert L. Brown
ISBN 0-87004-342-0 paper $14.95

Uphill Both Ways: Hiking Colorado's High Country
Robert L. Brown
ISBN 0-87004-249-1 paper $7.95

Telluride: From Pick to Powder
Richard L. and Suzanne Fetter
ISBN 0-87004-265-3 paper $9.95

For a free catalog of Caxton books write to:

CAXTON PRESS
312 Main Street
Caldwell, ID 83605-3299

or

Visit our Internet Website:

www.caxtonprinters.com

Caxton Press is a division of The CAXTON PRINTERS, Ltd.

WC

242